Deliberation & the Work of Higher Education

Innovations for the Classroom, the Campus, and the Community

Contents

Introduction

Creating New Spaces for Deliberation in Higher Education

Laura Grattan, John R. Dedrick, and Harris Dienstfrey

T hough it may not be widely recognized, American colleges and universities are home to robust cultures of innovation that are redefining our approaches to teaching, to research, to service, and to learning—and, in the process, reinvigorating the larger public and democratic purposes of academic life. Carmen Sirianni and Lewis Friedland have persuasively characterized these innovations as part of a broad civic renewal movement in the United States; institutions of higher education, college and university presidents, administrators, faculty, and students, are again embracing their roles as "architects of a flourishing democracy."

The most successful of these efforts variously involve students, faculty, and administrators seeking to connect their vocations and their personal interests with public life. Harry Boyte, in *Everyday Politics*, reports that his discussions with faculty and administrators, in fields ranging from family therapy to architecture, reveal a hunger to reconnect academic disciplines and professional practice with the "public work" of citizenship and politics. The Wingspread statement on student civic engagement, *The New Student Politics*, observes that many college students seek a "richly participatory" politics that ties their individual interests and experiences to the service of public problems. And Cynthia Gibson, in her report, *From Inspiration to Participation*, for the Carnegie Corporation, writes that the academy's four major approaches to civic engagement—civic education, service learning, youth development, and political action—all reflect higher education's efforts to "balance meeting the needs of youth with achieving larger educational, community, and societal goals."[1]

Given these trends, it is not altogether surprising that recent empirical evidence presents students today as more civically engaged than they were 15 years ago and savvier about their engagement. As the Center for Information and Research on Civic Learning and Engagement (CIRCLE) report *Millenials Talk Politics* argues, while college students remain ambivalent about politics-as-usual, especially in the forms they equate with media spin and polarized debates, many do seek opportunities to discuss public issues in what they would find more authentic terms and to organize people to address such issues. Many are finding what they consider the most reliable opportunities for engagement in their local communities.[2]

Yet large challenges remain. Tuition costs are skyrocketing, with the result that the requisite knowledge for today's information society is concentrated in fewer and fewer hands; parents and

---

[1] See Carmen Sirianni and Lewis Friedland, *The Civic Renewal Movement: Community-Building and Democracy in the United States* (Dayton, OH: Kettering Foundation Press, 2005); Harry Boyte, *Everyday Politics: Reconnecting Citizens and Public Life* (Philadelphia: University of Pennsylvania Press, 2004); Sarah Long, *The New Student Politics: The Wingspread Statement on Student Civic Engagement* (Providence, RI: Campus Compact, 2002); and Cynthia Gibson, *From Inspiration to Participation: A Review of Perspectives on Youth Civic Engagement* (New York: Carnegie Corporation, 2001). Other prominent voices joining in that conversation over the years include: Anne Colby et al., *Educating for Democracy: Preparing Undergraduates for Responsible Political Engagement* (San Francisco: Jossey-Bass, 2007) and Michael Delli Carpini et al., *A New Engagement? Political Participation, Civic Life, and the Changing American Citizen* (New York: Oxford University Press, 2006).

[2] These findings come from a CIRCLE study that convened focus groups on 12 four-year college campuses across the country. See Abby Kiesa, et al., *Millennials Talk Politics: A Study of College Student Political Engagement*. Peter Levine also documents and measures youth civic engagement trends in his 2007 book, *The Future of Democracy: Developing the Next Generation of American Citizens* (Medford, MA: Tufts University Press, 2007).

students who can afford higher education are therefore taking an increasingly consumer approach; and many colleges and universities appear content to capitalize on these trends rather than challenge them.[3] Any resurgence of civic engagement exists within a higher education environment that remains beset by the enduring problems of American democracy in our times—most notably, cultures of expertise and money and organized special interests that continue to sideline and estrange citizens.

For those who gain access to higher education, the new initiatives to reconnect with public life counter a prevailing culture of hyper-professionalism in the academy, which stresses career training and competition among students, while urging faculty into narrower and narrower paths of disciplinary research. These myopic aims are part of what William Sullivan identifies as the ethos of "instrumental individualism" that governs higher education today. Economic interests, he says, and the pursuit of individual advancement have largely replaced broader "questions of social, political, and moral purpose" among students and professionals who inhabit academic institutions and aspire to leadership positions in society. When complex issues are tackled within the walls of the academy, its entrenched "argument culture" rewards criticism and adversarial modes of discourse at the expense of real dialogue about ideas and values.[4]

The argument culture with its attendant polarizing discourse effectively excludes many students who do not see themselves in the stylized rancor of a politics that mirrors the popular vernacular of a world in which the public ethos is not about learning how to live together but about "voting off the island" those whom we dis-

---

[3] See the Public Agenda report, *Squeeze Play*.

[4] Boyte, *Everyday Politics*, 134-135; William Sullivan, "Higher Education and Civic Deliberation," *Kettering Review* (Spring 2000): 23-38; Deborah Tannen, "Agonism in the Academy: Surviving Higher Learning's Argument Culture," *The Chronicle of Higher Education* 46:30 (31 March 2000): B7-8; Public Agenda report, *Squeeze Play*.

like or disagree with. Such an environment leaves very little space and develops few alternative practices for serious engagement with concerns that are necessarily multisided and involve coexisting claims about what should be done. Nor does it guarantee the existence of spaces in which students can experience the deliberative and dialogic practices that offer a vital alternative to the reigning argument culture. Such spaces must be invented. The good news is that this invention is precisely what is happening on a variety of campuses.

This book is the product of a workgroup, convened by the Kettering Foundation, that involved faculty, administrators, and students who are experimenting with deliberation on their campuses. Meeting periodically between 1999 and 2005, participants in the workgroup tracked the major literature on civic engagement, taking a hard look at both opportunities and challenges, while simultaneously sharing stories, lessons, and outlines of successful practices from their own experiments with deliberative politics. Over time, as experiences, insights, and findings accumulated, the workgroup organizers came to believe that collecting some of the participants' stories in one place could provide a stimulating and helpful resource for others interested in experimenting with deliberative democracy concepts and practices. The result is this collection of primarily narrative accounts of what has been tried and learned, presented in the spirit of longstanding American traditions of experimentation and innovation. The intent of this volume is not primarily to survey current pedagogical practices or to render a social scientific documentation of the effects of democratic practices on students. Rather, the narratives presented here illustrate possibilities for experimenting with deliberative practices across a range of curricular and institutional settings.

Among the contributors are faculty who teach graduate and undergraduate courses, university administrators, and a recent college graduate now pursuing her law degree. Their venues range from a major research university in Virginia to a liberal arts college in New England, from a state university in San Diego to a historically black university in Ohio. And their concerns encompass the critical experience of the first year in college, students' efforts to address specific problems of the campus community, and the ongoing learning in and out of the classroom that is essential to the mission of higher education. In each instance, the authors experimented with deliberation in the context of specific issues that concerned them; and they did so in spaces where, for the most part, few people had previously considered such efforts to be productive or worthwhile.

One contribution of the projects reported here is that they illustrate several practical ways of creating space for deliberation in higher education—in classrooms, residence halls, fraternal houses, and local community settings—where students may learn and practice modes of reasoning and deciding together. These spaces allow students to practice collective decision making that draws on the multiplicity of their life experiences and concerns. The reports make clear that the students embrace this multiplicity in seeking collective understandings of common problems— of why *we together* should care about them and of what *we together* might do to resolve them. It is clear as well that students respond enthusiastically to the practice of deliberation, which is really a mode of democratic politics because it addresses their expressed interest in a more authentic engagement with issues and other people. It is an obvious counter to our polarizing argument culture.

The authors writing for this volume also speak to the contributions that deliberation can make to their own work as professionals and to the civic responsibility of the colleges and universities with which they are associated. For each of them, the practice of deliberation has enhanced the day-to-day academic or administrative work of educating college and professional students. The authors also understood deliberation to be a critical element of democratic politics—a public practice basic to the larger civic mission of higher education, which includes the responsibility of preparing citizens and potential leaders for their roles in our contemporary democracy. For them, then, deliberation is an innovative practice that bolsters civic renewal in higher education.

Each project described in this volume illustrates the practice of deliberative decision making as it has been exemplified in National Issues Forums (NIF)—a nationwide, nonpartisan network that includes among its participants community-based groups, K-12 educational institutions, colleges and universities, and faith-based and other civic groups concerned with public issues. The NIF network convenes locally sponsored and funded public forums in which citizens come together to deliberate over common problems, such as the high cost of health care, racial and ethnic tensions, immigration, violent crime, and the United States' role in the world. Forum deliberations center on three or four general approaches to the problem as outlined in nonpartisan NIF issue books. Participants explore the conflicting values embedded in each approach and the advantages, costs, and trade-offs of actions that might be taken—a process that often leads to finding common ground for action in their communities.[5]

The NIF network shares an approach to democratic politics that understands citizens as people who make decisions about their shared responsibilities together and do "public work" on important problems facing their communities and the nation. Such "public" politics is considered a necessary foundation for the legitimate functioning of formal representative institutions. In short, deliberative decision making among citizens provides the public judgments, suggests complementary actions, and provides the public permissions required for the effective functioning of institutional governance.

Our book begins with essays by two senior faculty members, whose many years of experience in higher education leave them troubled by the increasingly narrow paths down which today's students seem headed. Both hope that civic engagement through deliberative practices will help retrieve larger lives for their students. Michael D'Innocenzo, from Hofstra University in New York, reflects on the absence of strong intergenerational relationships connecting college students to the world outside what he

---

[5] For more about NIF forums and materials, visit the Web site at www. nifi.org.

calls, their "youth ghettos," and reports on encouraging signs from campus-community deliberations that have fostered respect across generations. Lee Ingham, from Central State University in Ohio, writes of his current hopes for—and disappointments about—the civic engagement of African American students. He recounts the challenges and opportunities he has encountered in his efforts to foster engagement by introducing NIF deliberations into the school's first-year seminar requirement.

The next three essays take deliberative pedagogy in the humanities classroom as their point of departure. Each of the contributors to this section has found deliberation integral to his or her work as an educator. Each has also found deliberation to be at the center of a relationship between advancing the pedagogical aims of their disciplines and building linkages between the classroom and the civic mission of training citizens and leaders for democracy. Joni Doherty, from Franklin Pierce University in New Hampshire, describes the transformative role deliberative dialogue has played in her own development as a learner and a teacher; and she reports on promising signs that deliberative experiences in her first-year seminars help students overcome barriers to learning that stem from their fears of confronting different ideas and perspectives. Maria Farland, from Fordham University in New York, chronicles the empowering impact of deliberative practices on students in her writing classes and she argues that deliberation can be a core component of active-learning pedagogies promoted by many humanistic disciplines at higher education institutions. David Cooper, from Michigan State University, details his experiments in "cross-fertilizing" deliberation with service learning and other active-learning techniques, reflecting on the concrete challenges and possibilities for practitioners of deliberative pedagogies in the classroom.

The next two essays report on the authors' experiments in using deliberative pedagogy to train professionals. The authors find that deliberation can help students meet the challenges they will face as professionals. Cristina Alfaro, at San Diego University, argues that deliberation can help new teachers move more easily into today's high-stakes public education environment. By switching to a deliberation in her own classroom and introducing to her students the skills to integrate deliberation into their K-6 classrooms, Alfaro has helped new teachers negotiate and adhere to state and federal standards while also creating spaces for these teachers and their students to experience agency in the classroom. Larkin Dudley and Ricardo Morse, at Virginia Tech University, document their efforts to train public affairs graduate students in deliberation—both as a way of understanding democratic politics and as a set of skills to practice it. They make the case that deliberation is a crucial competency for professionals interested in more democratic engagement with citizens.

In the next section, we move from the classroom to the broader campus community, with two essays by university administrators who experiment with deliberation to enhance learning and problem solving outside the classroom. These administrators have found that deliberative decision making can help bring about more democratic ways to address the problems of administrators, faculty, and students on campus and, at the same time, contribute to broader processes of active learning and cultural transformation. Douglas Walters, writes of his experience as dean of students at the University of Charleston in West Virginia when his university entered a period of intensive institutional questioning about its identity and mission, which opened a door for the systematic adoption of deliberative ideas and practices both in the curriculum and in cocurricular activity. Dennis Roberts and Matthew Johnson tell the story of a "fraternal futures initiative," in which fraternity and sorority students around the country are using deliberation to reevaluate their cultural purposes and organizational missions. They chronicle the opportunities and challenges they faced as administrators, working with students at Miami University in Ohio, to develop an issue guide, to help them convene and moderate forums, and subsequently to pilot the initiative on campuses across the country—and they report on the project's results thus far.

We close with two essays that chronicle from different perspectives a four-year experiment integrating deliberation into the curriculum and beyond and the effects of this on the civic attitudes and engagement of 30 college students known as "Democracy Fellows." Katy Harriger and Jill McMillan report on the findings of their research at Wake Forest University. They argue that different contexts— classroom, campus, and community—all contribute differently to making deliberation an effective practice for civic education. Allison Crawford, a former Democracy Fellow, provides a forthright assessment of the learning opportunities and challenges of deliberation as she experienced them in the three contexts of classroom, campus, and community, finally drawing connections between these formal deliberative engagements and other aspects of her undergraduate experience.

We have chosen to conclude with these reports from Wake Forest faculty and one of their students because, to date, the work in which the authors were engaged is the most comprehensive effort to document how deliberation practices can affect the development of college students' public skills, attitudes, and aspirations and what is entailed for faculty and students alike to commit to learning and practicing deliberative democracy. The entire collection of essays offered here provides evidence that Wake Forest's hopeful message is not only the capstone of an impressive scholarly experiment but, more important, that deliberative dialogue can be a cornerstone, reconnecting and revitalizing higher education with larger public and democratic purposes.

As the authors writing in this volume testify, in college classrooms and cocurricular settings on a wide variety of campuses across the United States, the idea and practice of deliberative democracy make a powerful contribution to meeting the civic purposes of higher education in America. Deliberation is challenging students to take ownership together for learning to think critically, for making collective judgments about their communities, and for building their capacities to contribute to democratic society in whatever career paths they chose. It is also offering them meaningful intellectual and public spaces. Finally, deliberation is providing faculty

and administrators with a means to move in the direction of accomplishing the democratic aspirations that prompted so many
of them to become higher education professionals when they stood
where their students do now. That inspires them to continue experimenting and innovating as educators and researchers.

The practice of deliberation is proving valuable to our contributors, at least in part because it provides them a way to bridge their
personal concerns and intellectual passions with the fundamental
challenges that are presented to citizens in contemporary democracy.
They are discovering that deliberation is much more than a pedagogical technique: it is a practice integral to strong democratic
politics; it is a practice that puts the public back into the public's
business. We hope that readers of this volume will also find these
narratives to be useful for their own purposes and perhaps even
inspirations for further experiments and innovations in an institution—higher education—that is critical to the functioning of
democracy in the United States.

*Laura Grattan is a doctoral candidate in political theory at Duke University.
Her research examines the politics of imagination in the context of grassroots
social movements in America, and she is actively engaged in a variety of
efforts to build campus-community relationships in Durham, North Carolina.*

*John R. Dedrick is director of programs at the Charles F. Kettering Foundation.
He has been closely associated with the work of the National Issues Forums for
more than 15 years.*

*Harris Dienstfrey is an editor and writer. He is the coauthor
(with Joseph Lederer) of* What Do You Want to Be When You Grow Old?
(Bantam 1979) and Where the Mind Meets the Body *(Harper Collins 1991).*

SECTION I
Deliberation and Enlarging Student Perspectives

Chapter One

From "Youth Ghettos" to Intergenerational Civic Engagement: Connecting the Campus and the Larger Community

Michael D'Innocenzo

The goal of transforming "youth ghettos" is a project of the Hofstra University Public Policy Institute. Our 15 years of experience with National Issues Forums have made us increasingly aware of age separations in our society. While we explore reasons for age separations, our principal focus is on fostering intergenerational relationships that are built around the deliberative framework of National Issues Forums. We have also taken care to be inclusive in regard to the racial and ethnic diversity of the changing demographics at our university and in our region. From these early intergenerational endeavors have come most encouraging responses by people of all ages (many of whom seldom, if ever, seem to cross the generational divide in their daily lives). Our experiences, illustrated by a variety of our projects, show that intergenerational endeavors foster more attentive, informed civic engagement and a level of respect, empathy, and appreciation among the different age groups.

Hofstra University is located in Hempstead, New York, a Long Island suburb 25 miles east of midtown Manhattan. Hempstead is in Nassau County, and Nassau and the adjoining county of Suffolk are among the most structurally segregated areas of the United States. Together, they have a population of more than three million people. Political observers have noted that if these two counties were a state, they would be the 23rd largest in the nation.

Since 1993, Hofstra's Public Policy Institute has devoted itself to increasing civic engagement by bringing people together in deliberative forums. From our university base, we have had the opportunity to develop a wide range of relationships across campus and community institutions. These endeavors have succeeded in fostering ongoing relationships of mutual encouragement and contributed to revitalizing democracy in the surrounding communities. Our programs take place in university classrooms, through partnerships between college and high-school students, and through relationships with public libraries, elder programs, and community organizations. Connecting campus and community in the name of democratic revitalization is challenging and difficult work. It requires patience and openness on both sides and institutional spaces and commitments through which those relationships can become sustainable. Folks who participate even in a single deliberative forum uniformly celebrate that deliberation offers a different kind of talk, which is community building. Too often, however, deliberation happens in isolated groups of folks who look alike and have similar experiences in terms of age, race, and ethnicity.

In the course of our activities, we have sponsored more than 300 forums, at Hofstra and in the Long Island community. Only gradually did we realize that nearly all of our forums involved people in the same age and racial groups. As we became increasingly cognizant of the age separation in our communities, we saw how little interaction there was among younger people and their elders. We were particularly struck by the extent to which high schools and, especially, colleges have become functional "ghettos" for young people.

We saw age separation and the lack of interaction between the young and the old as a societal loss for all age groups. Because young people seldom discussed public policy issues beyond their own peer groups (and only rarely with them), they missed the chance to develop shared assessments with folks older than themselves on issues facing our society and on how they might be addressed. We recognized that associations across age divides held the potential for mutual affirmation of civic engagement, a process that could be empowering, as it also worked to connect generations. We realized, of course, that to some degree, age separations have always occurred. (An important question is the extent to which current situations are different from the past.) Nonetheless, it still seemed possible that older people could model constructive civic awareness and engagement for the young and that the idealism and spirit of youth could energize and encourage older folks. We subscribed to the assessment of Urie Bronfenbrenner, a psychologist who focused on human development and family studies, that a key gauge of any society is the extent to which one generation genuinely cares about the well-being of other generations.

With these considerations in mind, an increasing focus of our Public Policy Institute has been to bring both college and high-school students together with adults in settings structured around National Issues Forums (NIF). Our goal is to foster intergenerational associations and to help these mixed-age groups deliberate about important public policy choices. Our efforts so far have been modest but very encouraging. We intend to build on these early experiences so we may offer models for civic engagement that span and connect the age spectrum. In this report, I share our (sometimes impressionistic) findings, not only about the age separation that seems so widespread in our society but also about the satisfactions and positive effects that younger and older folks derive from talking to each other about serious concerns of the day.

Why Do We Have Youth Ghettos?

As we delved more deeply into the geography and conduct of youth ghettos, it was not hard to grasp some of the key reasons why they function as they do. It is natural for young people to want to associate with peer groups who share their interests and value similar kinds of activities. Music, in particular, often represents a huge cultural divide among age groups. It is also understandable that during their teens and early 20s, young people are in the process of establishing their own individuality and that this usually involves some separation from adults, including their own parents.

But other, less obvious, factors are also at work. The physical space in which many young people spend much of their time has a large impact. This is particularly so on college campuses, where undergraduates spend only 15 hours a week in class, and then share the bulk of their days and nights with the fellow students with whom they reside. In the dorms and the dining halls, as well as in social activities, the presence of an adult is rare. (Circumstances are somewhat different for commuter students who live at home and who may have part-time jobs. But even in those situations, young people tend mostly to associate with peer groups and seldom have discussions about substantive public policy issues with adults.)

While students in high schools are not residentially sequestered as they are on a college campus, they spend a lot more time in classes, and peer group associations and pressures still command the prime energy and engagement of most teenagers. For high-school students, age ghettoization is not only a matter of charting how much time teens spend with different age groups but also a matter of assessing how teens regard the quality and importance of the time spent with adults in comparison to time spent with their peers. It is true that parents today often are more attentive to their children than were previous generations of parents. For example, the term used to describe parents always worried about their children —*helicopter parents*, meaning "parents who always hover over their children"—is now applied not only to parents of children in the vulnerable phase of middle school but to parents of high-school and college students as well.

But this genuine parental caring about sons and daughters falls far short of modeling sustained concern about the responsibilities of citizenship. An important part of the problem is the "busyness syndrome" that afflicts many parents as more and more husbands and wives have comparable educations and career involvements. Under these conditions, it is not easy for adults to have even "quality" time for their growing children—or often, for that matter, for each other. *The Juggling Act* was the title of a recent series on National Public Radio about the busyness of parents. In Hofstra's suburban area, many parents commute to New York City to work, and some spend as many as four or five hours on congested roads or crowded trains. As P. M. Forni explains in *Choosing Civility* (2002), "purposeful poise" is not always easy to achieve or sustain for people who lead pressured lives and who experience what sociologists call "time poverty." (Forni also argues that the decline of good manners undermines the ability of people to develop connections with each other.)

Another factor contributing to the creation of a youth ghetto is the huge numbers of hours that young people spend watching television—*The Other Parent*, as the title of James P. Steyer's book characterizes it—either alone in their own rooms or with other youngsters. This can happen at college too. For example, one college makes available to every student, at no cost, 92 cable television stations, including 5 HBO channels and all sports channels, thereby forcing on the students a particularly acute form of the challenge of "time discipline." Part of the concern with student TV viewing is that much of it appears to be solitary rather than social. The question is, to what extent do young people discuss with fellow students and adults what they watch, particularly if they tend to do their watching alone?

To the possibly isolating effect of television, add the rise in both high school and college of "pod people," students who are literally plugged in to music they have downloaded into their mp3 players. High-school students boast to us that they often listen to music while teachers are conducting classes. Students with long hair can easily hide the small plugs in their ears, while others creatively arrange their collars and shirts to cover the players. More and more young people are "connected" no matter where they are and where they go. But to what extent are they connected with each other, much less to any adults, in their listening preferences? On a recent early morning college bus trip that was to take 4 hours, within 10 minutes of starting *every one* of the students had his/her earplugs attached and was deep into the solitude of self.

Life and Politics Inside the Youth Ghetto

During the fall 2005 semester, we began tracking a small freshman group of 14 students, using initial surveys and focus-group discussions, and we have received many insights about life and political attitudes inside the youth ghetto. This group of students is now invited to forums each term. In future semesters, we plan to institutionalize more systematically forum involvement of a segment of the freshman class from their first semester through their senior year. We hope to follow the effects on the students of their deliberative experiences as they move through their college years.

We were not surprised that all 14 students had television sets in their rooms (though one set was broken). We found that, on average, the students watched television an average of two and one-half hours each day. Our sampling of TV habits among other students shows that the pattern of TV watching in the focus group was representative of most of their peers.

We asked the members of the focus group how often, on a daily and weekly basis, they talked with adults other than their parents and professors. Only two (14 percent) said they had such conversations. One was in touch with adults about 30 minutes a day (mostly on the Internet, via e-mail or instant messaging); the other student was in contact with adults 90 minutes a day during her part-time job. Several students said, "There is no opportunity at Hofstra" to interact with adults outside of the classroom.

It is true that all 14 of the students reported that they spoke to at least one of their parents every day, from less than 5 minutes a day (a student from Colorado) to more than 1 hour a day. But as one might expect, it appears that most of these conversations, nearly all of which took place on the telephone, often on cell phones as students moved from one destination to another, were "personal" rather than "social," in the sense of being concerned with current events.

Most relevant to our purposes here, we probed our group about their interest in politics and civic life. We learned that only 3 of the 14 read a newspaper "fairly frequently, even if not every day"—notwithstanding the fact that two newspapers, the *New York Times* and *Newsday*, are available on campus free of charge every day (including Sundays) at more than a dozen locations. Twelve of the fourteen said they did not follow current events closely. Ten said they occasionally got news from TV. Only one student reported reading any magazines regularly (*Time* and *Newsweek*).

When we asked our group whether they knew the name of their congressional representative, 10 said, "No," and 4, "Yes." When we asked whether they knew which political party controlled the state legislature in their state, eight said, "Yes," and six said, "No." Only 6 of the 14 indicated that they were registered to vote, and only 2 out of the 11 who were old enough to have voted in the 2004 presidential election did.

In follow-up discussions, the students said that their cohorts were either thoroughly absorbed in current events or else not involved at all. The latter situation seems to suggest an "adolescent moratorium" on dealing with adult issues. We found other signs of such a moratorium. Members of our focus group, as well as dozens of other students who have participated in our forums, indicated that they feel they do not have the time or experience or power to do much regarding public policy issues now, but that when they finish college, get jobs, and have families, they will be ready to be civically and politically engaged.

These responses seem to reflect the general level of political awareness of college students on our campus and perhaps elsewhere. In 2005, the American Bar Association, greatly concerned about the public's lack of basic knowledge about American democracy, named former Supreme Court justice Sandra Day O'Connor and former senator Bill Bradley, to cochair its Civic Education Commission. This effort is one of several, recalling not only the earlier report, *A Nation of Spectators* but also Harvard's ongoing "Vanishing American Voters Project." In all of these endeavors, special attention is given to the lack of knowledge and lack of engagement of young people. Political analysts frequently refer to the "Goldmine of Youth," indicating a rich civic "vein" that might yet be tapped.

Hofstra students (like many others who have been studied in our nation) have made generous commitments to volunteerism and various kinds of service learning; they assist in hospitals and in residences for the elderly; they mentor younger children, especially those with disabilities; and after Hurricane Katrina, many gave up college vacations to go to New Orleans to help with clean up and restoration projects. However, they seldom express any connection between these direct (and rewarding) personal interactions and larger societal structural issues of law, politics, and attitudes. In a sense, they act mostly "in the moment," doing good works that have some immediate benefit to those being assisted. As Jane Addams observed more than a century ago, while it is fine to take satisfaction in such service, the personal needs to be connected with the social and with long-range educational reform and politics to produce structural changes that improve attitudes, conduct, and opportunities.

Many of our views of students were powerfully reinforced by the fieldwork of anthropologist Cathy Small, who enrolled as a college freshman in order to get a sense of what students experienced during their first year. Her book, *My Freshman Year* (2005), published under the pseudonym Rebekah Nathan, highlighted how busy students were (many had part-time jobs) and how difficult it was for them to juggle classes, work, and campus life—much less have a sustained interest in politics and public policy. They simply did not have enough time to do all that they were required to do.

Many Hofstra students who participated in intergenerational forums said essentially the same thing when they maintained, sometimes defensively, that retired elders could be more attentive to news and politics than students, because older folks did not have as many demands on their time or as much need to keep proving themselves.

The Young and the Older in Intergenerational Deliberation

We have been expanding our emphasis on intergenerational forums during the past 4 years and hold as many as 15 in a single year. We are happy to be able to report that these forums have produced interesting, encouraging results, including signs that the civic interests of the elders (nearly all of them retirees) have been taken as a model by some young folks. Still, the process has not always been easy for the students.

Where the Generations Meet to Talk

Regardless of the amount of preforum preparation, young folks often approach the intergenerational gatherings with some reserve. When the gatherings use National Issues Forums books and the students have had previous forum experience, they have a greater feeling of competency and more of a sense that they are entering a level playing field (in terms of shared information and a defined, inclusive process), which often facilitates a more rapid and more effective interaction. However, in some cases, even when students have participated in many forums, they still have tended to sit together in the rear of the room, or to cluster in their own arc of a circle of chairs (unless one of the moderators intervened and orchestrated more random seating). Clearly, the physical arrangement makes a difference. It is natural to be more attentive to someone who is seated next to you than to a person across the room or several rows away.

The challenge for young folks is increased, at least at the outset, when we have a plenary town meeting format involving 100 to 150 people, for in such situations the students are outnumbered by elders 3 or 4 to 1. Worse for the students is when we have taken one or two college or high-school classes to a public library to engage with a group of adults who meet there regularly. In these circumstances, students, in addition to being outnumbered, face adults many of whom know each other, are friends, and often have the further bond of deep interest and knowledge about the topics to be discussed.

It should be noted that many of the elders have had more sustained involvements in forums than our students (often once a month, even every two weeks). In addition to forums, the adults have also participated in film-and-discussion series about leaders and historical periods, often leading to assessments of the pros and cons of alternative approaches that might have been available at the time—in effect, a retrospective deliberation process. Most important for many of the elders is participation in "Current Events in Perspective," a PPI series of town-meeting-type forums, where there is a great deal of interaction about what is happening in the United States and the world and what should be done about it. While some of our students have also participated in the current events town meetings at public libraries, they have not done so as often or as regularly, and one of our goals is to expand student intergenerational involvement in these kinds of programs.

Our intergenerational meetings always are best when all the participants have had previous forum experience, when the groups are small (not more than 25), and when the seating is random. In these circumstances, a mutuality of appreciation becomes evident during the forum and in the immediate aftermath, as people remain to talk before leaving. Unfortunately, we do not always have the option of arranging for smaller groups. The opportunity to use the space in libraries, the usual setting for small groups, is limited, and we always need to accommodate ourselves to ongoing programs.

In the best of circumstances, which are increasingly frequent, people linger in small, multigenerational groups, extending the policy discussions or developing closer associations with each other. In a number of smaller forums, folks of different ages expressed the view that they recognized common ground for continuing action and associations. This was most impressive, considering that most of the people had never met each other prior to the forum.

Until 2004, we used adult moderators for our forums. But in 2004, we began using students as moderators, both in forums with other students and for intergenerational groups.[1] Despite some initial apprehension, students feel a sense of empowerment and competence when they serve as moderators. In intergenerational forums, student moderators have also elicited admiration from the elders.

The success of intergenerational forums depends, in part, on what we might call informational and deliberative equality. Just as some

---

[1] We always have student comoderators—often two people for each approach in an issue book. This gives more folks the experience of being a facilitator and, especially when the moderator is a young student, reduces the anxiety of a single person having all the responsibility.

students are quick to excuse their ignorance about political matters by saying that older people have the time to learn about politics and to be politically involved, and they, the students, don't; other students—most notably a group of high-school students who took a semester-long course on deliberative democracy—complained that when adults have come with little or no formal forum experience, they tend to speak more than anyone else and to be less attentive to a spirit of inclusion. On such occasions, the comment we hear is that "these old people don't know how to participate in forums."

How the Young Respond

In recent years, intergenerational forums for the most part have been highly successful, particularly with regard to the process of deliberation. Like most other folks who have experienced NIF deliberative forums, both young folks and elders are virtually unanimous in praising the experience and value of these sessions. The spirit of inclusion, fairness, the importance of hearing different perspectives, of carefully weighing pros and cons of different approaches, and recognizing the difficult task of working through trade-offs to reach policy decisions and directions are acknowledged as highly important features of a democratic, inclusive society. Students particularly praise the role of the nonpartisan moderator (as opposed to a lecturer, still the central figure in most of their classes). All appreciate the opportunity for everyone to participate and to raise questions in a nonadversarial way.

Students who kept journals about their forum participation were uniformly positive when they evaluated the deep commitment of elders and when they spoke about how these forum experiences significantly affected their thinking and actions, particularly on the need to be civically engaged. Sue, a junior, who intends to become a teacher, said she was inspired to register to vote and pay more attention to politics because of the intergenerational forums. Paul, a senior film major, wrote: "The most encouraging element of the meeting was the level of care that the townspeople had. It became clear during the meeting that our government does not do nearly enough listening." Gina, a junior sociology major, reflected the visual shock of all students when encountering a gathering almost entirely of retirees:

> I did expect to see at least a few people under the age of sixty. The most pleasant surprise of the meeting was how informed everyone in the library was on the important issues in our country and around the world. Everyone who raised concerns had facts and figures to back up what they were saying. It seemed like the college students were the least informed people in the library that day.

Pat, a junior political science major, remarked, "Listening is a key element in the process of deliberation." He reflected on the forum experience this way:

> The gap between the level of interest in the political process among younger people and the elderly was on my mind after the forum. Perhaps it is because the elderly have more time to educate themselves on the issues. However, since younger people are usually in school, the question could be asked, "Why are they not being taught?" It occurs to me that our educational system needs to do a better job of teaching our young people the basics of American government and politics.

In all of these sessions, there is a growing respect and friendship among the generations, mostly because the elders have not acted as know-it-alls, condescending toward the young. Despite the film stereotypes of *Grumpy Old Men*, and Deborah Tannen's gender admonitions about long-winded, slow-talking, older men, our elder male participants, for example, have almost always been self-restrained (clearly our format and guidelines help), and they have actively sought to include younger folks so that their voices could be heard. In their own way, the elders themselves are ghettoized and welcome the opportunity to share views in a meaningful context with young people.

Perhaps the most positive effect of our intergenerational forums on students is this: that there was a demystification of the old that came from actually hearing people 30 or 40 or even 50 years older than themselves and learning that they were so caring about society and about the young.

How the Elderly Respond: Herb and Lou

The long-range effects of these experiences, as elders and students return to their regular daily lives, are not easily tracked. We have ample evidence that adults enjoy the discussions with the students, that they welcome the opportunity to work together and that they are enthusiastic about returning for more forums. We also know that these intergenerational experiences have stimulated some adults to change their own priorities, as they come to feel an increased obligation to the young and to encourage their civic engagement. The stories of Herb and Lou are good examples.

Herb, a World War II veteran, who participated in what was one of our first (unplanned) intergenerational forums in 1993, not only volunteered for many subsequent forums but also came to Hofstra regularly for other forums, talks, and cultural programs. All of this emerged from that first forum experience and led to his friendship with faculty and students. Herb, at age 83, was so eager to assist young people in reaching their potential and having an influence on public policy, that he became active in the Nassau Democratic Party (something he had not done previously). More striking was the focus of his civic activism, offering to coordinate projects to reach out to high-school and college students to bring them into the political process.

There was a definite charm in having a white 83-year-old volunteering to go into high schools and colleges to work with young people, particularly schools where as many as 90 percent of the students were African American or Hispanic. But Herb was not quixotic about this project; he developed a long-range plan for youth involvement, and he met with, and helped to revive, community Democratic clubs so they might more effectively take on this role.

Stimulated by his deep involvement with our university, and with people, older and younger, whom he met there, Herb wrote "A Citizen's Manifesto," which he self-published to convey his passion and commitment to others. He then became an advocate at public library programs for greater civic involvement among and more intergenerational activity for his retiree peers, telling them that they had a responsibility to leave the world better than they found it. Herb regularly, and publicly, admonished his peers that it was in their own best interest to avoid age segregation and to actively seek interactions with young people, which could be enjoyable and stimulating.

Lou was a New York City firefighter, who, at 55, retired as a lieutenant from the fire department. He began auditing courses at a local community college and became a voracious reader. Although Lou has been participating with us for 4 years, we only recently learned that he had been a 16-year-old high-school drop out, who later got an equivalency diploma in order to enter the fire department. "I didn't pick up another book until I had a chance to take the officer's test." Not withstanding his lack of a college degree, Lou certainly is among the best informed, most attentive and widely read of our regular adult participants.

Although Lou was clearly on his elder activist trajectory before he joined our projects, he, like many others, shows a deep concern about the civic engagement, education, and well-being of young people. He also recognizes, more than most adults, the challenges and the need to deal with the changing demographics in our area. He speaks with the knowledge of an insider. One of his recent efforts has been to reverse the decision of the Parks Department in his community to close the public handball courts. Lou's concern, reflecting his city youth, is that handball courts are places where people come together to play regardless of age, race, or ethnicity. The closing of the handball courts in his community, Lou asserts, is an obstacle blocking intergenerational associations. Sharing the game, according to Lou, takes priority over your race, ethnicity, and age.

Such civic engagement stories among the elderly adults who have worked with us can be repeated many times over.

An Array of Intergenerational Projects

The projects above were designed to be intergenerational deliberations. But ever since we became aware of the common age divide, we try whenever possible to provide an intergenerational element in ongoing projects. Here I describe several of our most productive efforts.

The Present in Perspective

Perhaps the most successful introduction of an intergenerational element into an ongoing project has been "The Present in Perspective: The Impact of Deliberative Democracy and Leadership in American Society," a special course developed by a senior New York State assemblyman, Thomas P. DiNapoli (a Hofstra alumnus); retired Long Island social studies teacher, Leon Hellerman; and myself. The students are mostly young undergraduates, who have had extensive experience in NIF forums and who have learned to serve as moderators. The course most notably includes a trip to Albany where the students meet with major leaders of the state legislature from both parties, affording an up-close opportunity to observe deliberative processes in our law-making bodies.

As a regular part of the course, forums are held among adults of different ages (though mostly retirees) and students, who not only participate but who also serve as moderators. The course's most powerful intergenerational forum used the NIF book *At Death's Door*, regarding approaches to terminal illnesses. Our elder participants had extensive experiences with death and dying, and the students came away with new and deeper appreciations of the travails of aging, often with a keen emotional feeling about what they had heard. These deliberations caused young people to think about public policy issues like physician-assisted suicide, which simply had not been on their radar screens. The intergenerational forums on "New Challenges of American Immigration" and "Racial and Ethnic Tensions" also revealed experiences and perspectives that generated lots of reflection for both the older and younger participants.

Former course students, who recently have gone into teaching careers and returned to the university to tell us they are using NIF materials and deliberative approaches that they learned in "The Present in Perspective," also emphatically state that the experience in this course inspired them to register to vote and to become more active in politics and their community. They emphasize that the deliberative experiences continue to shape how they interact with others, particularly with older folks with whom they had little prior interaction and for whom they now have appreciation and respect.

Deliberation and Candor in High School

Through our years of work with high schools, introducing their students to the techniques of deliberation, we developed a special relationship with the West Islip School District, which afforded us new perspectives on intergenerational relationships. At first, our work involved only the faculty. We conducted a Public Policy Institute over a period of two months for members of the Social Studies Department, teaching teachers the principle of deliberative forums and giving them the experience of being moderators and participants in forums. Several teachers then incorporated the use of NIF books and deliberative forums into their classes.

With the enthusiastic encouragement of Steve Lenowicz, the chairperson of the West Islip Social Studies Department, as well as of other faculty members (several were Hofstra history major alumni with whom, in some cases, we had relationships spanning over three decades), we then decided to work on developing a new course for the high school that would satisfy the New York State 12th grade "Participation in Government" requirement, using National Issues Forums with the students. We designed some forums to include both teachers and students. In several respects, this turned out better than we ever could have anticipated, and we gained additional perspectives on spanning the age divide.

One intergenerational forum with teachers and students was especially dramatic in its impact on the adults. The topic was drinking and alcoholism (for which we used the NIF issue book *Alcohol: Controlling the Toxic Spill*). Because of the forum's conducive framework, students felt free to express candid views about drinking practices and problems in high school, and, indeed, about disturbing experiences in middle school. All 15 of the adult (teacher) participants were stunned by the teenagers' revelations about what they and their peers did or observed on a regular basis. I consider myself fairly attuned to the lives of young people, but these disclosures were also surprising to me. They included students putting vodka in water bottles during the school day, and teens noting that they seldom ask each other, "Why are you breaking the law by drinking?" Instead, the more common question is, why aren't you drinking like everyone else? All of the adults were struck by the unanimity of the teens' views that few adults set effective parameters for their conduct regarding alcoholic beverages, and that, even when adults set boundaries, they did not pay attention to what was happening. It seemed to the young people that adults did not really want to know.

This particular intergenerational forum was a robust example of the insights that could be gained when people felt safe and affirmed in a deliberative context. Teachers said they had never had such candid interactions with high-school teens, and the students said they had never felt so invited—that their views and opinions were important to others.

Another significant development from the West Islip intergenerational work was that 12th-grade students who learned how to do issue framing working with adults, then took ownership of their projects by preparing their own issue books. Over the period of 3 years—each class lasted only 1 semester (16 weeks)—the high school published 6 student-generated issue books, beginning in the fall 2002 term: (1) *Iraq: Is It Time for War?* (2) *Iraq: Who Is Going to Clean Up?* (3) *Illegal Immigrants: Helping or Hurting the U.S.?* (4) *Hazing: Responsibility and Resolution*; (5) *Drink Up: The World Under the Bottle*; (6) *Raised … in America*. These books have now been used in high-school, college, and intergenerational forums. The West Islip students were the first to serve as moderators for their own issue books. The leadership of the high-school students was so outstanding that several newspapers wrote about the project and students were interviewed on National Public Radio.

We were also delighted to learn from West Islip high-school students that as a result of their involvement in deliberative projects, including the framing of the issue books, they discussed the issues much more extensively with their friends and their families. Many students said that taking an active role in issue framing and in forums enabled them to be catalysts for public affairs discussions with parents and peers, discussions they had not previously had.

Intergenerational and Diverse

Some of our best community forums have not only been intergenerational but also have been interracial and ethnically diverse. We have taken forums to the African American History Museum in Hempstead, the largest minority community in our county. In addition to our effort to involve people of color of all ages, one of our cosponsors has been a major regional Hispanic organization, Circulo de la Hispanidad. In these cosponsored forums, as well as in two dozen others throughout the county, we have focused on the NIF books *Racial and Ethnic Tensions* and *The New Challenges of American Immigration*.

These issue forums, as one might easily imagine, were highly charged. Many participants had a strong personal stake in the issues and in the direction of U.S. policy. Also, some participants were immigrants who had not entered the United States legally. To accommodate the illegal immigrants, we promised confidentiality as to their identity and their status; and because some were still learning English, we held some of the forums in Spanish and others with bilingual translations. Among the major exchanges were discussions raised by African Americans about whether new Hispanic immigrants were being accorded more respect and opportunity than people of color who had been here much longer.

The five forums that were part of this special program had the greatest diversity of any forums we conducted, in terms of age, racial, and ethnic groups. The younger people and the older folks each had their own take on the forums. Younger people commented that they were optimistic about the future because they believed that their age cohort was more tolerant and accepting of racial and ethnic diversity than were the adults. Older folks were impressed by the upbeat views of high-school and college students, many the children of immigrants or newcomers to the United States, who believed that their own hard work and commitment to education would still be an "open sesame" to acceptance and success in America.

Still, the "elephant" in the room was the same elephant that usually turned up in other NIF deliberations about immigration—the question of illegal immigration. In this case, several people of *all ages* defended the right of people to seek better lives in the United States and explained the contributions that illegal immigrants made to American society, often under enormous anxiety regarding the future and safety of their families. Others, *again of all ages*, while sympathetic to the desire of people for personal advancement, believed that disrespect for the law was harmful to society and unfair to those who were seeking to enter the nation legally.

Readers may also be interested in an unusual feature of an extensive two-year project, in Long Beach, a suburban city with the greatest diversity in our county. In addition to conducting intergenerational forums, we went a step beyond and created a "theater of the community" in which young people and adults role played alternative approaches to dealing with racial, ethnic, gender, and age issues that emerged from our deliberative meetings. I describe the project more fully in "Connections: Community Building in Diverse Areas" published in *Traditions, Transitions, Transformations in a Global Community: Proceedings of the Organization Development Network* (2001).

What Now?

As we look to the future, we anticipate having a wider and more sustained impact from our intergenerational projects. Our best news is that the work we have done so far has contributed to efforts to establish a Center for Civic Engagement at Hofstra University. This new focus on our campus will involve a broader array of faculty and students and will reach deeply into the metropolitan New York community. We will also be able to tap more extensively Hofstra alumni, who, like the graduates of most schools, are a valuable resource (and one that can be highly motivated and engaged, as its full potential is often untapped for purposes other than fundraising). The decade and a half of our Public Policy Institute endeavors, along with the institute's close association with the Kettering Foundation, have played a key role in the planning for the new Center for Civic Engagement.

As our Public Policy Institute developed, like most such groups around the nation, it faced the challenge of how to involve broader segments of the university community and use the talents and ideas of a diversity of faculty and students; now, we are poised to do that more effectively. With the emergence of the Center for Civic Engagement, we have been given a strong boost in this direction in 2006 by a grant from the Herman Goldman Foundation of New York City to help us focus on intergenerational civic engagement, with particular attention to the new demographics of our region and to the suburban-urban nexus.

One focus of our work will be coordinated activity with the university's Center for Suburban Studies, established by Hofstra's president, Stuart Rabinowitz, out of the awareness that Long Island, one of the nation's oldest suburbs, has been in the vanguard in dealing with accumulating challenges. We will work closely with the center, because many of its issues address concerns about an aging population, what it means in terms of supporting taxes for schools and the prospects for young people in an area where the median house price is now $400,000. One part of our expanded work will be to establish an intergenerational Web site where Web-comfortable youth can more effectively be connected with adults, many of whom are energized as they become more adept in using the Internet. We will continue to seek additional "safe places" (especially public libraries, but also schools, community organizations, and public facilities) where people can meet regularly for intergenerational forums and meetings. The more frequently people participate in deliberative forums, the more confident they feel about their own civic capacities; the ties among participants also become deeper and more lasting.

We will expand our local effort to engage more students and adults in a joint process of issue framing, particularly developing issue books that address the concerns of our region and our population. In these respects and others, we hope that Hofstra might become a model for effective intergenerational associations. We are eager to expand our direct work with schools (there are 100 school districts in Nassau and Suffolk counties); more of these schools and communities can benefit from the kinds of intergenerational projects that have already been modeled at West Islip High School.

Building on our ties with thousands of Hofstra alumni who are teachers, principals, and superintendents, we also intend to set up round tables in schools, which will bring in constituents from what used to be referred to as the PTA. While we have found that it is best to separate students and their parents for small discussions/ deliberations, our experience is that when they have addressed the same issues separately, they are very likely to compare their views afterward and continue the discussions in their own homes.

As our new center expands, we are considering making intergenerational NIF a regular part of the initial semester experience for entering freshmen at Hofstra. We have a contingent of nearly 300 retirees who meet regularly on our campus (many of whom have been regular participants in our past programs). Our larger challenge is to try to expand the age span so that it includes more people from mid 20s to 60. A major intergenerational aspect for our future endeavors is to take account of the expanding ethnic and racial diversity on our campus and in our region, and to address the gaps in perception and experience among folks in our connected (but often uncomfortable) urban-suburban nexus. Increasing numbers of our students are coming from New York City even as a love-fear attitude toward the metropolis continues to exist for many suburbanites—ironically, often among older folks whose own parents migrated to suburbia in order to escape the metropolis.

As for our research agenda, it will keep evolving as our experience with intergenerational deliberations grows. In regard to the effects of intergenerational forums, we look forward to assessing (1) how people of different ages view each other, before, during, and after these activities; (2) how they feel about the value of intergenerational contacts, not only in terms of age differences, but also with respect to the growing diversity of people in our schools and community; and (3) the extent to which these experiences lead to changes in the participants' level of civic engagement, including ways in which they approach complex issues, how they go about weighing pros and cons of different approaches, and the degree to which they feel confident that they can make informed judgments that can help to shape public policy.

In regard to the youth ghetto, we aim to investigate a central question: at some point does a deprivation of effective adult role models intensify the inclination of the young to turn more and more exclusively to their own peer groups?

We plan to do more tracking of the extent to which values of deliberative engagement are sustained over time. Part of the continuing assessment will include a focus on the impact of the intergenerational and diversity aspects of the forums.

An ongoing inquiry for us is how much involvement and experience is enough to have transformational value for the way people approach effective civic engagement. We are mindful of the observation of David Mathews, president of the Kettering Foundation, that "deliberative democracy is sort of like going to a gym for physical fitness—participating once or twice is not likely to do much good." Because our intergenerational programs will also bring together people who, because of age and ethnic and racial diversity, do not normally associate with each other during a typical day, we hope to move towards fulfilling Dr. Martin Luther King Jr.'s dictum: "We go farther faster when we go together."

Michael D'Innocenzo is a professor of history and The Harry H. Wachtel Distinguished Teaching Professor for the Study of Nonviolent Social Change at Hofstra University. A recipient of Hofstra's Distinguished Teaching Award who has also served as Speaker of the Faculty, D'Innocenzo for 15 years has been codirector of the Hofstra Public Policy Institute. He has specialized in bringing deliberative experiences to high-school and college students, as well as leading monthly "Current Events in Perspective" programs at five public libraries. He has been a newspaper columnist, a candidate for Congress, a founding member (and first chairperson) of the Long Island Alliance for Peaceful Alternatives (1985-present), national chairperson of United Campuses to Prevent Nuclear War (1985-1986), and served for 20 years on the board of directors of the Health and Welfare Council of Long Island and the New York Civil Liberties Union. Making use of the Wachtel Archives at Hofstra, D'Innocenzo is currently completing a study, "The Impact of the Nobel Peace Prize on Dr. King: Highlighting the Triple Evils of Racism, Poverty and War."

Chapter Two

Introducing Deliberation to First-Year Students at a Historically Black College/University

Lee Ingham

This essay describes the effort to introduce first-year students to deliberative democratic practices at Central State University, a Historically Black College/University (HBCU) in Wilberforce, Ohio, and one of a few HBCUs in the midwestern/northern area. Its students primarily come from large cities, and most first-year students have little or no experience in deliberative democratic practices. Using the civil rights movement as a model of student civic engagement, this paper focuses on the First-Year Seminar, a required, three quarter course sequence, which devoted one quarter to the Kettering deliberative issue guide Politics for the Twenty-First Century: What Must Be Done on Campus? *Supplementing this classroom work was a series of campus deliberations based on issue books from National Issues Forums (NIF). The objective of introducing first-year students to deliberative democratic practices was achieved, and a small group of students were enthusiastic about the possibilities of being civically engaged on campus, locally, and globally. The effort now will be to build on this foundation and increase the receptivity to NIF-oriented deliberations and the interest in and commitment to civic engagement.*

Introduction

In the fall of 2002, when I was a member of the Diversity Committee of the Southwestern Ohio Consortium for Higher Education, an organization dedicated to advancing higher education in the region, I participated in an NIF forum on affirmative action, along with representatives from several other member colleges and universities. My participation not only afforded me the opportunity to share in the vigorous discussions and exchange of ideas on the topic, but it also introduced me to the experience of a deliberative forum and to knowledge about NIF and its activities on college campuses. As an instructor in critical thinking at Central State University (CSU), a historically black college/university in Wilberforce, Ohio, the entire experience gave me the sense that the NIF deliberative model could help our students develop their argumentation skills and also help them become civically engaged in important social issues. I was in full agreement with the basic idea behind NIF: that the democratic process works best when citizens are knowledgeable about, and actively participate in, the deliberative processes that ultimately determine the policies that impact their well-being.

For some time, I had been quite concerned about our students' apparent lack of interest in political and social issues that had relevance to both their own lives and the life of the country. I very much wanted to find a way to use their educational experience at Central State to awaken in them a spirit of civic awareness, which I hoped would lead to civic engagement.

So, during the fall quarter of 2002, I arranged for three trained moderators from nearby colleges to conduct on the Central State campus three separate but simultaneous NIF forums about affirmative action. The forums were targeted for Central State's three Learning Communities cohorts, each consisting of 25 first-time students. I chose these particular students because I worked with them and had some control over their activities.

On the day of the forums, we found that one third of the students did not appear. I was quite disappointed. I was new to the forum experience and have since learned that even though, as I saw it then, *only* 50 of the 75 Learning Community students came, this turn out represented a more than respectable number and percentage. But I had hoped for more, and I might say, I still do. For better or worse, I have a strong desire to assist as many students as possible in developing an interest in and concern about the civic life around them.

Given fewer students than we expected, we conducted a single forum with three moderators, and I was pleasantly surprised at the results, especially when the moderators commended the students and congratulated them for their interest in and insightful comments on affirmative action. Seeing the enthusiastic participation of our students, I definitely felt that we could build on this positive reaction to promote civic engagement by bringing the NIF deliberative experience to our campus.

For two years now, the university has sought to introduce its first-year students to deliberative democratic practices. The presumption has been that at least some of these students would be inspired by their experience and would become advocates and practitioners of deliberative democratic processes on the campus and then, after they had graduated, beyond it.

The project is obviously at an early stage. In this paper, I describe what we have accomplished so far, the challenges that lie ahead, and some of the thinking and experiences that have fueled our efforts.

The Campus, Its Students, and the Need for Civic Education

The identity of CSU and the demographics of its current students are part of the story.

Central State University is Ohio's only public, predominantly African American institution of higher learning, with 97 percent of its approximately 1,600 students African American and the remaining 3 percent non-black or Hispanic students. One of the more pertinent facts about the student body is that 91 percent of it now comes from the nation's large cities and approximately 80 percent are identified as low income.

The conditions of our students' lives and their educational opportunities are such that one would suspect that not many have had any regular experience with deliberative democratic processes. The discussions I had with students supported this notion.

What I observed was part of an ongoing trend. I have been employed at Central State for several years, and over this period, I have witnessed, sadly, the steady erosion of student awareness of and commitment to social and political issues. I saw NIF deliberative forums as a "come back," so to speak, which, in its own way, could use the civil rights movement as a model for student engagement and involvement.

With the support of several faculty members who volunteer to teach the First-Year Seminar courses—at that time a year-long sequence of three one-hour courses that were required of all entering first-year students—I was able to get one full quarter dedicated to civic education. A questionnaire given to the students on the first day of the class confirmed our suspicions that they lacked knowledge of the formal workings of politics and lacked experience in deliberative democratic practices. The responses indicated that most had little knowledge about or even interest in policies that might improve their lives.

As far as those of us who were interested in bringing deliberation to Central State were concerned, this was all the more reason the university should make sure that when its students graduate, they are better informed, participating citizens of the world. Indeed, Central State's mission statement says as much. The statement commits the institution to "nurturing its students within a value-based environment focused on excellence in teaching and learning, and public service by academically preparing students with diverse backgrounds and educational needs for leadership and service in an increasingly complex and rapidly changing world."

Central State is not alone in the need to make such a commitment. According to Suzanne Morse, in her foreword to the issue guide *Politics for the Twenty-First Century: What Must Be Done on Campus?* most institutions of higher education *used to* (my emphasis) include civic education as an integral part of the educational experience. Morse writes, "Historically, colleges and universities have seen their role in society as preparing men and women for their private and public lives. Graduating well-educated responsible citizens was a clear mission that was articulated in both word and action." She goes on to explain that that mission is no longer so clear. "In the last half of the twentieth century,… the public part of the mission has found itself in competition with other aims and directions."

Today, educators and community leaders alike have called on our institutions of higher education to address the need to help our students engage in the public realm and to help them understand the murky societal processes that seem to eschew democratic debate while embracing the sophist philosophy of "go along to get along." The events of the last few years—the Supreme Court's involvement in the 2000 presidential election; September 11, 2001; the corporate scandals involving Enron and WorldCom; the continuing military engagement in Iraq; the attacks on affirmative action; and the recent natural disasters, including the Katrina debacle and its aftermath— have intensified the debate about the need for citizens to become engaged in public politics and the need for higher education to promote the civic engagement of its students. What better place and time to begin than in the students' initial foray into higher education?

Some Personal Reflections and the Civil Rights Movement as a Model

My own strong views about the purposes of a college education, along with my personal background, are clearly important sources of my efforts to bring NIF deliberation to the Central State campus. My highest hope for a college education is that it can and should be transforming. At a minimum, I believe that a college education should help students to know themselves and something about the world in which they live and to help them see the possibilities that lie ahead as a consequence of this knowledge.

In preparing citizens *for* the world, institutions of higher learning should not only help their students maneuver through the difficulties of attaining a college education but also help them become civically engaged. The requirement imposed by Congress, that institutions of higher learning that receive federal funds should observe Constitution Day, is one sign of the perceived need that such institutions should play an active role in producing an informed citizenry.

Although I have become aware of the work of NIF only recently, as I reflect on my experiences as a young person, deliberative democratic practices were exactly what were going on all around me, even if that was not what they were called.

I grew up in the Caribbean and came to believe that education is the key to any future success. I believed that then, and I believe it now. The education I experienced included learning about the important discussions of the day. And one of the hottest topics of the 1960s in British-ruled Caribbean island-countries was independence from British rule. While I was not of voting age at the time—I was only in my teens—I can remember the trepidation that some of us had about so dramatic a change. As the debates and discussions, pros and cons, went on, we wanted to know whether gaining independence would have a negative impact on our educational opportunities. I was present when two former British colonies lowered the British flag and hoisted the flags of their now independent countries. These events have left an indelible imprint on me.

In the late 1960s, when I came to the United States to attend college, I brought with me the curiosity I had developed about issues of the period. This curiosity was nurtured in college, and it was heightened as I gained knowledge about the civil rights movement.

I was not a participant in the activities of the movement. In fact, apart from recognizing the obvious reasons for these activities, I was largely ignorant of the events leading up to them. I became a keen observer, however. Martin Luther King Jr. was assassinated during my first year of college. That event, coupled with some of my experiences attending a predominantly white, private, southern Baptist college, resulted in my voraciously reading everything that I could find on the African American experience.

When I came to Central State University in the late 1970s as an instructor in the Philosophy and Religion Department, I was pleased to find a student body that was relatively engaged in the burning issues of the day. I believe this atmosphere was partly fueled by the weekly "Convocations," which brought nationally and locally known political, social, and academic leaders to speak to the student body. However, over the years I saw the student population become less and less interested in discussions on civic and political issues. This attitude was most lacking especially after the critical years between 1995 and 1997, when there was quite a bit of media attention focused on the "crisis" at Central State, fortunately not realized, about its demise as a state-supported institution of higher education.

It is the engaged, active atmosphere of the 1960s that I think NIF-oriented forums and discussions can create again. I do not see this as looking "mournfully to the past," but as a way to use the civil rights movement and Central State University history to serve as catalysts for motivating our students and demonstrating to them the real-world effectiveness of student-led deliberations.

From a historical perspective, the involvement in the civil rights movement of young people in general and African American young people in particular stands out as a *prima facie* example of civic engagement on college campuses. During this period, African American college students were civically engaged as they involved themselves in a struggle that had local, national, and global ramifications. Somewhat like myself, even those who weren't physically engaged were led by the very nature of the movement to become cognitively engaged in the impact their peers were having on American society.

Campus activity in the 1960s gave birth to several local, grassroots civil rights groups that became national in scope and, consequently, brought to the forefront several young, talented individuals with charismatic leadership styles, who gained national and international prominence because of their engagement in civic matters. Individuals like H. Rap Brown, Angela Davis, Julian Bond, Fred Hampton, and the late Kwame Toure (Stokely Carmichael) fueled the minds and imaginations of African American youth and were instrumental in changing the political and social fabric of American society. They imparted a belief that everyone was a stakeholder in determining the future of American society and that each individual could make a difference by becoming civically engaged.

In organizations such as the Student Non-Violent Coordinating Committee, the Congress of Racial Equality, and the Black Panthers, and from lunch counter sit-ins in North Carolina to the Freedom Riders in the southern United States, African American students took up the challenge. The students who "sat in" at the Woolworth lunch counter in Greensboro, North Carolina, in 1960, and demanded to be served in spite of their color, were freshmen at North Carolina Agricultural and Technical College. The Student Non-Violent Coordinating Committee came out of the halls of Shaw University in North Carolina and was the driving organizational force of sit-ins across the South. James Farmer founded the Congress of Racial Equality on the campus of the University of Chicago, following student discussions about discrimination. Based on my reading, the members of these organizations often came to their decisions through a deliberative process. One might say the stakes were too high not to.

The findings of the survey we conducted of first-year students might suggest that the entering students of Central State do not have even minimal knowledge about politics today, much less offer the possibility of giving rise to charismatic leaders. I see the situation differently.

I think it is fair to say that however factually uninformed about politics the students who come to Central State may be, many of them have some knowledge of or experience with political events, whether local, national, or international. What they lack, however, is careful reflection on the meaning of their knowledge or experience. This is why we want the students to think, reflect, and deliberate about issues that are so important. At this point, even as we keep in mind the civil rights movement as a model for a large body of actively engaged students, it seems clear that the initial impetus for student involvement at Central State has to come from those of us who value it and who then secure administrative and faculty support to sustain the opportunities for such involvement over the long run.

An essay by W.E.B. DuBois, "The Field and Function of the Negro College," written more than a half century ago, in 1954, is relevant here. DuBois wrote: "We hold the possible future in our hands but not by wish and will, only by thought, plan, knowledge, and organization." He continues, "If the college can pour into the coming age an American Negro who knows himself and his plight and how to protect himself and fight race prejudice, then the world of our dream will come, not otherwise."

This is still the challenge. As Gary Paul, a political scientist at Florida A & M University, itself an HBCU, states very clearly, "Historically Black Colleges and Universities ... must work harder to engage students more fully in democratic processes." He goes on to say that "more needs to be done to meet the challenge of growing distrust, apathy, and frustration among college students." I think Paul is correct in his analysis of the lethargy and malaise that seem to be pervasive on HBCU campuses. These are the institutions that were the "hotbeds" of student activism during the years of the civil rights movement.

Still, as Paul and DuBois before him remind us, the challenge is not only to the "Negro college" but to all of us trying to help students create a "brave new world" by becoming civically engaged.

The NIF Project at Central State

I recognize the ambitiousness of these thoughts. I also recognize that ambitious projects are built bit by bit. A process of this sort has occurred at Central State.

In the 2001-2002 academic year, CSU began to require all of its first-year students to enroll in the yearlong series of courses collectively called the First-Year Seminar. The broad aim of the courses was to help these students make a smooth transition from high school to college. The students were made aware of the resources available to them on campus, taught to develop study skills that would enhance their chances of being academically successful, and aided in understanding the relationship between the major discipline in which they chose to concentrate and their desired career path.

Later in 2002, the school started a new program, the Learning Communities initiative, to explore whether a more concerted effort would increase the students' ability to meet the demands of college. That fall, on a first-come, first-serve basis, 75 first-time students were enrolled in the new program and were placed in cohorts of 25. These students were given various kinds of "special" attention. They were clustered together in their classes, they lived together, studied together, and had opportunities to attend off-campus cultural activities. Their professors met on a regular basis to discuss the performance of the students and, in some cases, integrated their syllabi for collaborative student assignments.

It was during the same year, via the Learning Communities, that NIF deliberations became part of the larger effort by Central State to address the needs of first-year students and to widen their intellectual and civic horizons. Learning Community students, using an NIF issue book on affirmative action, conducted the first deliberation forum on campus. Since that time, all subsequent forums have been especially directed toward this group, even though campus forums are open to all first-year students.

Two years later, in the spring quarter of 2004, one full First-Year Seminar course was devoted to civic engagement. (See page 55.) The following description states the rationale for the course:

> As part of its mission, Central State University "academically prepares students with diverse backgrounds and educational needs for leadership in an increasingly complex and rapidly changing world...." The final course in the three-course first-year sequence is an attempt to remain faithful to the mission principle through an exploration of the state of civic engagement on college campuses, including Central State University, and its implications for the larger society and the world.

The text for the course was the Kettering Foundation issue guide *Politics for the Twenty-First Century: What Should Be Done on Campus?* which presented four alternative options for developing in students "the skills necessary for participation in a democratic society." (The four options are public service, acquiring deliberative skills, democratizing the campus, and a well-educated citizenry.)

The course was conducted as a seminar. The instructor's primary function in each of three classes was to serve as a moderator and to guide the students, who basically were responsible for conducting the classes.

A class consisted of about 25 students, who were divided into groups of 5 or 6 persons. Each group was responsible for presenting one of the four options in the text and for entertaining questions about it from the instructor and the other students. While this format is not a precise replica of the standard NIF forum, it offered our students an in-depth exploration of and deliberation about the issues.

To supplement the experience of the classroom deliberative experience, faculty, staff, and students conducted a series of evening NIF forums. These forums were public events, offered to the campus at large, and most First-Year Seminar instructors took forum attendance of their students into account when grading them.

Because the First-Year Seminar is a class, many of the students treated it as such. These students did what was required of them with little or no particular interest in the issues or the deliberative process. Other students actively participated and became "hooked" on the issues and the process and took part in evening forums. In one instance, three students agreed to moderate an evening forum on "Terrorism," which turned out to be one of the most successful evening forums—attendance was high, and interaction between students was more animated than usual. Another example of being "hooked" occurred when several CSU students watched one of the 2004 presidential debates and then, via video conferencing, participated in a deliberation with students at Kent State University on "Americans' Role in the World." One of the CSU students was so enthusiastic about the experience that she went on to moderate an evening forum on the same topic.

From my vantage point, attendance at most of the evening forums was modest (and low in one case), though again I need to say, I have high expectations. The following table contains the figures.

National Issues Forums 2004-2005 and Fall 2005

Winter Quarter	Attendance
January 11, 2005: "Alcohol: Controlling the Toxic Spill"	34
February 8, 2005: "Crime and Punishment"	38
March 15, 2005: "Terrorism"	37
Spring Quarter	**Attendance**
April 26, 2005: "News, Media and Society"	4
May 3, 2005: "Public Schools: Are They Making the Grade?"	11
May 24, 2005: "Americans' Role in the World"	19
Fall Semester	**Attendance**
October 18, 2005: "Alcohol: Controlling the Toxic Spill"	26

However one rates the levels of attendance, it is noteworthy that many of the students were "repeaters" who attended more than one forum. In fact, it was from these repeaters that we were able to draw on students to become moderators for subsequent forums. One student moderator put her experience this way:

> Before coming to Central State University I was unaware of forums. My freshman year of college was very new to me. I was very soft-spoken and really did not have much of an opinion about anything. The professor of my First-Year Seminar class made it mandatory for students to go to campus forums and express their feeling about various subjects or should I say problems that the American society is faced with today. Last year I began to be so involved in forums I volunteered to host a forum about the tragedy of 9/11.

I believe Forums helped me grow as a person. Over the past year I began to be more concerned about campus issues and I am very much involved in many organizations around campus. Forums gave me the ability to be more open about situations and helped me express my inner feelings in a more professional manner. I remember learning at a forum that the reasons why college students do not complain about many issues is because they are not aware of how powerful their voices can be. I decided right then that I was never going to allow my voice not to be heard.

As a teacher, even one such testimony helps make the hard work of bringing deliberation to campus worthwhile.

Still, it seems fair to ask: What is the appropriate measure to evaluate our deliberation program? Is the glass half full or half empty? In the midst of this effort, I am of two minds.

One could say that in the first two years of the program, we had only a single course to introduce our first-year students to deliberative concepts and practices. This meant an hour of classroom a week for approximately 12 weeks. But one could also say that this was a *full* course, not just a single class or two, and is far more than exists on many campuses. Further, the course was supplemented by the extracurricular forums, which instructors recommended to the first-year students. If we did not have a bonfire of deliberation, we certainly had a spark.

Still, the number of students who became attracted to deliberation was relatively small. I, of course, had hoped for many. But, on the other hand, we had repeaters, we had students who volunteered to moderate, we had students who found a new power and authority in themselves from the process of deliberating. Perhaps I can best sum up my own feelings by saying that I hope that in the not too distant future, students will become directly involved in the whole deliberative process of sponsoring, moderating, and creating campuswide forums. We definitely have taken a step in that direction—but we definitely have steps to go.

Currently, we face a new challenge. Because CSU has moved from a quarter to a semester academic year, it has reduced the required First-Year Seminar courses from three quarters to one semester. As a result, only two weeks are devoted to the issue of civic responsibility. We hope to meet this obvious challenge by conducting more forums outside the classroom (some forums will use NIF issue books) and making participation in them a condition for being in the Learning Communities.

Conclusion

Whatever the challenges, other faculty members and I plan to continue this effort to get our students thinking about civic responsibility and the deliberative democratic process. We will continue to use the limited time allowed in the First-Year Seminar class and supplement that with regularly scheduled evening forums. We are still very interested in seeing whether and how students will use deliberative practices in other classes. But our primary objective now is to get students intricately engaged in deliberative practices and policies in their campus life. Our long-range objective is to see how participation in these deliberative activities translates into greater participation among the larger student body.

Lee Ingham is currently the executive director of the Center for Student Academic Success at Central State University, where he works primarily with first-year students, helping them to make a smooth transition from high school to college and providing resources and opportunities for their academic success. Prior to his current position, Ingham was an instructor in the Philosophy and Religion Department at CSU, where he is a tenured faculty member. Formerly an adjunct professor at Antioch and Wilberforce universities, he received his BA from Carson-Newman College, his MA from Howard University, and has completed work toward a PhD at Vanderbilt University and the University of Cincinnati. He has been involved with the Kettering Foundation's Deliberative Democracy Seminar for the last three years.

COURSE DESCRIPTION

FYS 103: First-Year Seminar "Civic Engagement"

Required Text: *Politics for the Twenty-First Century: What Should Be Done on Campus?*

RATIONALE: As part of its mission, Central State University "academically prepares students with diverse backgrounds and educational needs for leadership in an increasingly complex and rapidly changing world." FYS 103, the final course in the three-course first-year sequence, is an attempt to remain faithful to the mission principle through an exploration of the state of civic engagement on college campuses, including Central State University, and its implications for the larger society and the world.

OUTCOME: Upon completion of FYS 103, the student should have a greater appreciation for the importance of civic engagement and how student involvement and leadership on campus has and still can contribute to democratic processes and outcomes.

COURSE STRUCTURE: The course will be conducted as a seminar. Students will be divided into four groups. Each group will be assigned an "option" from the text for which it is responsible for presenting the argument of that option and leading the classroom discussion on the assigned day.

The course is intended to provide a comfortable and stimulating environment that encourages each student to be an active participant by raising questions, presenting viewpoints, giving and taking constructive criticism without fear of being ridiculed. The in-class time will be used primarily for cooperative learning, discussions, and presentations.

Chapter Three

Individual and Community: Deliberative Practices in a First-Year Seminar

Joni Doherty

Deliberative dialogue has been part of the academic experience at Franklin Pierce University for the past eight years. In this essay, the author describes her experiences with integrating deliberative democratic theory and practices in the first-year seminar as part of an initiative designed to teach students about diversity and how to communicate effectively across differences. She also reflects on her own education as a teacher.

I came to teaching somewhat later in life than most of my colleagues, propelled in part by the need for meaningful and sustained connections with other people. Before I returned to school, I had spent 12 years working as a book designer and artist in my own studio in a rural setting, a relatively solitary working life. Out of this came a deep curiosity about my relationship—or apparent lack thereof—with the community in which I lived. What was my relationship, personally and professionally, with the communities that surrounded me? Driven by a combination of social desires and intellectual curiosity, I began taking graduate-level courses in gender and cultural studies. I loved being part of an academic community and the sense of being engaged with others in a common and purposeful enterprise. Based on this experience, and with the encouragement of my academic advisors, I decided to shift my professional focus, change my profession. As the director of my program put it, "It's clear you love being in school, so why not make a career of it?"

I Become Educated

In 1998, when I was hired at Franklin Pierce, a four-year, coeducational, liberal arts college in Rindge, New Hampshire, I knew very little about pedagogy. My approach was based on what I had observed as a student and my experiences as a teaching assistant and an adjunct. Franklin Pierce University was very attractive to me, in part because of the size of the undergraduate college (its annual enrollment is currently about 1,600 students, most of whom live on campus), and because I was intrigued by the theme of the core curriculum, "Individual and Community," which obviously resonated with my personal and professional interests. After all, the desire to be engaged in a meaningful way with a community was what had caused me to continue my education.

According to our mission statement, the hallmark goal of Franklin Pierce education is "to prepare its students to function well as citizens and leaders of a democratic society." All of our programs are "designed to help students achieve goals organized around three themes: tolerance and community; content literacy and integration with critical analysis; and holistic preparation for leadership and lifelong learning." Many colleges and universities articulate similar goals. Indeed, some see these goals as characteristic of a "liberal education" designed to instill in students the capacity and resolve to exercise leadership and responsibility in multiple spheres of life.

I soon became aware that many students had educational goals that didn't prioritize acquiring the knowledge and skills necessary for leadership, citizenship, and civic engagement. Instead our students' priorities are in sync with those of many other people their age from across the country. In 2004, a U.S. Department of Education study found that the top priorities of high-school seniors planning to attend college were getting a good job (91 percent) and a good education (89 percent) (Ingels et al. 2006). For many of the Franklin Pierce students I spoke with, the two merged. They measured the quality of their educational experience by how relevant courses were to their career objectives.

The priorities and expectations of these students corresponded with the Department of Education survey in other ways as well: only 20 percent of high-school seniors from across the country believed that working to correct social and economic inequality is important, and slightly less than half thought being an active and informed citizen was a priority (Ingels 2006). These students weren't necessarily opposed to being active in their communities, but it wasn't a priority or, oftentimes, even seen as an option. They believed that they had to become established in their careers and achieve some level of financial security first. Some students even believed that they probably wouldn't be able to become actively engaged in their communities until retirement—in other words, for another 40 or 50 years!

Given such views, it isn't surprising that it was difficult for many of them to connect in personal and specific ways with the university's mission statement, as much as they might agree with its general principles. Genuine enthusiasm for the core curriculum and its "Individual and Community" theme was too often lacking. For a time, I accepted this as an intrinsic part of the challenge of teaching. In retrospect, I wonder how I could have forgotten so quickly that the reasons that drew me back into school were deeply embedded in *my personal goals* for connection and companionship and in *my professional interests*, which were clearly affirmed by the core's theme and the university's mission. As I look back, I wonder that it took me so long to realize that for students to be deeply committed to learning, authentic connections must be made between *their interests* and course content. In some important sense, my own diversity education fundamentally began when I truly understood the need to bridge these kinds of differences.

The teacher-centered approach within which I was operating didn't stop at content. I now see that I used the same pedagogical style that had always worked for me as a student, a seminar-style approach in which most of the class period was spent discussing the assigned readings. How repetitious it must have seemed to too many of my first-year students! However, it had worked for me, so that's what I did. Sometimes I would start by asking whether anyone had any questions about the reading. They rarely did. I am an avid reader, as are some of the students, but it quickly became clear that many did not fall into this category. Sometimes class discussions were lively, but too often they fell short of my expectations. It often seemed that I was working much harder than my students were.

It was right about this time that I came across "Contemporary Understandings of Liberal Education," an article by Carol Geary Schneider and Robert Shoenberg, which discussed a variety of "hands-on, inquiry-oriented strategies," including collaborative inquiry, experiential learning, service learning, research- or inquiry-based learning, and integrative learning (Schneider and Shoenberg 1998, 7). My own strategies suddenly seemed remarkably uninspired, but I wasn't certain how to implement what they described. In an effort to become a more effective teacher, I enrolled in a summer workshop on something called "deliberative dialogue," led by the New England Center for Civic Life, at the time a relatively new academic institute at Franklin Pierce. The workshop brochure promised that it would teach faculty ways of improving class discussions. That sentence alone was enough to get me to sign up.

As I participated in my first deliberative forum, I immediately realized it was rich with concepts and practices that I could integrate into my teaching. The storytelling that occurred during the "personal stake" period at the beginning of a forum creates a bridge between each individual's life experiences and the subject-at-hand. The inclusion of beliefs and priorities along with the analysis of factual information created more entry points for participants. I was also intrigued by the unexpected intersections between deliberation and the theoretical approaches of deconstruction and feminism, which are important in my own scholarly pursuits. In all three, acknowledging the value of multiple perspectives, some of which may be competing or even contradictory, serves to create a rich array of interpretive possibilities. All of these theoretical approaches recognize the inherent value of diversity and resist the impulse to define difference solely in terms of conflict. For example, Jacques Derrida once simply described deconstruction as "openness to the other" (Derrida 1998, 124). Both feminism and deliberative democracy depend on inclusive practices so that the various and sometimes competing concerns of all stakeholders can be considered. Furthermore, as a feminist, I appreciated the value placed on finding a balance between subjectivity and objectivity in deliberative practices. Rita Gross, a religious studies scholar and a feminist, has written that after genuine objectivity, empathy is "the most central and critical value." Empathy, she wrote, is "mentally entering into the spirit of a person or thing and developing appreciative understanding." Gross has identified four essential values that are required for the development of this perspective: objectivity; empathy; finding, fostering, and promoting genuine pluralism; and a critical stance (Gross 1993, 313). I have found the same qualities are essential for any successful deliberation. (I note for the record that Gross does not promote cultural relativism, nor do the practices I describe in this essay eliminate the necessity of making and abiding by well-informed and ethical judgments.)

Deliberative practices contain a range of practical pedagogical approaches that offer concrete means of involving students in active and engaged learning situations in and out of the classroom. I began to realize that creating a learning-centered environment was much more complex than simply moving from lecture to discussion. Deeply impressed by what I had learned at the workshop, I was ready to begin relinquishing my newly acquired "sage on the stage" status for that of "guide on the side." (I am still learning how to get out of the way.) In this essay, I reflect on my deliberative experiences in the classroom and my work with colleagues in the Diversity and Community Project, an initiative of the Center for Civic Life, which seeks to integrate deliberative practices into the higher-education environment. I am committed to assisting students to develop a sense of agency and the capacity to articulate their ideas in a manner that has intellectual integrity and compassion. I do not want them to be silenced by the fear that speaking openly will create conflict, but instead to understand that appreciation for diversity and the ability to communicate across differences are essential for realizing our democratic ideals.

The Diversity and Community Project

The Center for Civic Life developed the Diversity and Community Project to reduce tensions that arose after several racial conflicts on campus and to foster an awareness of and respect for diversity. Using deliberative practices patterned on those developed by the National Issues Forums (NIF), we held forums on topics related to gender, race, ethnicity, and sexual orientation. We also used the Sustained Dialogue model developed by Harold H. Saunders, director of international affairs at the Kettering Foundation. As a result of these activities, a continuing place for deliberation on our campus in academic and student life has been developed and sustained. Since 1999, the Diversity and Community Project has been part of Franklin Pierce's first-year program.[1]

The basic challenge we faced was how to develop ways of engaging the predominantly-white campus community in meaningful discussions about diversity. Today, the project has three interrelated components:

> *First-Year Seminar Deliberative Dialogue Initiative:*[2] This integrates deliberative theory and practices (which include participating in deliberative forums and exploring content related to race, ethnicity, gender, sexual orientation, and socioeconomic class in course readings) into the Individual and Community Seminar, which is required for all first-year

---

[1] The project was adapted on other campuses in northern New England through the Northern New England Diversity and Community Project, a collaboration between the New England Center for Civic Life and Vermont Campus Compact. Both were funded in part by grants from the William and Flora Hewlett Foundation and the Institute of Museum and Library Services and received substantial support from Franklin Pierce University.

[2] At Franklin Pierce, we use *deliberative dialogue* to refer both to forum-based discussions and to classroom discussions that follow the same principles of discourse as those used in the deliberative forums. (See box page 67.)

students. Instructors can decide whether and to what extent they want to incorporate this initiative into their courses.

Deliberative Forums Initiative: Throughout the academic year, the center convenes six sets of forums that address diversity topics. Three topics are presented in the fall and three in the spring. Depending on the level of interest in each topic, three to five forums will be held over a one-week period, with 18 to 20 participants at each site. Participants include students who are fulfilling course requirements and others—including faculty and staff—who are drawn because of a particular interest in the issue being addressed. In addition to the campus forums, some instructors hold forums in their classrooms during regularly scheduled class times. Each set of forums may be fulfilling curricular, cocurricular, and extracurricular interests. In a typical fall semester, approximately 400 participate in the forums. These are primarily first-year students, some of whom may participate in more than one forum. All forums are comoderated by a team comprised of a faculty member and a "Civic Scholar," the third interrelated component of the Diversity and Community Project.

Civic Scholar Program: Each year up to 10 upper-class students become Civic Scholars. These students learn how to moderate deliberative forums and participate in a year-long program. Civic Scholars collaborate with the center's faculty, who mentor them. Both the faculty and the Civic Scholars participate in planning and assessing projects and activities, in addition to convening and moderating deliberative forums.[3]

When we developed this project our plan seemed straightforward. We would use deliberation to bring the issue of diversity to first-year students. But we soon found that we first had to teach

---

[3] Some Civic Scholars volunteer to be "peer leaders" for first-year students, who are divided into "peer groups" of 18 to 20 students, to ease their transition to college. Each peer group receives a peer leader—who in some cases is a Civic Scholar—and a faculty advisor.

deliberative theory and practices and develop an atmosphere of trust before we could explore diversity.

Deliberation and the Individual and Community Seminar

Integrating the project's Deliberative Dialogue Initiative into the required first-year seminar, with its Individual and Community theme seemed a natural fit. The seminar is designed to assist students to:

- Become familiar with the Individual and Community Integrated Curriculum, including the Goals of the Student Experience at Franklin Pierce;
- Develop critical-thinking skills;
- Accept the academic challenge of college-level writing and oral communication;
- Learn collaborative skills;
- Become actively involved in the community;
- Explore issues in modern America that challenge us to integrate our rights as individuals with community responsibilities; and
- Understand the evolution of concepts, such as free choice, beliefs, values, independence, and autonomy, in the context of their relationships to community standards.

In addition to typical course requirements, such as reading and writing assignments, class participation, and exams, all students are expected to complete a civic engagement project. Each student is expected to work approximately 10 hours during the semester on a community-based activity and then make an oral presentation about the experience to the class. In addition, some instructors require a written report.

The deliberative version of the seminar integrates the theory and practices of deliberative democracy with the study of diversity topics. In addition, the use of curricular and cocurricular forums extends the learning environment beyond the classroom into the surrounding community to assist students in making connections between theoretical concepts and real-world experiences. In short, the goal was, and remains, to have students engage in experiential civic education focused on diversity.

Today, the deliberative version is used in approximately one third of the 30 or so of the first-year seminar sections taught each fall. In most cases, the faculty teaching the deliberative dialogue sections have attended at least one of the NIF workshops led by the center, at which faculty are introduced to deliberative theory and practices. Those who integrate the Deliberative Forums Initiative into the first-year seminar do so to different degrees. Some simply use the classroom ground rules for deliberation developed by faculty associated with the project. (See accompanying box.)

Ground Rules for Classroom Deliberations

This is a dialogue, not a debate.

Everyone is encouraged to participate. No one person or group should dominate.

Treat all participants as equals.

Listen to each other with empathy. Disagree respectfully.

Listening is as important as speaking.

Examine your own assumptions as well as the assumptions of others.

Explore the advantages and disadvantages of each position.

Speak from direct experience, not hearsay.

Our goal is to move toward greater mutual understanding of the issue.

Try to imagine what others who are not present might say.

Other instructors ask their students to participate in one or more forums during the semester. The forums are intended to assist students in developing two key skills: expressing themselves clearly and listening attentively (which is measured by the ability to state the viewpoints and perspectives of other speakers). Deliberation also makes explicit the ethical nature of the issues under consideration. Through participating in forums, students acquire an appreciation for diversity and a more sophisticated understanding of the complexity of the problem being addressed.

A handful of faculty incorporate a fully integrated approach, which includes assigning course readings that explore diversity, using the classroom ground rules for deliberation during class discussions, and asking students to participate in several forums, both in and out of the classroom. In some courses, students learn how to moderate forums or develop their own discussion briefs. Some faculty develop a single civic engagement project for the entire class, such as teaching students how to moderate forums or creating a discussion guide. In other sections, each student works individually on a community service project. The group project further develops students' ability to work collaboratively and it provides them with a common experience to reflect on. The array of interpretations that can arise out of a seemingly common experience is a surprise to many students. They begin to see that each one is based on a particular set of assumptions and experiences, that these are different for different people, and that finding common ground requires analysis and communication. Obviously, the more diverse the group, the richer the experience will be.

Assessing and Modifying the Diversity and Community Project

I need to take a step backward now and explain why, in our original conceptualization of the project, the forums did not always work according to our expectations. Initially, the forums were integrated into course requirements but never scheduled during class time. Instead, they were held at various times and locations across the campus and open to the entire university community. Students from each class were directed to various forum locations so they would not be with their classmates. In this way, the students presumably would engage in dialogue with other members of the campus community and thus would gain a wider range of perspectives which they could share with each other when they were back together in the classroom. Sometimes there were as many as 50 participants in a single forum, ranging from first-year students to seniors. In the planning stages, this all seemed to be very well thought out. However, throughout the past six years, I have regularly had cause to reflect on a question once posed by a colleague: "This all sounds fine at 30,000 feet. What does it look like on the ground?" And the answer turned out to be, "Unpredictable!" The forum experience was —too often— intimidating and silencing for the first year students.

Each year, during our annual retreat, the center's faculty reviews the past year and makes modifications based on what we've learned. We realized that the complex skills we were aiming to develop in students simply required more time and practice than initially anticipated. We learned that we needed to explicitly identify the differences between the skills necessary for deliberation and the content we hoped to introduce about diversity, and to be sure both were being properly taught and accurately evaluated. We learned that we sometimes were placing students in situations they weren't prepared for. We learned that we needed to create and maintain an atmosphere of security to facilitate the risk taking necessary for students to develop new skills. We learned that if we were to gain and maintain faculty and administrative support, we had to be clear about the goals and expectations of the deliberative journey of the first-year seminar. We came to see that if a group of first-year students was learning how to deliberate, the quality of critical thinking and communicative skill was going to reflect just that. It takes time and practice to develop the ability to listen attentively, process what has just been heard, and respond in a thoughtful manner. In other words, we needed to teach skills as well as content, not simply provide course content about diversity and then expect the students to be able to engage in open and thoughtful deliberation.

The rough spots were most obvious at the campuswide forums. Many students found these forums to be positive learning experiences, whether or not they actually spoke. Some first-year students always felt comfortable about speaking up in this venue; upper-class students regularly participated. Feedback from reflection papers and anonymous postforum questionnaires indicated that the first-year students were being exposed to new perspectives regarding diversity. Some indicated surprise that other students their own age had had so many different experiences and different opinions. There was general agreement that holding public discussions was beneficial because it got everyone thinking about important issues. All this was on the positive side. However, too often, too many would sit quietly and listen to the handful of the more outgoing— or courageous—voices, who ended up dominating the forums. We were exposing our students to new ideas, but it was not at all clear that those who did not already feel comfortable with speaking in a group setting were learning how to do so as a result of their deliberative experiences.

During our first few years, some faculty and administrators were fairly critical of the quality of students' contributions in terms of both content and manner of expression. The harshest comment I heard came from a faculty member who stated, "It's just a bunch of kids sharing what they don't know with each other." One forum visitor recommended that we simply replace the forums with small interactive workgroups to ensure content was mastered, completely dismissing the value of any public dialogue. And so we learned it was important to be clear about the dual, but closely integrated, goals of (1) teaching students how to deliberate with each other about (2) potentially divisive issues related to diversity. We were not simply attempting to convey information to them but to engage them in an experiential way. We believed that deliberation, in and of itself, is the practice of diversity, because it is based on the assumption that the only effective way of addressing persistent and difficult ethical issues is to communicate effectively across differences. Therefore, we did not want to divorce practice from content.

But even as these doubts and concerns were being voiced, it seemed that in an amazingly brief time everyone on campus had heard about deliberative dialogue, and many were familiar with what had been discussed in the forums, even if they weren't present. During a student/faculty softball game, when someone quipped that we needed to deliberate about a controversial call, it was clear that the Diversity and Community Project was becoming part of our campus culture.[4]

Developing Forums for Peer Groups

Our students helped us reorganize our program. During the classroom debriefing sessions after a forum, students often asked if we could hold class forums rather than participate in the campus-wide series. It was becoming increasingly obvious that separating students from their peer groups for the campus forums and expecting them to speak publicly about potentially divisive issues with a group of people they didn't know, was profoundly discomforting, if not downright terrifying for them. This may seem like an exaggeration, but I believe I am not overstating the intensity of the feelings expressed by some of my students.

Possibly their sometimes-extreme discomfort was partially fueled by the transition from being seniors in high schools to being the newcomers on campus. As first-year students, they were anxious to fit in and make new friends. Terms like *clean slates* and *fresh start* were regularly used in the essays on their college goals,

---

[4] This indeed has happened. We have attempted to have deliberative sessions during our faculty meetings. Although we have not yet done this in a systematic and consistent way, we are still working on it! Deliberation has been used to address a range of issues by both faculty and students over the years, including administrative challenges like core curriculum review and prioritization, and issues related to academic and campus culture.

which they all wrote at the beginning of the semester; they were focused on not making "mistakes," either socially or academically. So, while teaching citizenship skills and diversity content were priorities for us, for many students the first priority was to find a place for themselves in a new social structure, and they weren't about to blow it by saying what might not be well received in a public setting in front of people they had just met.

The students worried about potential teasing afterwards if they didn't express themselves skillfully or voiced a perspective that wasn't generally accepted by the other participants. In an essay reflecting on a forum experience, one student wrote, "I would rather talk in front of judges and teachers any day than be in front of my peers. Speaking in front of students my own age and even younger makes me nervous because I feel like they are judging me." Another student summarized her reluctance in this way, "After you finish teaching, you go home. I live here." Others indicated a reluctance to say anything for fear of hurting someone else's feelings unintentionally; one student said, "Whenever it's about race, I'm afraid to say anything."

In response to the repeated requests from my students, I began holding forums during class time. These were comoderated by the group's peer leader (assigned during orientation weekend at the beginning of the school year, when the peer group is formed) and me.[5] Just as someone learning to ride a bike seeks out a quiet road rather than a busy street, so students who are learning and practicing new deliberative skills often prefer an environment that feels stable and secure—which for many means being with a small group of people who already know and accept them. Students are familiar with their peer group, and hopefully they trust their peer leader and know what to expect from me. Some of my colleagues may view this as "hand-holding" or, worse, lowering academic

---

[5] I have been very fortunate that most of my peer leaders have also been Civic Scholars. However, we do not have enough peer leaders who are also Civic Scholars for the number of faculty using the deliberative versions of the Individual and Community Seminar.

expectations. However, what I am describing here is neither thera-
peutic nor remedial, but simply meeting students where they are
to create the conditions necessary for them to excel academically.

During class discussions, we sit in a circle so each person can see
the face of everyone else in the room. Although this may seem
like an insignificant detail, I have always been struck by how it
ensures that the quality and tone of the conversation remains respect-
ful, even if there is strong disagreement. Since my seminar meets
twice a week and each session is 75 minutes long, I set aside two
class meetings for the forum to allow plenty of time for the story
telling, which is a particularly important part of the deliberative
experience for first-year students. Then we spend a third class
meeting debriefing, being sure to cover both process and content.
Depending on how the class has progressed in learning the practices of deliberation, about one half to two thirds of the way into
the semester, I will ask students to participate in a campus forum,
presenting it as a challenge for which they are well prepared. The
focus on teaching deliberative skills in an environment that builds
confidence has resulted in both higher participation rates and more
thoughtful deliberations in the public forums.

In retrospect, all this seems amazingly obvious, but it took us
some time to learn that breaking up peer groups was not the most
effective way to teach first-year students how to develop deliberative and critical thinking skills and to cultivate the habit of public
deliberation. Today, the students remain in their own peer group
for the first forum—that is, they have their own forum on the
chosen topic in their own classroom. The group is then split in
half for the second and any subsequent forums they participate in
outside of class. We also make a great effort to limit the forum size
to 18 to 20 participants, the same number of students in a typical
peer group. Half of the participants in a forum will come from
one peer group, ensuring plenty of familiar faces. In addition, the
familiar size of the group will encourage repeated participation by
everyone present, thereby reducing the intimidation factor caused
by a large group of unfamiliar participants. The other 50 percent
of forum participants may be from another section of the first-year

seminar a course offered by a major or minor program (most typically, American studies, criminal justice, English, history, mass communication, philosophy, sociology, or women's studies), or the general campus population.[6]

Preparing to Deliberate

As we were restructuring the Diversity and Community Project, we were also adjusting the way deliberative practices were integrated into the course. Initially, we had put a tremendous amount of energy into developing good moderators in the belief that this would result in good deliberations. But, we discovered that although a forum might have a successful outcome in terms of increased understanding of the topic, this wasn't our only goal. Remember, we were trying to teach students how to communicate across differences and be active participants and leaders in their communities. Clearly, achieving this was going to require much more than simply asking them to attend a forum. And so we began to consider how we could develop a set of practices designed specifically for teaching the theory and practices of deliberative democracy to first-year students.

I began to spend more time in class identifying and practicing the skills needed for deliberation, and asking students to look at how it differed from discussion and debate. My intention was not to promote one over another, but to get students to begin thinking about different modes of communication, and how one might use a particular style depending on the situation. To use a rudimentary comparison, just as some projects require a hammer and others a screwdriver, there are times when debate may be the best choice while at other times deliberation may be needed. To develop more awareness about these different modes, we now spend one class

---

[6] Careful coordination is required between the Center for Civic Life and the faculty using the Deliberative Dialogue Initiative to ensure that we have sufficient locations and moderating teams lined up and that students are directed to the correct location for their peer group.

session on an exercise adapted from NIF moderator training. Pairs of students are recruited to discuss, debate, or deliberate about the same question. Between each role-play, the entire group reflects on the differences in body language, tone of voice, and the style and content of each exchange, and how that affects the relationship between the two people and the outcome.

I also ask students to keep a log that lists all the different styles of communication each utilizes during the course of one day and to note how these shifted depending on the context. When students report back on their observations, the whole class explores the various situations they encountered. During this reflection period, we consider questions such as:

- When did you feel comfortable expressing your ideas and opinions?
- When did you feel constrained?
- What was the relationship between content and style of communication?
- Did whom you were speaking with influence what you said and how you said it?
- What were the differences between content and style depending on the context (the dorm, the classroom, a student club meeting)?

Not only have these experiences provided a foundation for understanding the theory and practices of deliberative democracy, they have led into an examination of more abstract concepts such as power relationships and the conditions necessary to exercise the right of free speech. All of this is solidly grounded in the students' own personal experiences, not only in the classroom but everywhere on campus.

During class discussions, sometimes I asked students to "say back" what the previous speaker had said before making the next contribution. To do this successfully requires comprehension, interpretation, and integration into the next comment in fairly rapid succession, so initially the pace of the discussion slows down. The content, however, immediately becomes more substantial, especially with regard to relevancy and more in-depth commentary. At other times, each person is asked to explicitly integrate some aspect of what had been said by the previous speaker into the following contribution to the discussion. (The goal is to confirm that the current speaker heard and understood the previous comment, not to foster consensus or agreement.) Both exercises demand attentive listening, a skill that is not emphasized enough in education, or in our culture overall. As one colleague pointed out during one of the center's retreats, "Listening should be recognized as one of the liberal arts." These exercises foster the consideration of other perspectives, sharpen critical thinking, and assist in the development of the skills needed for thoughtful public deliberations.

Introducing Diversity

So far, I have concentrated on the practices and conditions that foster and support deliberation. What about diversity, the topic we want to explore through deliberation? Depending on their particular disciplinary expertise, faculty members who are teaching the seminar address the theme of Individual and Community—and diversity—in different ways. For example, diversity may be explored through socioeconomic class, gender, sexuality, race, ethnicity, religion, as well as on local, regional, national, and global scales. There is also a fair amount of faculty choice in selecting readings and developing writing and other course assignments, including the civic engagement projects.

Early in the semester in my classes, when students are still getting to know each other and me, I have found it productive to introduce the exploration of diversity with a forum on a subject that the group doesn't perceive as divisive. Although my choice may seem counterintuitive, one topic that I have used successfully is the NIF discussion guide *Violent Kids: Can We Change the Trend?* During the class forum, we explore how violence affects middle- and secondary-school children, a focus that chronologically has the advantage of being one step removed from the students' current peer group and environment, yet is filled with familiar reference points. Another topic that has worked well, because everyone in the room has just engaged in a sustained exploration of this very issue, is *What Kind of Education Do We Need After High School?* The diversity connection becomes apparent as we examine the effects that socioeconomic class have on how one defines the issues-at-hand and how the resources of individual families and communities affect options for addressing the problem.

Not only is our campus population predominantly white, as I noted earlier, but most students have grown up in the Northeast—in New England, New York, and New Jersey. Many are the first generation in their families to attend a four-year liberal arts college. In spite of this apparent homogeneity, there are significant differences among them because of their different hometown environments (rural/suburban/urban) and their different socioeconomic classes. They tend to attribute educational and financial success—or failure—solely to individual effort, with little awareness of the impact that larger social structures, group membership, or even their family's socioeconomic status may have had on their lives. So, this is where we begin, with the diversity that already exists in the room. Only after students have acquired some skill and comfort with their deliberative practices, and with each other and me, do we move on to additional diversity issues that may be outside of their direct experiences. Course readings, primarily autobiographical, bring additional perspectives into the classroom. Texts like *Revere Beach Elegy* by Roland Merullo, *Honky* by Dalton Conley, and essays from *Beyond the Whiteness of Whiteness* by Jane Lazarre act as a bridge between more familiar personal experiences and new perspectives. *White Privilege*, edited by Paula Rothenberg, provides the historical and theoretical foundation. "The Possessive Investment in White-ness," an analytical history of structural racism in the United States by George Lipsitz, frames the central question of my seminar: What are the effects of social, cultural, and economic structures on indi-viduals? How do these assist or block individuals from realizing their personal goals? (Indeed, how do they influence the very definition of those goals?) The dream cherished by so many—that personal effort and will power can overcome any obstacle, and that success is the result of an individual's effort—is challenged in the following passage from Lipsitz's article:

> If we believe social life is the sum of individual actions, we define racism as an individual act of hostility. Systemic and collective behavior becomes invisible and past and present systems and actions that channel rewards and resources toward one group and away from another do not appear racist, yet these systems and actions reinforce racial identity and white privilege. They give "people from different races vastly different life chances" (Lipsitz 2004, 77).

This essay challenges students to consider within a public context an issue that many of them see as personal. This lies at the very heart of the Individual and Community theme. Many students are unaware of the ways racial discrimination is integrated into our social structures. Instead, they often perceive it as a problem caused only by individuals who are either hateful or who behave badly. Racism then becomes solely a problem of appropriate personal behavior. Through a combination of course readings and forums that ask them to consider an array of personal and public approaches to addressing racism, students begin to see the deep ties that bind the personal and the public realms.

Because deliberative experiences make students aware of significantly different life experiences among their peers (who seem similar to them on so many levels), they become more open to considering the impact of cultural, economic, and political structures on the lives of even the most motivated individuals. These insights can be extended to other areas of difference, including religion, socioeconomic class, gender, social orientation, and ethnicity. Once the students become more sensitive to the wide range of human experience that exists in even an apparently homogeneous group, they recognize the consequences that differing life experiences can have on individuals or groups. Even though they may not have personally experienced discrimination, or at least may not be aware that they have, because of the stories shared during the forums, they realize that it still exists. Instead of dismissing discrimination and social inequity as "something that was taken care of in the 60s" or "a problem for your generation, not for ours," their engagement with these issues is more complex and dynamic. In this context, we consider questions like:

- What can be achieved by individual effort? What are the limits?
- Are there cultural, economic, and political structures that enhance an individual's likelihood of success?
- Can the same structures that provide some with advantages present obstacles for others?
- Can you identity the factors in your life that enhance or limit your options?
- What, if any, is your responsibility to others?

Although not all my colleagues would agree with me, I see important distinctions between civic education and partisanship. For example, when we hold a forum, we are not advocating for a particular outcome or simply seeking to promote tolerance. Instead, our intention is to create an environment in which individuals who may have fundamentally different values and priorities can engage with each other in a dialogue that results in everyone having greater respect and understanding for each other and a more comprehensive understanding of the issue. If we can achieve this during the deliberation, the outcome is bound to be just. Therefore, I believe it is my responsibility to create a deliberative environment that fosters the acquisition of knowledge and skills needed to make well-reasoned judgments about ethical issues, and not to advocate for particular outcomes.

I would add two related points. First, most of the forums conducted on our campus and in our classrooms do not result in actions; instead, students are asked to make judgments together about the best possible approaches for addressing the problem-at-hand. Second, in an academic environment, the development of knowledge and skills can be considered very respectable outcomes for a deliberative forum.

The Civic Engagement Project: Engaging Diversity

Each fall, my class participates in a group civic engagement project (though any student who wishes to develop his or her individual project is encouraged to do so). These projects have provided students with valuable firsthand experiences regarding diversity. During the first several years, the seminar students held forums for seventh-graders and ninth-graders in Fitchburg, Massachusetts, using the *Violent Kids* discussion guide. Teams of three college students moderated forums for 16 or so younger students during an hour-and-a-half session. Each member of the team takes a turn at moderating.

Although Fitchburg is only 20 miles from our rural campus, it is quite different in its ethnic and economic diversity and its urban environment. Our college students work closely and collaboratively with these children. What up to that point was a fairly academic and abstract study of diversity topics now was suddenly embodied in the facial expressions, gestures, and voices of a very lively group of middle-school and high-school students. Convening and moderating these forums was quite demanding for the first-year students. Not only were they required to think critically, listen carefully, and facilitate a dialogue, but the energy level of the younger students was intense, and attention spans tended to be brief. The first time we visited the schools to hold forums, I feared I had gone too far—asked too much. I was wrong. Both sides loved the experience.

The college students learned that the younger students were able to propose actions for addressing problems beyond those presented in the discussion guide. For example, one Fitchburg group came up with the idea of having students keep a journal and setting aside a little time each day to express anger or frustration through writing and drawing rather than acting it out in classrooms and hallways. Another group proposed giving class credit for participating in clubs or other structured after-school activities. They believed this would help kids who have trouble with social skills or whose family or neighborhood environments are not safe. Since most of the college students had come from much more affluent socioeconomic environments, many of the stereotypes they had about so-called "inner-city" kids were shattered. They were deeply impressed by the resilience and irrepressible energy of these younger students and by their pragmatic solutions to difficult problems. And I discovered that learning could take place in a noisy and, at times, chaotic environment.

Seminar students have also moderated forums on immigration and the quality of public school education for high-school students in Peterborough, New Hampshire. Demographically speaking, this school district is more similar to the high-school environment of many of our college students. Although the actual age difference is only one or two years, the college students marvel at how "young" the high-school students are. This "maturity gap" highlights for them how much they have already learned in one short semester at college. That they are now back in a high-school classroom in a leadership capacity is something most had never imagined they would be able to do so soon in their lives, if ever, and is a great confidence builder.

Although the student moderators often are extremely nervous during the days leading up to the forums, they are exuberant about the experience on the ride back to campus. Here are some characteristic statements:

- Every time that I have had to make a presentation in front of a class, my face would turn red.... I feared that would happen again. But I was wrong. I will admit that I was nervous at first, but then as we got to the first choice, I began to relax. Then to my own surprise, I said something.... I learned that I do have the courage and ability to speak in front of people.

- After participating in this forum, I feel more confident in myself. I get very nervous when I have no reason to be. I have always been a well-prepared person.... Once I heard their comments during the other choices, I changed my whole approach.... I threw away my note cards and asked questions that directly affected them.

After the forums, each team writes a group report summarizing the outcomes, and analyzes participant responses using quantitative data from pre- and postforum questionnaires and qualitative data from comments recorded during the forums. In addition, each team member is asked to write a personal reflection. The following are typical comments based on the students' experiences:

- I think that having to lead a discussion on the subject made me learn more.
- You want to know the topic well enough to not make a fool of yourself.
- When I approached the forum, I wanted to learn all sides of my choice and learn a lot about the other choices too. That way I could keep the discussion on my choice and not allow it to wander.

Based on this civic engagement experience, a number of students decide to become Civic Scholars, and the following year they find themselves teaming with faculty to moderate forums in Franklin Pierce classrooms and across campus. Others become active in the Student Government Association or other service-oriented clubs. In the few short months of the semester-long experience, their long-held assumptions about the need to prioritize personal success over community engagement has been reconsidered. The two are now seen interwoven.

Several years ago, the first-year seminar faculty voted to change the name of this requirement from Community Service to Civic Engagement because we wanted to emphasize the mutually-beneficial and educational nature of the exchange, rather than as one group providing a service for another. Integrating deliberation into the projects is one way to ensure that this will occur. For example, one student moderating team's report about a high-school forum described the reciprocal nature in this way:

As a civic engagement project, we were successful in raising an important issue to members of the community, even though they were younger. They had interesting opinions to share with us, and we did a good job of taking those opinions and producing an insightful discussion.

The college students here are engaged in a form of public scholarship, which has been carefully crafted to maximize opportunities for them to learn content and develop skills in addition to engaging the younger students. It is clear to me that everyone (including me) learns a great deal from these kinds of projects.

"An Education of Lasting Value"

One of my goals as a teacher is to provide access to knowledge and skills that will help my students acquire a public voice and to realize that they have valuable contributions to make to the communities in which they live. My desire to help others do the same is unquestionably informed by my own experiences as someone who, for many years, was fairly isolated from the life of my community. I did not believe I had the power to speak in a meaningful way to public issues or to be active in ways that were personally meaningful. The issues seemed unapproachable, and I felt ineffectual and disengaged.

The changes I have experienced in my life have much to do with the open exchanges, based on trust and reciprocity, that I now regularly enjoy with many colleagues and students. Trust and reciprocity, it seems to me, are essential for acquiring a public voice— or, as it is sometimes called, free speech. As Jane Tompkins writes in her powerful memoir, *Life in School: What the Teacher Learned*, "Most people work most happily when they belong to a community of people who are there to support, encourage, and appreciate them." But these conditions, she claims, do not exist in most higher-education environments because people are often isolated through too-busy schedules, competition for resources, and the "absence of a culture of conversation" (Tompkins 1996, 188-191). Tompkins concludes her meditation on the isolation of academic life with a warning: "If the places that young people go to be educated don't embody the ideals of community, cooperation, and harmony, then what people will learn will be the behavior these institutions do exemplify: competition, hierarchy, busyness, and isolation" (Tompkins 1996, 194). The same competitive and fast-paced environment experienced by faculty also exists for students. As I reread her words, I am reminded of the statistics that I cited at the beginning of this essay. Numerically, they paint the same picture—a society in which each person is focused on individual success, disengaged from community life, and detached from concerns about the social and economic well-being of others.

When students are reluctant to express their views in a public forum or the classroom, they sometimes defend their behavior as "politically correct." This understanding of political correctness— as an impulse to withdraw—is fueled by a desire to maintain group solidarity. They do not want to rock the boat. Somewhat ironically, the reluctance to speak about controversial issues springs out of caring deeply about relationships with others. Talking publicly about issues, particularly those connected with diversity, may damage one's standing in the group, or is seen as only deepening the problem. Therefore, silence. Yet to have free speech, everyone must believe that they are free to speak. The culture of conversation— public conversation—is the foundation of community. How can we create the necessary conditions for students to exercise their right—even their obligation in a democratic society—to speak?

The answer lies in fostering an environment in which students can rely on the respect and trust of their peers, just as we faculty need to rely on the same from our colleagues. Deliberative dialogue seeks to create spaces where people can safely remain open to new perspectives, be self-reflective, and examine their underlying assumptions. The ground rules used in deliberative dialogue call for the cooperation Tompkins finds so lacking in most academic communities. At one and the same time, deliberative pedagogical practice explicitly validates the experience of each student (and each faculty member) while asking for additional perspectives. In this context, differing views are understood as an opportunity for inquiry, not conflict. Only at such a moment can we and our students begin to develop perceptive and open-ended questions and truly engage each other. This is the beginning of learning— not only to have enough trust in the group and confidence in one's self to share ideas, but also to wonder genuinely what others are thinking.

In closing, I want to comment briefly on the relationships between deliberative democratic pedagogical practices described in this essay and the recommendations for the reorganization of under-graduate education made by the Association of American Colleges and Universities (AAC&U). In *Greater Expectations: A New Vision for Learning as a Nation Goes to College*, the AAC&U urges that institu-tions of higher education foster learning-centered environments in which the increasingly diverse student population now attending college can acquire the knowledge and skills needed to "meet the emerging challenges in the workplace, in a diverse democracy, and in an interconnected world" (National Panel Report 2002, vii). It is clear that what the report recommends is what faculty associated with the New England Center for Civic Life at Franklin Pierce have been doing since 1998. Five of the eleven "Organizing Educational Principles" the AAC&U endorses are characteristic of deliberative pedagogical approaches:

- Values collaborative work,
- Links critical thinking to real-life problems, often involving contested values,
- Interprets education as an informed probing of ideas and values,
- Develops creativity by valuing personal experiences, and
- Celebrates practical knowledge
  (National Panel Report 2002, 44).

In short, the AAC&U believes that institutions of higher education are becoming increasingly diverse and that students need the skills and knowledge to live in a diverse democracy and an interconnected world. One way of realizing these goals is to integrate deliberative democratic practices in the classroom, in institutional decision making at every level, and in civic engagement and public scholar-ship projects. The deliberative practices developed for first-year students at Franklin Pierce meet the challenge posed by *Greater Expectations* in affirming diverse perspectives, values, and life experiences as essential components for "an education of lasting value" (National Panel Report 2002, vi).

Not only does the use of deliberative dialogue help to create an atmosphere of open communication that fosters inquiry and an appreciation for the value of community and diversity, but it is also an essential habit of mind for people who live in a democratic society. As Terry Tempest Williams writes in *The Open Space of Democracy*: "The human heart is the first home of democracy. It is where we embrace our questions. Can we be equitable? Can we be generous? Can we listen with our whole beings, not just our minds, and offer our attention rather than our opinions?" (Williams 2004, 83). We must attend to the emotional as well as the intellectual life of our students by creating environments that ensure all of our students are truly free to speak and to be listened to with respect and attention. For me, as for many of my colleagues at the New England Center for Civic Life, deliberative pedagogies, such as those I have described here, help that to happen.

Joni Doherty is director of the New England Center for Civic Life and teaches in the American Studies Program at Franklin Pierce University. She is editor of the College Issues Forums, *a series of discussion guides developed in collaboration with students and faculty at Franklin Pierce and directs the Diversity & Community Project, an initiative developed to foster awareness of and respect for diversity.*

References

Derrida, Jacques. *Of Grammatology.* Trans. Gayatri Chakravorty Spivak (Baltimore, MD: The Johns Hopkins University Press, 1998.

Gross, Rita M. *Buddhism After Patriarchy: A Feminist History, Analysis, and Reconstruction of Buddhism.* New York: Albany State University of New York, 1993.

Ingels, Stephen J., Michael Planty, and Robert Bozik. "Seniors' Values and Plans." *A Profile of the American High School Senior in 2004: A First Look.* U.S. Department of Education. 2006. http://nces.ed.gov/pubs2006/2006348.pdf.

Lipsitz, George. "The Possessive Investment in Whiteness." *White Privilege: Essential Readings on the Other Side of Racism*, ed. Paula S. Rothenberg. New York: Worth, 2004.

National Panel Report. *Greater Expectations: A New Vision for Learning as a Nation Goes to College.* Washington, DC: Association of American Colleges and Universities, 2002.

Schneider, Carol Geary and Robert Shoenberg. "Contemporary Understandings of Liberal Education." Washington, DC: Association of American Colleges and Universities, 1998.

Tompkins, Jane. *A Life in School: What the Teacher Learned.* Reading, PA: Addison Wesley, 1996.

Williams, Terry Tempest. *The Open Space of Democracy.* Great Barrington, MA: Orion, 2004.

Chapter Four

The Deliberative Writing Classroom: Public Engagement and Aristotle in the Core Curriculum at Fordham University

Maria Farland

This essay argues for the value of deliberation in the introductory writing classroom. Focusing on a first-year writing course taught at Fordham University, the author describes the use of democratic forums and issue-framing exercises as tools for improving the logic and rhetoric of student assignments. She reports on a range of writing assignments that invited students to connect their oral arguments in deliberative forums with writing strategies in the classroom. In the concluding section, the author reflects on the wider applications of this deliberative approach to the classroom, suggesting links to higher-education initiatives concerning institutional mission, active learning, and student engagement.

"[T]he essential need is the improvement of the methods and conditions of debate, discussion, and persuasion. That is the problem of the public."

John Dewey, *The Public and Its Problems* (1927)

Nearly a century after Dewey's observations on "the problem of the public," many Americans share his sense of the importance of public deliberation and better public engagement. Most U.S. universities state their commitment to educating students for citizenship and civic life, and yet many agree that civic engagement —whether measured in terms of voting, democratic participation, or membership in associations—is on the decline. The 2000 Higher Education Research Institute's annual survey of college freshmen confirmed this assessment, reporting that student interest in politics was at an all-time low for an election year.

To explain this political alienation among young people, some critics cite what linguist Deborah Tannen terms "the argument culture"—an all-too-common tendency towards agonistic debate, and an unwillingness to engage with other views, particularly when uncomfortable issues are at stake. Students, for their part, frequently adopt a pose of uncritical apathy and ironic detachment. As columnist David Brooks observes in a recent article about students at top universities, "When it comes to character and virtue, these young people have been left on their own."

As a response to the decline in civic engagement among the young, a number of figures working in the field of civic renewal have focused on the value of deliberation, citing the positive effects of opportunities to deliberate about public issues, especially within the campus community. Theorists like Benjamin Barber, Jane Mansbridge, and Robert Putnam argue that meaningful public talk and deliberation can combat cynicism and alienation among the young and can empower citizens to believe that they can affect change in their communities. Barber terms this approach "strong democracy," suggesting that it will transform both disempowered citizens and communities and apathetic campuses.

It is my belief that such deliberation and engagement can also empower students in their writing. When writing takes place against the backdrop of a series of deliberative forums in which students come together to examine in a broader public conversation the issues addressed in their writing, students' firsthand experience of the complex value choices inherent in each topic allows them to write from a position of authority and knowledge. In particular, the debates surrounding each issue provide writers with "motivation," both in the everyday sense and in the sense specific to the study of rhetoric and persuasion. For scholars and students of rhetoric, motivation designates the "intellectual justification, rationale" or the "facts and arguments used to support a proposal" (Williams and Columb 2003, 45-73). Foremost, student writers must learn the importance of motivating arguments, which involves both making readers care about them and making readers see the logical steps, facts, and justification that might lead someone to support them.

Undergraduate core courses—particularly writing courses—provide a rich context in which to make available opportunities for reasoned disagreement, productive dispute, and practices of democratic deliberation. Deliberation encourages what one practitioner in the field of freshman writing calls "the give-and-take of reasons, where the history of a disagreement and the various positions taken in response to it are treated critically and justly." Deliberation is committed to exploring the range of positions taken in response to difficult social problems. Various positions are treated critically and fairly, and each approach, or "choice," is presented neutrally and without prejudice. In this way, deliberative approaches stand in stark contrast to the culture of professional expertise in which the role of the academic professional is to employ specialized knowledge in order to endorse a particular pragmatic or conceptual solution. Beyond the clear and concise presentation that we expect of students' oral and written arguments, the deliberative classroom invites students to situate and differentiate claims; to establish the logical soundness of arguments and evidence; and to justify the reasons for an action or belief. It builds on and complements existing methods for teaching rhetoric, persuasion, and logical clarity and invites students to link these skills to debates within the community, both on the campus and beyond.

This essay details an experiment with deliberative pedagogy in a first-year seminar at Fordham University taught in spring of 2005 and spring of 2006. Like other seminars in Fordham's writing program—anywhere from 40 to 50 seminars each semester—the course examines the rhetoric and ethics of academic argument. My approach situates the teaching of argument within the framework of a deliberative approach to analysis of social problems that have no easy or straightforward answers. These problems include (but are not limited to): concerns about our treatment of crime and the nature of punishment; the debate about race in America; the growing concern about the state of our environment; America's changing and uncertain place in the world; concerns raised by the news media and popular entertainment; and issues surrounding world peace and ethnic conflict resolution. Kettering Foundation President

David Mathews calls such problems "wicked problems" (from a paper by Horst Rittel and Melvin Weber), and their very intractability makes them particularly suited to the first-year core curriculum, in which the goal is to introduce skills in moral deliberation and intellectual debate.

"Talking About My Generation"

Each seminar in Fordham's writing program develops its own unique content. In my seminar, the focus is the problems and challenges facing today's generation of students as they are portrayed in a number of formats—the essay, the documentary, the newspaper and television editorial and news story, and the historical monograph. In responding to these issues in the seminar context, students draw on their own experiences, concerns, and observations about student life and community. The broad goal is to provoke reflection and deliberation on the main issues of concern to today's students, including the kinds of difficult social problems that reverberate from the wider community onto the campus. Reflecting this emphasis, the seminar is titled "Talking About My Generation"—a title that makes reference to the current generation's opportunities for public engagement with issues that affect them directly.

As in any writing course, the primary aim is to refine students' writing skills through frequent written assignments and exercises. Employing Aristotle's five rhetorical strategies (or *topoi*) of invention, about which I will say more presently, students develop their writing skills in a series of brief three-paragraph essays. Each essay foregrounds one of the five topoi: identifying and describing; comparing and contrasting; exploring relationship; examining circumstances; and using authorities and sources. Students also develop related skills—such as note taking, researching, outlining, and revising—that are crucial to successful writing. Seminar workshops treat specific writing skills through exercises and examples from Joseph Williams and Gregory Columb's *The Craft of Argument* and from student papers, which are excerpted (anonymously) and distributed for discussion. Assignments progress from shorter, inductive tasks to longer, research-based term papers.

Students read a range of popular and scholarly texts produced in response to the earlier-noted difficult social questions raised about their generation. The deliberative classroom involves student writers in meticulous research, sophisticated thesis formulation, balanced evidence gathering, and an evenhanded consideration of a range of possible counterclaims, weighing alternative inter-pretations and comparing analyses that have been made or that might be made in response to the issue under scrutiny. Most of all, the deliberative classroom highlights the importance of reasoned argument, when argument is understood as driven by a set of underlying values and value tensions, and when, after closely reading and confronting a range of formulations and evidence, effective argument involves accounting for and weighing the trade-offs involved in different approaches to an issue.

Aristotle's Topoi and Deliberative Pedagogy

Traditional approaches to writing instruction frequently stress variations on Aristotle's topoi, the rhetorical strategies of invention made famous by the Greek philosopher. Karen Gocsik, director of the Dartmouth Writing Program, describes the topoi as Aristotle's effort "to formalize a system for coming up with, organizing, and expressing ideas," observing that they provide "a series of questions that you might ask of a text—questions that might lead you to interesting paper topics." Gocsik usefully summarizes the topoi:

1. Use Definition
2. Use Comparison
3. Explore Relationship
4. Examine Circumstances
5. Rely on Testimony and Authorities

In today's undergraduate writing curriculum, the topoi frequent-ly make their appearance in the familiar compare-and-contrast assignment, or in exercises designed to prompt critical thinking on difficult logical operations, such as the relationship of causation. At times, the very familiarity of these exercises can make them predictable and stale (few classroom exercises are more reviled than the compare-and-contrast assignment). Yet the logical and rhetorical operations contained in the topoi are indispensable to virtually every form of academic and nonacademic writing. Claims about causation, claims about circumstances, and claims about precedent—to take three elements in the third category of Aristotle's topoi (explore relationship)—arise in nearly every situation in which persuasive speech and writing are required. In our times, as in ancient times, they are indispensable to persuasive writing and speech, and yet all too frequently they are devoid of connection to broader social questions.

For the topoi to function with maximum effectiveness and persuasiveness in today's classroom, they must be reconnected with their origins in deliberative and democratic practices. In Aristotle's time, rhetoric described the art of speaking persuasively and in public. The topoi provided a set of ideas or guidelines for using language so as to persuade others, and the setting for such persuasion was the *agora*, or "public square." *Rhetoric* was the body of rules to be observed by a speaker or writer in order to express himself with eloquence and persuasiveness. Our most venerable techniques for elegance in writing thus have their ancient roots in situations when elegance of speech was paramount.

In the modern classroom, as in the ancient agora, the teaching of writing can benefit from the reanimation of rhetoric's origins in forms of public engagement. This reanimation of the settings of Aristotlean rhetoric does not demand nostalgia for Athenian democracy, or, as has become popular among some conservative critics of liberal arts education, an emphasis on "great books." In the Middle Ages, rhetoric was considered one of the seven "liberal arts," taking its place, with grammar and logic, in the *trivium*. Rhetoric's strategies were not confined to elevated or arcane subjects, but were seen as useful—much as basic grammar is useful—to everyday situations.

The Everyday Issue of Alcoholism

For our deliberative writing classroom, I focused our attention on social issues that were actively present in the campus community and part of a larger social community as well. One example of this kind of direct connection to students' daily life can be seen in a series of writing assignments dedicated to a central campus issue: alcohol consumption and policy.

In keeping with our deliberative focus, we began with a deliberative forum on the alcohol issue. Students used the issue guide, *Alcohol: Controlling The Toxic Spill* (Kendall Hunt, 1998). Published as part of the National Issues Forums discussion series, the issue book provides a framework for deliberation concerning the $145 billion worth of problems caused by alcohol consumption in our society.

Building on our work in the forum, we explored the alcohol issue using Aristotle's ideas for invention. For example, a discussion of alcohol that employs Aristotle's dictum to "use definition" might seek to define *alcoholism*, perhaps with the intention of showing that many people who believe themselves to be social drinkers may in fact be alcoholics. Similarly, a definition-driven discussion might use division or taxonomy to consider the range of types of alcoholics or stages of alcoholism. An alternative use of definition that employs contrast might examine the similarities between alcoholism and other forms of addiction, such as drugs or gambling, or between alcoholism and mental illness. Other modes of contrast involve observing difference. For example, attitudes toward consumption of alcohol differ from culture to culture (a fact that is almost uniformly noted by students). Contrast can also be employed to stress *degree*. Arguments might consider whether it is better for students to consume alcohol than marijuana; whether it is better to ban alcohol or to encourage responsible use of alcohol; or whether alcoholism is better understood through medicine or criminology. Across this range of approaches, student writers employ Aristotle's dictum to use definition to consider aspects of the alcohol issue as it affects their campus community.

Aristotle's topoi also direct writers to explore relationship. Perhaps no relationship is more complex than causation, and student deliberations regarding alcohol provide an ideal context in which to explore the validity of arguments about antecedents and consequences. For example, many experts believe that the causes for alcohol consumption are genetic; others believe they stem from psychological inadequacy, or a weakness of the will. Surprisingly, student opinions in Fordham forums have taken issue with the notion—expert testimony notwithstanding—that alcohol abuse can be traced to genetic or innate biological causes. But the very question of whether alcoholism is a disease raises broader questions surrounding antecedent and cause. Is it possible to be a recovering alcoholic? If alcohol is known to damage unborn babies, should alcoholics who are pregnant be considered criminally negligent? Claims about antecedent and consequences are always complex, but in the case of alcohol, that complexity is often very readily apparent within campus culture.

From these thorny questions surrounding claims about causation, students moved to consider an issue relating to an alcohol policy that may be unique to Fordham: Does the university's scheduling of classes affect alcohol consumption? In 2004, a Fordham task force concluded that the university's relative lack of Friday classes had been the leading cause of binge drinking on and around campus. The administration moved to overhaul the system for class scheduling, instituting a schedule of Monday through Friday classes, in the belief that this change would reduce alcohol consumption on campus.

In the spring semesters of 2005 and 2006, my students responded to this policy in a written assignment on causation, employing peer interviewing to assess the validity of the policy's assumptions about causation. Student writers concluded that the policy was based on a "conclusion [that] fails to account for the many reasons college students drink." Rejecting the administration's notion that class schedule has a causative effect on drinking habits, students offered fascinating accounts for the multiple causes for rampant alcohol use on many U.S. campuses. "[T]here is big business in providing eager underage drinkers," wrote one class member. Others agreed, citing the ways in which local businesses compound the problem: "In the Bronx, it seems that unless you look twelve, all you need to get a bottle of liquor is a twenty dollar bill," one writer observed. "It's easier to buy alcohol in the Bronx than it is to find flashcards to study for a test." Interestingly, several student writers cited "heavy workload" and "academic pressures" as reasons for drinking. "Many students drink because they are emotionally distressed," explained one paper, citing the widespread campus use of beer as a stress reducer and sleeping aid.

Careful consideration of campus policy allowed students to confront Aristotle's final topoi: "use testimony and authorities." The alcohol policy pointed to the kinds of testimonials, statistics, maxims, laws, and precedents to which writers and speakers have recourse when they employ the testimony of authorities. Do our rules regarding alcohol make sense, given scientific evidence that tells us that alcoholism is a medical condition? Do our rules regarding alcohol hold up under scrutiny, given that alcohol is a leading killer? Such questions arise in the context of a consideration of causation and the challenges of establishing causation. But they also raise the question of the uses and misuses of expertise and expert testimony, and the ways in which we establish laws based upon contested evidence.

What is at stake in these kinds of written and oral deliberations is not so much the question of how certain policies might affect alcohol consumption, but rather the question of the difficulties and challenges that inhere in making claims about causation and antecedents. Broadly speaking, the use of deliberative techniques in the classroom allows students to see the broader set of choices that might arise with respect to a complex social issue like alcohol and drug use. Paired with the Aristotelian topoi, these techniques foster more rigorous "methods and conditions of debate," to employ Dewey's phrase, in which students assess the logical and rhetorical effectiveness of their claims.

Such assessment does not confine itself to an issue like alcohol. Properly introduced, issues like affirmative action, or ethnic and racial conflict, have direct bearing on campus culture and events. The use of deliberative discussion guides (such as the National Issues Forums guides), as in the example of alcohol policy, can forge creative connections between national and campus issues, in ways that allow students to use examples from their personal experiences as a link to engage with issues of larger political significance.

Apathy and Student Engagement

Deliberative approaches stress the range of possible positions that can be taken in response to challenging social problems. Such evenhandedness stands in sharp contrast to many forms of debate within the ivory tower. They also provide an important antidote to widespread assumptions of faculty "bias," whether in the sense of prejudice toward a particular political party or toward a particular methodology or viewpoint. Beyond this emphasis on balance, deliberative frameworks blend conceptual and pragmatic approaches to motivating arguments, in ways that alert students to the subtle interplay of practical and interpretive elements within most real-world debates.

As noted earlier, motivating arguments is a central issue in the study of rhetoric and composition, and most handbooks in rhetoric and composition divide modes of argumentation along lines of practical and interpretive problems, as seen in Williams and Columb's guide, *The Craft of Argument*. (See Figure 1.)

Figure 1

Pragmatic Problem: What must we do to change this?

Conceptual Problem: What must we do to better understand this?
(Williams and Columb 2003, 46)

As the authors explain, most argumentative writing addresses itself to one of these kinds of problems, and much academic writing divides itself along similar lines. In traditional, expert-based academic approaches, researchers frequently separate the conceptual from the pragmatic. Moreover, their chief aim is to endorse a particular pragmatic or conceptual approach, and professional culture often resembles the zero-sum game of interest-group politics. In deliberative approaches, by contrast, writers strive for neutral, evenhanded presentation of the full range of both conceptual interpretations of a social problem and the pragmatic solutions that reflect these different understandings. Practical and interpretive dimensions of a problem are considered together, rather than separately, and each choice presents both a unique view of the problem-at-hand and a corresponding solution reflecting the values and motivations that underlie the approach.

In our seminar, students confronted the problem of motivating arguments through the problem of student apathy. This emphasis on student motivation—or the perceived lack of it—brought the problem close to home, while also inviting students to employ the devices of Aristotle's third topoi, causation and relationship. In an early assignment, students were asked to assess the validity of the claim that "today's students are apathetic." To kick off this assignment (see Figure 2), I distributed a series of newspaper

---

Figure 2
Assignment #5: Student Apathy

Each year, it seems that fewer and fewer students vote, while more and more people express disenchantment with politicians and the American government. Based on your research, address the following questions:

1. **Paragraph #1:** Apathy. Why has this transformation taken place? What caused this disenchantment? Be as comprehensive and specific as possible.

2. **Paragraph #2:** Consequences. What other problems does it create?

3. **Paragraph #3:** Causality. Based on what you have written, come to some conclusions about cause and effect and the challenge of finding causes for problems. Think about how you determine responsibility and blame. In light of what you have concluded, how do you arrive at solutions?

---

editorials on student disengagement (they seem to be especially plentiful during election years) culled from major newspapers. The assignment models itself on the classic three-paragraph assignment.

In subsequent writing assignments, students employed research (in the library and on the Internet) to assess recent trends and patterns in civic engagement, comparing the trends among today's students with changes in the population as a whole. The goal of these assignments, an exercise that makes use of Aristotle's "use definition" and "use comparison," was to reassess the stereotypical view of students as apathetic. In my experience, students respond strongly to any attempt to label them as a group. Building on this strong reaction, I have incorporated related assignments in which, for example, students assess the validity of a series of newspaper articles labeling their generation as "Generation Debt." While the labels change from year to year, the urge to label each generation as less caring than the last seems to persist.

Yet there is ample evidence to counter the labeling of today's youth as indifferent and apathetic, and my students' recent research has revealed that some forms of public engagement are on the rise. Popular campaigns like MTV's "Rock the Vote" and Sean Coombs' "Vote or Die" suggest a countertrend towards political engagement, particularly surrounding elections. The rise of community-service programs, especially programs on college campuses, and the rising participation in such programs, provide vivid illustrations of the kinds of engagement characteristic of the current generation.

I also allow students to compare their generation to previous generations through a screening of the film *Berkeley in the Sixties*, a documentary based on extensive footage of the Free Speech Movement and other collective student action during that decade. Following a viewing of the film, students employed techniques of compare and contrast, as well as techniques of classification and taxonomy, to assess the validity of claims about their disengagement against the tangible visible evidence of the activism of past generations. Students argued eloquently against the apathy thesis, with many suggesting that campus policies—especially policies restricting free speech on campus—have a chilling effect on public engagement. One student wrote eloquently of a roommate who "did not engage in voicing her own beliefs because she was afraid of getting in trouble." She quoted a student leader at the University of Memphis, who observed that, "There's no action, nothing. You're not allowed to do any sort of political activity without approval." Campus newspapers prove particularly useful for the research component of these assignments and are available through the Lexis-Nexis University Wire, which can be found in most university database libraries.

In the examination of student apathy, as in the study of student alcohol use, my seminars incorporated deliberative forums, most of them made available through the National Issues Forums discussion guides. Our discussion of student engagement employed a guide produced by the Kettering Foundation, *Politics for the Twenty-First Century: What Should Be Done on Campus?* The guide addressed the problem we examined in our "apathy" unit: student disengagement. Employing a deliberative framework, the discussion guide highlights four approaches to fostering civic engagement among today's college students. Apathy is approached both conceptually (what causes it? how might we better understand it?) and pragmatically (what can be done to counter it? how can we provide concrete venues and techniques for fostering public engagement?). While different approaches to this issue are motivated by a shared sense that student apathy is a problem for our society, they differ in their specific motivations and their specific sense of what drives the problem and its solutions.

In considering their discussions around *Politics for the Twenty-First Century*, seminar participants grappled with the guide's four perspectives or "choices" concerning the social problem of student apathy. Some critics share my students' sense that restrictive campus policies—such as censorship—result in apathetic, disengaged students. They argue that such policies act as a powerful deterrent to student engagement. If authoritative administrations are the source of student apathy, they argue, we must democratize the campus, affording opportunities for students to make genuine contributions to the way in which the campus is run. Opponents of this approach counter that it is unrealistic to implement power sharing on today's campuses. Universities and colleges are complex organizations, and students are transient populations who cannot be expected to master the intricacies of campus finances and long-term planning. While more robust student participation in governance may be desirable, the critics continue, the idea of student-run campuses (in the style of institutions like Berea and Antioch colleges) is clearly ineffective, as demonstrated by the financial insolvency of these institutions. Moreover, opportunities for student engagement should be structured and monitored. Many who hold these views believe that community service provides a superior format in which to allow students to gain experience in public engagement and confront real-world political problems. Though differing in their specific recommendations, both of these approaches—democratizing the campus and engaging in community service—share a belief that student-citizenship skills are best promoted from outside the curriculum, or in the cocurriculum, in student government or student programs.

In response to those who argue that campus activism—or community service—are the most obvious locus for student engagement, other members of the academic community view the curriculum itself as the optimal place in which to inculcate citizenship. They cite the tradition of the liberal arts—and its links to the civic arts—as the most valuable preparation for public engagement. Only by learning skills of reasoned argument, logic, and moral deliberation, will students develop the skills necessary for participation in democratic community. From this perspective, community service, while laudable, does not provide adequate intellectual training in the critical-thinking skills necessary to foster robust citizenship. Only rigorous academic training—coupled with training in a particular discipline—will make strong citizens and a strong democracy. Proponents of this approach argue that strong academics are the best preparation for citizenship.

By considering a range of perspectives on how college campuses could train a more robust citizenry, students were forced to go beyond the simple palliative of "service learning," and responded with genuine enthusiasm to the questions raised by their deliberations. To quote one student paper, "American students need to recognize the importance of being represented in government. A lack of concern in the little issues that affect young adults on campuses can lead to a lack of concern in bigger, more significant issues." The sentiment was echoed across a range of student writings, in which writers voiced enthusiasm for greater engagement and concern about the long-term consequences of disengagement from citizenship. Many students wrote with passion about the kind of world they envisioned and the kinds of contributions their generation might make to the world of the future.

My Generation—Who Are We?

As the capstone essay for this course, students were asked to propose a name for their generation. (See Figure 3, page 104.) Mirroring the catch phrases that are often applied to generational trends ("the Lost Generation" or "Generation X"), these invented names allowed students to codify their hopes (or fears) concerning their generation's prospective legacy.

Among the fascinating names students devised for their generation, one of the most intriguing was "Generation Thumb." "Youth today," its creator observed, "depend on their thumbs to operate every bit of technology from cell phones to keyboards." Whereas older generations "use their index figure" to "dial a number" or program a microwave oven, today's students "use their thumbs instead." The trend reflects the pervasive technological innovation that has shaped the younger generation:

> We thrive on the use of cell phones, the Internet and any other device that becomes more efficient though the use of our "thumbs." Technology has revolutionized the world that we live in, increasing convenience and maximizing potential. While this reality is not unique to our generation, we mark the transition from the development of such tech-

nologies to the incorporation of technology into common existence. Technology is now an extension of ourselves and it is beginning to shape what we value and what entertains us. It is for this reason that technological innovations define our generation and its trends.

Figure 3

Generational Trends: Talking About My Generation

For this essay, you will use library research to define your generation. To reach this definition, consider works of art, journals, advertisements, and articles describing current events—any form of cultural output between the date of your birth and the present.

Make sure you come up with a name for your generation, along the lines of the names others have before you (the Lost Generation, the "Me" Generation, Generation X, Generation Y). Make sure you use diverse sources—don't use all articles from the *New York Times*, for example. Make sure that one of your sources comes from the Internet; that one is a visual item; and that another derives from music or video.

Organization

You might organize around a theme or topic that relates to the name you propose. Or, it might help to use a chronological approach. The goal is not to provide a synthetic historical account of the era in which you were raised, but to provide an engaging analysis that explains some key feature of your generation. You may write in the first person, using *I* and *me*, or you may write in third-person narration.

Complete this essay in a series of stages

1. First, consider a trend that you and your fellow students used to follow when you were younger. (A trend, in this instance, is defined as any practice or fad that enjoyed brief popularity: a particular TV show, style of dress, a type of music, an activity. It could be a widespread phenomenon, or one that was unique to your school. Be creative.) Explain the trend. Provide a background description of

it, and tell your readers something about its origins: how and why did this become a trend in the first place?

2. Offer an analysis as to how this trend represents something about your generation.

3. Repeat this for three trends or events that you see as important for your generation.

Make sure your transitions between paragraphs explain why you are moving (logically) from one paragraph to the next paragraph. Make sure you explain your reasoning as you explain how these events, trends, and experiences may have defined your generation.

The student also lamented the "alarming ramifications" of technology's rampant proliferation, cautioning that in the world of video games actions remain separate from their consequences. For Generation Thumb, acts like war and urbanization—two themes common in today's video games—assume an unreal, gamelike quality. While Generation Thumb was a whimsical name for a generation steeped in technological advances, such as the cellular phone and the BlackBerry, this student had learned to weigh the pros and cons of these developments, and his written discussion reflected an ability to deliberate concerning their implications for his world.

As we completed our work, I asked students to look ahead to their distant future, again employing deliberative forums to frame their learning. In response to the 2005 *Village Voice* series "Generation Debt"—which argued that today's students face unprecedented indebtedness and financial pressures—I asked students to consider an unlikely subject: their future retirement from the workforce. Employing the NIF discussion guide *The National Piggybank: Does Our Retirement Need Fixing?* we considered the future of Social Security and its ramifications for their futures. In a series of forum deliberations, students were able to confront their own past, present, and future and to chart the kinds of choices and forms of fiscal policies that might shape their lives. By considering a range of approaches to how the system of Social Security might be fixed (through privatization, fiscal reform, or reassessment of the system itself), and beginning to confront the trade-offs, benefits, and values inherent in each approach to reforming Social Security, students weighed the consequences of these choices for their own families and futures. The deliberative process informed them regarding current events and political issues, and also informed them of the wider political implications of their personal decisions regarding their financial management and strategies. Students came to see the wider political reverberations of that most individual of domains, personal finance.

Teaching the Conflicts versus Using Deliberation

Deliberative approaches to written and spoken exchange are not the only ways to prompt these sorts of reflections about past and future, but it is my belief that they are particularly valuable in combating the very apathy that was one of our subjects. Many students feel that the culture wars have had a "chilling" effect on the quality of campus debate, and some commentators cite "political correctness" as a further muzzle on intellectual exchange. Gerald Graff has argued that humanities educators must counter these trends by "teaching the conflicts," urging that only open consideration of the underlying ideological divisions that drive intellectual inquiry will counteract the slide towards disaffection. But such an emphasis risks replicating the same agonistic structure that has turned students away from academic debates and approaches in the first place.

Deliberative frameworks strive to resist predictable, partisan alignments. As such, they are particularly suited to the skepticism of undergraduates, who tend to view ideological agendas with suspicion. Deliberative approaches are especially promising for first-year and core curriculum courses, such as courses offered through freshman seminar and writing programs. These courses usually state their broad commitments to "critical thinking" and moral deliberation but nearly always lack a clear set of techniques by which to advance those commitments. Deliberative frameworks stress rhetoric, persuasion, and logical clarity, and they invite students to begin to use these skills to enter debates within the university's community and individual disciplines. In addition to the clear and grammatical presentation that we expect from students' written arguments, we expect they will be able to contextualize claims; to recognize the importance of qualification and modulation; and to assess the soundness of evidence and authorities. These skills are closely associated with the kinds of logical and conceptual operations that are built into deliberative frameworks. Such frameworks tend to minimize the kinds of ideological and methodological "conflicts"—to employ Graff's term—that may turn students against political and public engagement.

A common deliberative experience can also be valuable in setting the basis for a broader "unit" of assignments. In the case of our study of the problem of student apathy, our discussions and writings ranged far and wide, from narrow technical issues relating to voter registration and electoral fraud, to broader speculations regarding the hopes and aspirations of today's youth. Existing discussion guides on topics like affirmative action, terrorism, and the environment suggest a rich range of possibilities for implementing deliberative frameworks in introductory writing classrooms. Combined with other—and even more polemical or biased—texts and sources, these frameworks help students to see beyond the purview of a single perspective, and to begin to grapple with the kind of "enlarged mentality" that students of Immanuel Kant view as central to democratic politics.

Institutional Mission and Deliberation

I have focused on the core of the traditional curriculum—the first-year writing course—presenting three specific units—alcoholism, student apathy, and generation definition—in which deliberative approaches helped foster learning. But deliberative approaches have ramifications beyond this somewhat narrow context, and they have applications in the broader work of humanities professionals, particularly in work around institutional mission and in the cocurriculum. They also have immediate promise as a tangible way of enacting what many strategic planning initiatives have proposed as a central pedagogical goal for higher education: active learning. In this way, deliberative approaches promise to respond to broader institutional demands for active and mission-based classroom activity, while preserving the kinds of activities that have traditionally distinguished the liberal arts curriculum.

The deliberative approach demands that students are active, engaged, and empowered, not passive or bored. In the forum context, students engage in face-to-face discussion and assume their position as public actors, albeit within the somewhat narrow field of the classroom. Recent research in the field of education suggests that students learn best when they play an active role in their own education; that is to say, they absorb knowledge more efficiently and gain their intellectual independence through active engagement rather than passive reception. Deliberative pedagogy, with its emphasis on active participation in weighing the pros and cons of a range of solutions to a set of problems, serves to create an environment that encourages students to take risks and accept constructive feedback, and offers a dynamic, collaborative dialogue rather than a one-way transmission of knowledge from teacher to student. This dynamic, collaborative pedagogical style has long been the accepted norm in language teaching, where vigorous student participation is recognized as the most effective means of acquiring proficiency. The same principles hold true in other humanities courses, where the students are learning to name and describe the world around them, and the stakes are even higher, because the culture they are learning to participate in is their own.

Beyond the recent calls for more active learning in our university classrooms, many institutions have begun to demand greater overall coherence, demanding linkages between their institutional missions and classroom activities. (Such linkages often feature prominently in strategic planning or evaluative exercises linked to accreditation or legislative bodies.) Within these calls for greater

relevance, most institutional mission statements affirm our universities' commitment to preparing students for citizenship. Yet, as
indicated at the outset, most faculty and students agree that
public engagement—seen in participation in elections, voluntary
associations, or campus politics—is less robust than ever. In reaction,
numerous institutions (including Duke University's Kenan Institute
for Ethics, Loch Haven University's Democracy Lab, University of
Georgia's Honors Program, and Wake Forest's freshman seminar on
deliberative democracy) have begun to explore the potential of
deliberative democracy for strengthening learning and community
on their campuses. The venues range from freshman orientation
programs to extracurricular and service-learning programs. A
number of nonprofit organizations have joined this effort (Cynthia Gibson, Carnegie Corporation; Paul Brest, Hewlett Foundation;
John Dedrick, Kettering Foundation; Suzanne Morse, Pew Partnership for Civic Change). Deliberative forums have been used successfully in first-year orientation programs and honors programs at
numerous universities and colleges. Deliberative techniques have
also been used in conjunction with service-learning programs, where
reasoned debate about topics like homelessness, care for the
elderly, and medical care have allowed students to confront the
social problems that underlie the institutions in which they serve as
volunteers.

Despite their differences, many of the institutions that sponsor
deliberative programs state their commitment to training undergraduates for active citizenship and participation in public life.
The contexts vary. At my institution, a Catholic university in New
York City, there is a direct link between our unique institutional
mission and investment in public engagement. The relationship
between deliberative pedagogical techniques and the intellectual
traditions surrounding Catholicism, particularly in the United
States, is an important one. For many academic professionals at
Catholic institutions, the social-justice traditions associated with the
Catholic Worker and figures like Dorothy Day have abiding importance for an institutional mission seen as geared towards public
engagement (see Fisher). In fact, the 1960s movements for participatory democracy—particularly campus movements—were driven in

large part by a cadre of individuals whose grounding in the social-justice traditions of modern U.S. Catholicism was a central, if not always explicit, motivating factor.

When we consider the highly visible student leaders of the 1960s and 1970s, we see that many key players in that tradition were rooted in institutions of Catholic education, in ways that have not been acknowledged. Mario Savio, the leader of the Free Speech Movement at Berkeley, was a graduate of Manhattan College in the Bronx. Tom Hayden, the writer of the Port Huron Statement, and arguably the leading figure in the student movements of the 1960s, was Catholic-educated prior to his work at the University of Michigan and cited the Catholic concern with social justice as the root of his later—and often more secularized—political activism. The leading mentor of many of these figures, Michael Harrington, was a prominent Catholic intellectual. Though such instances are anecdotal, there is a powerful case to be made that Catholic institutions have a particular commitment and inclination towards democratic practices and institutions.

At other higher education institutions, including historically black and tribal colleges, unique institutional missions set the tone for different kinds of priorities and investments in deliberative practices.

But whether our institutions are regional, religious, vocational, or traditional in their orientations, most of us state our commitments to training citizens and to training students in the basic skills of oral and written expression. In the practices and techniques of the deliberative classroom, I have argued here, we find a useful set of practices for learning and teaching in these contexts. Whether in the curriculum or in the cocurriculum, deliberative techniques contain valuable elements that inculcate skills necessary to an active citizenry, or, for those less geared towards broader public engagement, to being active learners. Deliberative techniques have particular promise for first-year writing and core courses, and for the teaching of writing and argument in other disciplines, when the skills they inculcate are indispensable to making written and oral expression both more cogent and more compelling for the students and faculty who engage in them.

Maria Farland is associate professor of English and American studies at Fordham University in the Bronx. She has taught at Johns Hopkins, Columbia, Wesleyan, and Fordham universities and has published numerous articles on American literature and culture.

References

Barber, Benjamin. *Strong Democracy: Participatory Politics for a New Age*. Berkeley, CA: University of California Press, 1985.

Brooks, David. "The Organization Kid." *Atlantic Monthly* (April 2001).

Dewey, John. *The Public and Its Problems*. New York: H. Holt and Co., 1927.

Fisher, James Terence. *The Catholic Counterculture in America, 1933-1962*. Chapel Hill: University of North Carolina Press, 1989.

Graff, Gerald. *Beyond the Culture Wars: How Teaching the Conflicts Can Revitalize Higher Education*. New York: W. W. Norton, 1993.

Henry, Sarah and Maria Farland. *Politics for the Twenty-First Century: What Should Be Done on Campus?* Dubuque, IA: Kendall Hunt, 1992.

Tannen, Deborah. *The Argument Culture: Moving from Debate to Dialogue*. New York: Random House, 1999.

Williams, Joseph M. and Gregory Columb. *The Craft of Argument, Concise Edition*. New York: Addison, Wesley, and Longman, Inc., 2003.

Chapter Five

Four Seasons of Deliberative Learning in a Department of Rhetoric and American Studies: From General Education to the Senior Capstone

David D. Cooper

This essay describes a multiyear effort to infuse deliberative democracy and deliberative learning practices into three new humanities courses that the author developed and taught at Michigan State University. The courses range from a general-education writing requirement to an elective upper division American studies seminar. Each of the experimental classes is distinguished by a pedagogy that combines active-learning techniques—principally service learning—and deliberative democratic practices, including public forums, study circles, and civic engagement opportunities for students. Taken as a whole, the author's journey shows that the synergy between democratic deliberation and engaged learning can energize the undergraduate humanities classroom at all levels, even the senior capstone. The experience also reaffirms for the author Thomas Jefferson's important and enduring message to future teachers: a strong democracy requires nothing less than a diligent and purposeful education for citizenship.

From 2002 to 2005, I set out on a systematic journey to incorporate deliberative democracy and deliberative learning practices into a sequence of three new courses I developed and taught at Michigan State University (MSU) in an interdisciplinary Department of Rhetoric and American Studies. The courses covered a full gamut of undergraduate teaching assignments, from a general-education requirement to a senior capstone project. This essay is partly a description of some of the techniques I tried out along the way, partly a lab report on the outcomes of the experiments I conducted, and partly a travelogue about the highs and lows of the journey—the exhilarating discoveries I made, the company I kept, as well as the wrong turns I took and jams I got into.

Each of the experimental classes along that journey is distinguished by a pedagogy that cross-fertilizes active-learning techniques, principally service learning, and deliberative democratic practices, such as public forums, study circles, and civic engagement opportunities for students. Taken as a whole, my journey shows, I hope, that the synergy between deliberation and active learning can energize the undergraduate humanities classroom at all levels, even the senior capstone. Moreover, I bring away from these travels two key, but by no means original, insights into the value of deliberation and the challenge, as Daniel Yankelovich puts it, of "making democracy work in a complex world" such as ours. Democracy itself, I rediscovered, is fundamentally a rhetorical art. And deliberation, the discursive engine of democracy, can be a powerful, compelling, even transformative pedagogy that challenges students and teachers alike to connect principles, ideas, and critical reflection—the usual and venerable fare of the humanities classroom—to the crucible of lived community problems in which ordinary citizens conduct the extraordinary work of citizenship.

Setting Out: A Toehold in General Education

In the late 1990s, several colleagues and I organized the Service Learning Writing Project, an initiative in service learning and composition studies. By yoking together rigorous classroom writing instruction, critical readings in American civic culture, and real-world writing projects in community, municipal, and non-profit agencies, we found that students developed more complex understandings of the crucial role of language and critical thinking skills in the work of social and political change. We eventually established a new writing course in 1999—"Public Life in America"

—which fulfills a general-education writing requirement at Michigan State University and currently enrolls nearly 300 students a year in 12 stand-alone sections.[1]

During the last few years, inspired largely by my participation in a Kettering Foundation workgroup, my interest has turned to the relationship between rhetoric and democratic practices and, in particular, to how deliberative democracy techniques might be used for teaching, writing, and critical thinking. Through continuing conversations and alliances with the colleagues whose work also appears in this book, I learned that the best way to promote a robust democracy is to encourage public deliberation of controversial issues, foster strong communities, and help promote citizens' civic, rather than professional identities. In the case of our students and higher education, this meant that to strengthen what Harry Boyte calls America's "civic muscle" we had to practice deliberative democracy in our classrooms and on our campuses.

I began experimenting, then, with methods of connecting the rhetorical and critical-thinking requirements of MSU's general-education writing course with Kettering's traditions of deliberative democracy and with the particular methodology of public conversation and problem solving practiced in hundreds of National Issues Forums (NIF) taking place across the country.

All these strands came together in 2002 when my colleague Eric Fretz and I designed a pair of closely related experimental writing courses in the general-education sequence, which would provide students with opportunities to study techniques of deliberation and

---

[1] My colleague Laura Julier and I published a comprehensive curriculum development resource guide on this work, including a framing essay, detailed syllabi, student reflections, community-partner perspectives, a portfolio of community-writing projects, and a resource bibliography. *Writing in the Public Interest: Service Learning and the Writing Classroom* is available for free download at http://writing.msu.edu/content/wipi/c&j.html. For a more recent update, see "Public-Interest Writing Courses Help Students Connect Written Expression with Community Problem Solving" (*Muses* 18.1, Summer/Fall 2006): http://www.cal.msu.edu.

to practice both public dialogue and public problem solving. These two courses were not team taught in the traditional sense. Fretz was scheduled to teach a writing section with a focus on "Race and Ethnicity," and I was assigned a "Public Life in America" class with a special emphasis on education and youth issues. We each designed our own syllabus, although there was a good deal of overlapping of required texts, learning strategies, and writing assignments.

Our classes incorporated three active-learning components, which we designed to link the academic issues of the separate courses, foster a strong learning community between our classes and among our students, and practice democratic skills of deliberation, collaboration, and participation. The first component involved setting up a fairly traditional service experience for students, and the next two components required students from both of our classes to collaborate on organizing an NIF forum on youth violence open to the public and, later on, to moderate smaller deliberative study circles in class.

Students practiced public dialogue and public problem solving early in the semester by conducting in-class practice forums on topics like the future of affirmative action and the quality of public education. (In my class, students even framed and deliberated a class attendance policy.) We devised several writing assignments, often in consultation with students, that moved students away from typical arguments based on debate to arguments anchored in the looser soil of deliberation. Students also analyzed, evaluated, and presented arguments on topics of current concern to local audiences, an activity we called "grass roots democracy in action."

Next, students gained important insights into public problems through question and answer sessions with invited guests (including a circuit court judge) and by working and learning in community settings with a number of community partners, including several Neighborhood Network Centers located in Lansing.[2]

---

[2] Fretz and I explore that collaboration in detail in our article "The Service Learning Writing Project: Re-Writing the Humanities Through Service Learning and Public Work." *Reflections* 5.1/2 (Spring 2006): 133-152.

Our students then collaborated in a number of small teams to research, organize, and host the public forum on "Violent Kids: Can We Change the Trend?" Students designed and drafted a discussion guide for forum participants and worksheets and instructions for moderator assistants. Students also handed out and evaluated pre- and postforum questionnaires. They self-selected into committees that worked on timetables and deadlines for various stages of forum organization, communications, publicity, and background research on things like children's television, media violence, and effects of video games.

After the forum, one of the work groups assembled and organized all of the forum work from each project team into a comprehensive portfolio. Fretz and I drafted and circulated to all of our students an extensive portfolio assessment and evaluation memo that critically addressed the contribution of each work group—all of which led to a deliberation we had not anticipated.

Our students were generally ruffled by our C+ evaluation of the portfolio. The grade was assigned to each student, and it counted for a sizable portion of their final grades. We took advantage of our students' dissatisfaction and invited them to put together a small deliberative forum to take a closer look at the evaluation memo and to present point-by-point arguments in favor of a higher grade. A small student work group agreed to frame the issue and prepare three choices for deliberation. Another work group took responsibility for moderating the joint-class forum, another for postforum reflections, and so on.

To give a flavor of how our students thought through the issue and how well they had integrated the deliberative process into the learning ethos of the classes, here is the discussion guide they prepared:

Choice 1: The NIF forum collaborative grade of C+ is fair and equitable.

Prof. Fretz and Prof. Cooper's evaluation memo is thorough, well argued, and reasonable. While some students may nit-pick with details, overall the judgment is sound and the conclusions are justified. All the students in [each class] clearly knew well in advance that the forum work would be evaluated with a common grade. Sure, some students may have worked harder than others. But to insure the integrity and honesty of the forum project as an exercise in democracy and public life, students must be willing to accept the common grade.

Choice 2: Working groups that excelled deserve a better grade than C+. On the other hand, the evaluation memo suggests that other working groups may deserve less than a C+.

The working groups should be evaluated on a group-by-group basis. Prof. Fretz and Cooper should grade each group according to the arguments made in the separate committee sections of the evaluation memo. This grading procedure is ideal because it takes into consideration both collaborative work and individual effort. It is also more fair. The downside: all the work groups knew from the outset that the portfolio would be graded collaboratively. Is it ok to change that policy after the fact?

Choice 3: The common grade for the NIF forum work should be higher.

The evaluation memo grade is simply too low. Granted, the points are well argued. No one claims Prof. Fretz and Cooper are being overly unfair. However, the forum was hard work for *all* students. It took up almost a third of the course work. It was a successful public delibertion. The portfolio, measured by even the toughest standards, was an excellent piece of work. No one disputes these points. Prof. Fretz and Prof. Cooper need to raise the grade, and the class will accept without question the higher common grade.

Fretz and I were convincingly swayed by Choice 3, and we raised the common grade to a B.

After the public forum—and once the dust had settled from the mini-forum on grading—our students had an opportunity, during the last two weeks of class, to moderate study circle sessions on "Youth Issues, Youth Voices" and "Changing Faces, Changing Communities" based on material provided by the Study Circles Resource Center in Pomfret, Connecticut. Study circles are smaller and more intimate than the typical public forum, so they give students more opportunities to prepare for, actively engage in, and moderate public discussions. We required each student in our classes to moderate at least one study circle discussion. We felt it was important to provide even the most reticent of our students the chance to practice habits of deliberation, such as critical listening, asking leading questions, generating and sustaining discussions, staying neutral, and leading groups toward consensus.

Afterthoughts

Reflecting on our experimental classes convinced Fretz and me that engaging in public work in higher education means including students and their interests into the work and life of the classroom— even, and perhaps most important, in decisions about the syllabus and calendar, how to use class time and space, writing assignments, and evaluations. In an organic classroom like ours, where teaching/ learning techniques have to mesh with pedagogical philosophy, teaching in the traditional sense of disseminating knowledge and downloading students with information becomes transformed into a collaborative process in which professors and students work jointly toward a common goal.

We discovered that learning strategies that promote public work through deliberative pedagogy offer teachers rewards and fresh perspectives as well as posing difficult challenges. Organizing public forums, facilitating off campus community-based learning experiences, practicing deliberative strategies, and co-designing assignments with students thrust faculty into new, sometimes un-comfortable positions. No longer the "sage on the stage," teachers become facilitators and, in many ways, colearners with students— and co-workers, too. We no longer directed from the sidelines or articulated abstractions behind a podium. We found ourselves doing work right alongside our students.

As we became facilitators and colearners, we had to give up some expectations about what should happen in a college classroom. In the process, we found new ways of thinking about those questions that all of us in higher education ponder: Where does the learning take place? How can I ratchet up the learning curve? What do I want my students to take away with them? Through practicing democracy in the classroom, we are able to answer these questions in different and more interesting ways than we could have in a more traditional classroom setting. Students learned disciplinary knowledge (in this case, writing rhetorical arguments, thinking critically, connecting written argument to concrete public problem solving) through experience and practice. In addition, they began to experiment with ways of operating and effecting change in the public sphere.

For our part, we learned that the role of professor is both bigger and smaller than the ones articulated by the traditions and expectations of our academic disciplines. Our most challenging and prosaic role, for example, was that of project manager. We helped our students anticipate snags, identify community and university resources, solve problems, develop networking skills, and lay out efficient workflow—skills we felt were basic to the toolkit of citizenship. We also fetched envelopes and department letterhead, provided campus contacts to facilitate logistics for the forum, and arranged for the use of printers, fax machines, office phones, and computers.

For me, a striking and lasting consequence of adopting and adapting to a deliberative pedagogy was that I no longer considered myself a "teacher" in the conventional sense in which my colleagues understood, practiced, and peer reviewed the role. Rather, I became an architect of my students' learning experiences or maybe a midwife of their practices of becoming better writers and active citizens—or, perhaps more to the point, something like a forum moderator. In a public forum, successful deliberation is often inversely related to the visibility and presence—indeed, the knowledge and issue expertise— of the moderator. The same applies to a teacher in a deliberative classroom: you spend a great deal of creative intellectual energy listening to students and learning to get out of their way so they can take ownership of the subject, in the same way that forum participants must "own" an issue.

That fundamental role shift totally changed my experience of the writing classroom, from mundane matters like the physical arrangement of desks and the venues where learning takes place to epistemological underpinnings, ethical practices and boundaries, not to mention problematic relationships with more traditionally-minded colleagues who felt that I was cutting my students too much slack. In the annual department review, one of my colleagues criticized me, for example, for comments repeated on several narrative evaluations from students that "it was like the students were teaching the class." In the future, obviously, I need to do a better job of articulating a philosophy of deliberative pedagogy so my colleagues can translate statements like that as observations of practice and not criticisms of my teaching style.

The deliberative pedagogy that we employed demands a great deal of preparation and planning, but at the same time requires spontaneity and flexibility—and a certain degree of uncertainty. Our students' learning experiences encompassed complex and interlocking community groups, constituencies, organizations, and several offices and units at my university. Grounded in multiple learning partnerships, action research, and real-world contexts, learning became a dynamic social process —emergent, messy, edgy, relational, sometimes inconclusive, occasionally (though not often) painful and confused, frequently full of entanglements, and always, I hope, challenging. I found myself constantly pushing the class to a point of agitation, churning, and controlled chaos because that was where the real learning took place—at that threshold where students became present in, and took ownership of, their own learning experience.

Through the Gateway into the Professional Writing Major

Shortly after my experiments with deliberative democracy and pedagogy in the general-education writing sequence, my department expanded its mission by offering a new undergraduate degree in Professional Writing. The major is designed to capitalize on and complement our teaching, research, and outreach strengths in rhetoric and American studies. In addition to preparing students for careers in professional writing, the major lays solid foundations for graduate work in rhetoric, writing, technical writing, the teaching of writing, and the study of culture. From the outset, the Professional Writing Program has emphasized the organizational, disciplinary, and cultural contexts for writing. Students specialize in one of three advanced writing tracks: (1) technical writing and writing in digital environments, (2) professional editing and publishing, and (3) writing in cultures and communities.

I saw the new major as a good opportunity to take what I had learned about deliberative democracy and active-learning techniques in the general-education writing sequence and apply it to upper-division courses in the major. Along with several colleagues from the Service Learning Writing Project, I served as a consultant to the curriculum planning committee for the "writing in cultures and communities" track. I later designed and taught the first gateway course for that track, appropriately titled "Writing in the Public Interest," in which students explored various forms of public writing and their roles in democracy and public culture.

In this course, drawing on the history of civic culture in America, I used examples that highlighted the power and possibility of collaborative decision making. I saw these examples as case studies of deliberative democracy in action. They ranged from turn of the century women's literary clubs and the 19th-century Chautauqua movement and Lyceum system, to 20th-century settlement houses, citizenship schools, and the contemporary National Issues Forums. The study of these historical foundations helped prepare students to practice rhetorical conventions for deliberating and arguing in a democratic community. One of the important goals of the new course was to understand how language shapes community and democratic practices, and how, in turn, social processes and democratic traditions influence language.

Public writing and active learning were once again intertwined. Students worked with numerous local nonprofits and public advocacy organizations, from the Sexual Assault Crisis Intervention Center to the Ronald McDonald House, and for each practiced its particular conventions of public writing. Students compiled portfolios that were designed to get them "thinking rhetorically" about the groups with which they worked. They collected and analyzed examples of public writing. Students wrote essays about which forms of discourse were best suited to an agency or organization's public agenda, what messages were being communicated, what positions advocated, and at which registers of the public sphere the messages were aimed (local, regional, national).

Our reading and discussion revealed different intellectual and conceptual frameworks for "writing in the public interest." We examined case studies of what are called "rhetorical situations" and how they are bound up in issues of public interest. A rhetorical situation is an occasion that compels constructive argument in the public sphere. Such arguments—the rhetorical basis, it should be noted, for a deliberative forum—always take place within a social or public context, and within communities that define the relationships between writers/speakers, readers/listeners, and issues of shared import and concern. We looked, for example, at the way the Columbine High School shootings in Littleton, Colorado (April 20, 1990), created a rhetorical situation concerning gun control and youth violence which rippled across the country. Or how Janet Jackson's "wardrobe malfunction" at the 2004 Super Bowl prompted a rhetorical situation about decency, moral values, and the limits and responsibilities of broadcast media—issues we are still brooding over today.

A centerpiece of the course involved a semester-long project and partnership with the Michigan Campus Compact and the Michigan House of Representatives' Civics Commission (MICC), a bipartisan initiative dedicated to the proposition that the best way to teach civics is to engage students in the public work of the state legislature. My students researched and designed Web-based, deliberatively framed opinion polls for the commission, aimed at providing college students throughout the state with a new venue to learn about and express their opinions on legislative proposals that had some bearing on young adult issues—for example, public smoking bans, state control of universities, and tough new "Zero Tolerance" laws. In addition to posting polling questions, students framed alternative positions on the proposals, prepared comprehensive background information, and analyzed polling results distributed to Michigan legislators.

Students hammered out a uniform template, which they used to organize each of the 12 polls we posted to the MHCC Web site. The template called, first, for neutral, unbiased background information on the proposed legislation. "Does this information," students asked, "help in allowing poll participants to make educated decisions?" Next, each poll was preceded by a *highlights* paragraph, which presented positions on the bill and included a discussion of trade-offs associated with each position. "Make sure," students wrote in the poll-preparation guidelines, "to incorporate all sides—i.e., negative and positive facts [sic] because this is the last bit of information given before casting a poll vote."

Here is a sample poll students wrote for a proposed Zero Tolerance Bill on underage drinking:

> **CAST YOUR VOTE.** Under the Michigan Liquor Control Code, should the state give a person under the age of 21, who registers any level of bodily alcohol content (BAC), a misdemeanor with penalties that include automatic driver's license sanctions (for second and subsequent violations) and the possibility of a fine, community service, and substance abuse screening (at the violator's own expense) and/or substance abuse prevention or treatment services?
>
> 1. No. If an underage person is not physically seen consuming alcohol, it is unfair to enforce the same punishment as someone who was physically seen drinking.
>
> 2. Yes. Drinking underage should have the same consequences, regardless of whether people are physically seen drinking or not.
>
> 3. Yes. Underage drinking is illegal. Any Zero Tolerance law in Michigan should have no exceptions. A misdemeanor with these penalties is a very lenient punishment for underage drinking.

4. No. There should be some leeway with what a person under the age of 21 can have in their system, due to the fact that mouthwash contains alcohol, and accepting wine at church will make the BAC levels rise.

Notice the way that the polling project captures many of the basic rhetorical components of deliberation, including (1) the importance of naming issues in comprehensible public terms that my students' college-age peers could relate to, (2) recognizing that facts and information about the Zero Tolerance issue are important as a basis of deciding what is good for and valuable to the broader commonweal, (3) making choices that carry consequences, and (4) viewing individual behavior through the lens of public policy. To the extent that this poll and the others issued an invitation to college students statewide to be part of a public conversation, they became productive exercises in democratic decision making—especially for a generation of students for whom the Internet has become a dominant and accepted medium of communication, connection, and information gathering. "Deliberation," David Mathews and Noëlle McAfee remind us, has "the power to get people to take the first step to civic involvement. Deliberation also links these people to one another, creating a public, which is a body of people joined together to deal with common problems."

As with the general-education writing class, I wanted this course to include public creation, community action, and democratic decision making. I designed the course so my students and I, along with the MHCC, formed a purposeful learning community that *practiced* the subjects it was exploring. In fact, everything I learned in the general-education writing class about the learning practices of deliberative communities was reinforced and intensified— and often brought to my mind the well-known comment of Myles Horton, founder of the Highlander School. "When you believe in democracy," he said, "you provide a setting for education that is democratic."

My second season of democratizing the classroom suggested, like the first, that the sort of democratic pedagogy Horton has in mind must operate at multiple levels. It means, first and foremost, linking students' academic learning with experiences of democracy building and public work, learning that is rigorously situated in lived contexts and grounded in action. It also means trying to infuse the strategies and principles of democratic deliberation into every reach and recess of learning that takes place in the course, including, in particular, my own role as an active, engaged learner and a democratic practitioner. As a consequence, whenever I conduct a self-assessment of my courses now, I hardly ever ask, "How well am I teaching?" The critical questions for me are, what am I learning? and *am I getting out of my students' way?*

Destination: The Elective Seminar

The semester following the gateway course in the professional writing major, I was scheduled for an upper division "Special Topics" elective seminar in the American Studies Program. I saw it as another opportunity to continue experimenting with deliberative democracy and pedagogy. I also wanted to tackle some related questions that have troubled me since graduate school, questions that have roiled the field of American studies for the past 30 years, hounded the American democratic experiment since its inception, and continue to challenge our practices of deliberation and public decision making. Those questions were bluntly posed to my generation of American studies scholars/teachers by Harold Isaacs in the closing chapter of his 1975 classic *The Idols of the Tribe: Group Identity and Political Change.* Confronting the ethnic conflicts and dilemmas emerging in 1970s America, Isaacs warned, "The underlying issue is still: Can human existence be made more human, and if so, how?... How can we live with our differences without, as always heretofore, being driven by them to tear each other limb from limb?"

The Latin motto *E pluribus unum* ("One from many"), selected in 1776 for the Great Seal of the United States, has been a source of inspiration and pride and, especially in recent decades, a cause of shattering controversy in America. A central question that has long perplexed Americans and American studies is how—and *whether*—we should reconcile our many separate, communal, ethnic, and group identities with a shared identity we hold in common as Americans.

I called the American studies elective seminar "Civic America." In it we took a close look at concepts like pluralism, civic culture, social capital, and civil society; historical and social movements; and grassroots practices of American public life that seek to make the tension in our democracy between "the many and the one" creative and productive. Since service, public work, and citizen participation are key ingredients in nourishing civil society, interested students were invited to sign up for a volunteer placement in a local community service or municipal agency that would give them a firsthand look at the challenges of Civic America. Students who selected that option kept a separate journal in which they connected field experiences to seminar readings and discussions, and vice versa.

As I had done in the course on "Writing in the Public Interest" in the Professional Writing Program, I again embedded a strong emphasis on deliberation into themes and concepts of Civic America that could stand entirely on their own in any American studies class. We began with a groundwork of readings and case studies that vividly sketched out vocabularies and dilemmas of civic culture. We examined a series of grassroots portraits of democracy in action drawn from video vignettes produced by *The American Promise* series, including successful efforts to reintroduce wolves into Yellowstone National Park over the objections of local cattle ranchers, agitations by students at Gallaudet University to lobby for a new deaf president, and organizing efforts among largely Hispanic low-income neighborhood activists in San Antonio, Texas, for relief from chronic flooding caused by seasonal rains. We also winced through several examples of civic dysfunction, including political corruption in a small town on the Texas border

each approach? Looking back on the deliberations, what are the conflicts in this issue that we still have to "work through"? Where can you detect any shared sense of direction or common ground, if any, for future action?

I also gave the study circle participants permission to reflect personally on the following questions: How has your own thinking about this issue changed? What do we still need to talk about? Why is that so difficult to talk about? How can you use what we learned in our study circle?

Once again, I combined the written responses into a document that would serve, I hope, as a lasting contribution to the narrative life of the Civic America seminar.[4]

The practices of civic culture and some of the public policy issues raised in the Civic America seminar found even more traction in conversations simultaneously taking place in my department and across the university. That same semester our provost launched a series of intense and searching discussions about rethinking liberal arts education at Michigan State University.

Meanwhile, my department formed a task force charged with reexamining the general-education writing sequence. Its report took several positions relevant to the discussions we were having in the Civic America seminar over "the one and the many." The taskforce clearly favored *pluribus* over *unum* in its vision of a socially engaged writing curriculum. It strongly recommended, for example, that the required writing course emphasize readings and diverse cultural content that honored historically disenfranchised voices and heightened students' awareness of America's changing and diverse populations and our country's problematic history

---

[4] That document was posted on the National Issues Forums Web site on January 19, 2005, as part of a news feature on "Deliberative Study Circles Become Part of a University Course." http://www.nifi.org/news/news_detail.aspx?itemID=2845&catID=2871.

of adapting to cultural differences. One of the "Guiding Assumptions" the task force proposed to shape our thinking about a new writing course, for example, stated:

> **Respond to Changing and Diverse Populations.** It is imperative that a writing program be attentive and responsive to diverse populations. Academic discourse and standard written English have excluded a multiplicity of voices alive in the American discourse for centuries, and American academia now faces the challenge of addressing unprecedented global migration. In addition to addressing linguistic diversity in our students, we must also recognize the power and potential of historically excluded discourses of race, ethnicity, class, gender, sexuality and disability.

I was under the strong influence of the core question still percolating in the Civic America seminar: Should we reconcile our many separate, communal, ethnic, and group identities with a shared identity we hold in common as Americans? If so, how? After I viewed *Farmingville,* Isaacs' warning about dismembering the body politic was no theoretical abstraction to me. Perhaps, as Robert Frost admitted about his own habit of contrariness, it was the devil in me. In any case, I drafted a sharply worded memo to my colleagues and friends on the task force, in which I sought to counter their *pluribus* with a strong dose of *unum.*

> In a fervor to honor historically disenfranchised voices, we don't want to exclude cultural practices and rhetorical processes essential to making democracy work: for example, the power of public deliberation, or the rhetorical practices that diverse groups use to make hard choices together, gain clout and presence, achieve compromise, promote better understanding across lines of race, ethnicity, class, etc. Civic and public literacies, it seems to me, are far more challenging imperatives to respond to changing and diverse populations than merely opening up the canon in a required writing class and putting Frantz Fanon and Paulo Freire on our reading lists.

The key question for a socially engaged writing program, I asserted, is not how to recognize historically excluded discourses but what enables diverse voices to find legitimate courses of public action that are consistent with what is valuable to the community as a whole. Our students, to be sure, need to know how to see through glib ideologies of common sense that cloak the trappings of abusive power and the maintenance of the political status quo. The problem, I warned, is that students might be led to the conviction that powerlessness is a virtue, or that respect for cultural diversity is inconsistent with those habits of the heart that yearn to bridge group differences. In effect, I was urging the task force to shift their center of moral gravity from the other to *one another*.

I had just finished my third season of purposeful deliberative learning, and I shared with the task force what I had learned: the communities—rhetorical and real—where our students live their lives, and many of the actual rhetorical situations in which they find themselves as public writers, call on them to search for common ground, act through compromise, make decisions among imperfect and incomplete choices, and search for ways to achieve and maintain social cohesion and harmony amid the acrid smoke of group differences that hung over divided communities, such as Farmingville.

Arriving at the Senior Capstone

One advantage of using deliberative practices and active-learning techniques is that the impact of subject matter often ripples outside the classroom and beyond the usual tidy brackets of the semester calendar. That was certainly the case for Sarah W., one of the members of the Civic America seminar. After the semester was over, she asked whether I would direct her senior capstone requirement. Sarah wasn't particularly excited over the prospect of conducting a research project and writing a senior paper. She lit up, however, when I suggested, "Why don't you do a full-blown public forum on the study circle topic 'Who Is College For?' in our Civic America seminar last semester?"

Sarah hit the ground running. All I did was help connect her to the right campus and community networks and meet with her regularly to help keep her on track. She did everything: media liaison, letter writing, scheduling, study guide preparation, summary overhead transparencies, refreshments menu. Sarah was very nervous about moderating the forum, so I invited several colleagues and students to a practice forum at which Sarah diligently walked us through the choices, guided the conversation, and initiated reflection and next steps at the end.

"This event," Sarah wrote in a press release, "will give participants a rare opportunity to discuss the issue and work toward a common solution. It is not going to be a debate. Rather, it will be a chance to converse about an important issue that touches all of us, work toward understanding all viewpoints, and suggest some solutions." She was right. On April 12, 2005, Sarah held a small but successful deliberative campus forum on "Who Is College For?"

Afterward, Sarah submitted a bulging portfolio that chronicled her experience with the deliberative forum. The portfolio included several drafts of her evolving forum timelines, research and preparation materials, publicity kit (press releases, issue maps, posters), summary forum notes, participant evaluations, pre- and postforum questionnaires, and moderator materials (welcoming statement, transparencies, and so on). She also included a detailed reflection on her learning experiences. Here are some excerpts:

> Embarking on the Capstone Project was one of the most challenging assignments I have ever experienced....

> I went into this project blind, but I have come out feeling confident that if ever asked to do something like this again in my life, I will be able to use the skills I learned over this semester.

> ... I was able to take something I had learned in the Civic America seminar, and dive into it. Rather than simply participate in a forum and learn about the process, I was able to make the process available to the entire campus. The deliberative process is something that has become almost foreign to our society. People want to debate issues, not discuss them. Living in a democracy, it is so important that citizens are educated about their options when it comes to

deciding where they stand on issues.... I was able to be involved in educating the attendees on not only the topic ... but also on the deliberative process in general. The participants walked in with one or two opinions, and left having learned to both form new opinions and to change their existing opinions. More importantly, they were able to listen to the opinions of others and witness democracy at work.... This was an experience that I will look back on as being something that helped me to break out of my norm and learn new skills, while also impacting my community. I am really proud of my project, and I will always value the lessons I learned through this experience.

Some Postcards Home

I've come through these four seasons of deliberative learning with many more lessons, insights, and future challenges than I have the space to recount here. I briefly note the most important among them:

- One of the things I most admire about the NIF-style of public deliberation and its adaptability to the humanities classroom is the way it respects and elevates personal experience in the calculus of public problem solving. Whenever I have the privilege of moderating a public forum or when I participate in a forum like Sarah's organized by students, I am always amazed at how powerful personal stories can be and how essential they are to public creation. Asking participants how a particular issue impacts them personally or what personal experiences have shaped their perspectives on an issue ... these are absolutely crucial foundations for deliberation. The reciprocity between what people care about deeply and passionately and the hard work of hammering out the political will it takes to get people acting together is the greatest asset and the most daunting challenge of deliberative learning. In skillfully moderated forums, the power of personal stories—of people using their lived experience as a primary way of engaging social or political issues—is often a more fertile source of conviction and persuasion than formal modes or skills of rhetorical training and debate or perfectly framed choices.

- The same thing happens in a good personal essay. While experimenting with these seasons of deliberative pedagogy, I also edited an international journal of literary nonfiction—*Fourth Genre: Explorations in Nonfiction*—which kept me in touch with good writing and the extraordinary vitality of contemporary narrative and story telling. Reading literally thousands of essays submitted to the journal during that period reminded me daily that a writer's unique voice and the palpable sense of his or her unique presence in a piece of writing are essential hallmarks of the contemporary essay. It's interesting to me that NIF-style public forums are another discursive arena where story, voice, and personal presence matter. In this sense, *narrative* connected my work as a literary editor and my experiments in public conversation and deliberation in the undergraduate classroom.

- When I set out on my first experiment with deliberative pedagogy for the general-education writing course, I was much concerned about my students' anemic civic consciousness. Like many Americans, I thought it derived from their cynicism, apathy, indifference over conventional politics, or perhaps a sense of powerlessness at being left out of the political equation. Accordingly, in the course I posed such questions as: Why have we withdrawn from public association? Why have so many Americans, especially young people, lost faith in our common life?

Given the experience of doing public work alongside this generation through my seasons of deliberative learning and through the influence of my colleagues at Kettering, I'm asking different questions now. For example, how can I deepen my students' connections to the community through the kinds of experiences that move them from an awareness of issues into pragmatic problem-solving strategies? What forms of civic engagements best fit my students' *personal* motivations to get involved—especially their anger, their hope, and the realistic expectations they bring to the work of pursuing systemic social change? Does the university's lofty rhetoric of public service and being a good institutional citizen mask different realities that students experience in the local community—and, indeed, on their home campuses and especially in my classes?

And what traditions in the life of our civic culture can best sustain students' political engagement?

- By helping students learn to become better interpreters of their own lives, society, and culture, my home disciplines of rhetoric and American studies—indeed, the humanities-at-large—can become durable and enduring resources for democracy. With their traditions of rigorous inquiry, analysis, conversation, critical reflection linked to action, and humane questioning of the status quo, the humanities are indispensable to social and cultural renewal. The humanities' quest to find truth and knowledge, as English professor Maria Farland has observed, often originates in problems or challenges that should rightly be considered "public business," especially when that knowledge yields moral insight and ethical clarity or purpose into such pressing issues as mapping the human genome, preserving the natural environment, cloning controversies, reining in youth violence, balancing individual rights and social responsibilities in the wake of 9/11, and resolving racial tensions in our communities and schools—all legitimate terrain of humanistic inquiry and insight. In short, humanists can serve the public interest by sharing their deep understanding of the roots of public problems in ways that speak to everyday experience.

To fulfill that legacy, the humanities professoriate must do a better job of closing the gap between the world of ideas and the theoretical reflexes that animate faculty culture, on the one hand, and our students' preference for concrete applications of knowledge and for active methods of learning, on the other. We need to find new and more effective ways of aligning pedagogical techniques and practices so they better address the disconnect between action and ideas that, for better or worse, characterizes the current generation of undergraduates' predominant learning style and their practices of citizenship. Such pedagogical techniques and practices include the use of active and interactive teaching and learning practices, especially the deliberative pedagogy I experimented with, where the learning ethos of the classroom—syllabus construction and management, assignments, assessment, heuristics, architecture, everything—is modeled after a public forum, and my role as teacher becomes that of a moderator and my students become agents and participants in the productive public work of the course. We also need to better integrate into the curriculum active research opportunities for undergraduates—as in Sarah's capstone—instead of using the undergraduate classroom as a site where we download our research expertise. Students need to be viewed as active producers of knowledge and agents of democracy and not primarily as passive consumers of information. Above all, we have to attend to those features and flaws of the campus culture and its disciplinary arrangements that are detrimental to civic involvement—for example, the degree to which uncontested skepticism is valued and rewarded, the absence of idealism, or the disconnect between the university's professed "mission" and its actual relationship and behavior toward the surrounding community. The same call to urgency, consequence, responsiveness, and relevance that John Dewey issued to the discipline of philosophy 100 years ago applies even more so today to American studies, rhetoric, and the liberal arts generally. "Better it is for philosophy to err in active participation in the living struggles and issues of its own times," Dewey insisted, "than to maintain an immune monastic impeccability without relevancy and bearing in the generating of ideas of its contemporary present."

Four years ago, my first experiment with the "engaged classroom" was a reaction to an ache I felt to connect my scholarship in American studies and my teaching of writing to public issues outside of the academy. I invoked the voices of America's civic conscience—Tocqueville, Whitman, Jane Addams, Martin Luther King Jr., Robert Coles—in an effort to engage students in direct community service. I am still listening to those voices, and I continue to ask students to draw inspiration from them as well. As I have developed new ways of being in the classroom through upper-division courses, seminars, and capstone projects inspired by deliberative democracy, and as I continue to enter new seasons of reclaiming the public mission of the university, I also have to pay attention to the changing voices, challenges, and learning styles of students and not hold them hostage to the political instincts of my generation, the Boomer juggernaut.

The civic engagement and public work movement in the academy has allowed me to reimagine my role in the classroom and the working relationships I have with students, colleagues, and community partners. It has given me opportunities to combine the teaching of academic and public skills. It has challenged me to rethink the purposes and practices of academic scholarship in the humanities. Above all, it has renewed my hope that universities can play a dynamic role in fulfilling Jefferson's legacy and educating citizens to perform the difficult, necessary, and rewarding work demanded by a strong democracy.

David D. Cooper is professor of Writing, Rhetoric, and American Cultures at Michigan State University and University Outreach and Engagement Senior Fellow. Cooper received the Campus Compact's Thomas Ehrlich Faculty Award for Service-Learning in 1999. The editor of the journal Fourth Genre: Explorations in Nonfiction, *he is author/editor of several books—most recently,* Trying the Ties that Bind: Service-Learning and the Moral Life of Faculty. *He is founder and current director of MSU's Public Humanities Collaborative.*

SECTION III

Deliberation in
Professional Education

Chapter Six

Reinventing Teacher Education: The Role of Deliberative Pedagogy in the K-6 Classroom

Cristina Alfaro

Discussions about how best to prepare teachers for our nation's diverse classrooms, particularly those with language-minority and other minority students, usually revolve around the standards and best practices for addressing students' linguistic and academic development. Whereas this focus is important, an equally critical focus is education for civic engagement and decision-making citizens. This essay argues for using a deliberative pedagogy in teacher education and professional development. It examines two concerns: whether such a pedagogy, incorporating deliberative forums and the deliberative technique of issue framing, can be the basis of a curriculum methods course for K-6 teachers; and whether such a course can lead its teacher interns to create class room curricula with a strong focus on deliberative pedagogy.

After eight years of teaching a traditional history and social science methods course to pre-service teachers in California grade-school classrooms, I decided to "reinvent" what I was doing.

I had been frustrated by the course's narrow approach to teacher education. For the most part, it focused on implementing California state standards with a basically "one-size-fits-all" curriculum, which in no way recognized the mixed linguistic, cultural, sociopolitical, and economic conditions of the students. Further, much of what I did involved standards-based curriculum, classroom management, record keeping, tracking, and testing. In effect, I was training technicians for classrooms presumably filled with students all cut from the same mold—in California!

This single-focused approach to teacher education is not just peculiar to California. As careful education analysts have shown (Nieto 2002 and 2003 and Troyna and Rivzi 1998, among them), this approach can be seen in the methods courses, field experiences, and textbooks that college and university teacher education programs use throughout the United States.

That this traditional approach lacks awareness of the increasing diversity of the American classroom is obvious. Less often noted is the failure to consider the need for civic education in grade-school classrooms and for an education that explains the role of the citizen in a democracy. In California, for example, neither the California Standards for the Teaching Profession (the basis for education programs to prepare grade-school teacher candidates) nor the standards of the National Board of Certification (the basis for higher levels of teacher accreditation) say anything about developing a curriculum that focuses on democratic principles and civic engagement.

California is the most diverse state in the United States and one of the most diverse places on Earth. People from the entire planet continuously arrive, especially from Latin America and the Pacific Rim, bringing many cultures and languages to schools, businesses, and communities. For me, as a teacher of teachers, the educational task of responding to this diverse population was of a piece with readying it to engage actively in our democratic life. More specifically, it seemed clear to me that a revised K-6 grade history and social studies curriculum could have a profound impact on preparing students to become decision-making citizens, people ready to participate thoughtfully in the work of democracy.

My view of the democratic task of education comes in part from Dewey (1957), one of the first to advocate for educational renewal utilizing the experience of students—in other words, a bottom-up rather than a top-down approach.

> Education has to be embedded in the real life experience of the learner.... It has to connect with the past of the individual as well as propel him or her into the future.... Experience is

the product of the interaction of the individual with his or her environment.

Both Dewey and, more recently, Nel Noddings (1999) have recognized the need to empower young people as decision makers and have recognized as well that elementary classrooms offer excellent contexts for the practice of decision making. For Dewey, decision making should come through individual deliberation, which he saw as a process whereby individuals separately played out a series of choices in their imagination. This "dramatic rehearsal" would allow a student to make decisions about the consequences of a possible option without actually enacting it.

In "Renewing Democracy in Schools," Noddings identifies two elements of "political education" that are necessary for equipping students to be participants in democracy: choice and discussion. Thus, Noddings takes Dewey's ideas about an individual act of choosing and places it in a group context. Instead of weighing options alone, members of a group weigh options together, informed by the sharing of beliefs, experiences, values, and opinions. This effort to reach a collective understanding lends itself to collective choice.

Paulo Freire's (1985, 114) concept of "conscientization" has also influenced my thinking. In explaining this concept, Freire writes:

> If the type of consciousness that recognizes existing knowl-
> edge could not keep searching for new knowledge, there
> would be no way to explicate today's knowledge.

I take this to mean that educators must keep searching for different ways to teach students from diverse backgrounds. Freire challenges educators to raise their level of consciousness to go beyond commonly accepted existing knowledge as the center of the school curriculum and to supplant it with "multiple centers," based on considerations like class, gender, language, and race. This multidimensional perspective—an important aspect of conscientization—is the necessary first step in creating a new curriculum.

I was drawn to the work of Dewey and Freire in particular because these authors spoke so directly to my experience. I had come from a minority community, and in school my voice was never heard, invited, or valued by the members of the majority community who taught me. Further, in higher education, especially graduate school, as I was being trained in the social sciences and in education, I became committed to a positivistic mode of inquiry, believing that critiques of society that were based on just one individual experience would contaminate "objectivity." As I put it now, I was immersed in the traditional method of teaching the social sciences, which treats the society around us as if we were not participants in it. It was the work of Dewey and Freire that, in essence, brought me to myself; that injected me with a healthy dose of self-criticism, skepticism, and an attitude of challenging the business-as-usual conditions of society; and that ultimately led me to the deliberative pedagogy I propose in this paper for teaching the social sciences to school-age children.

Another factor in deciding to change my approach to teacher education has been the process of reflecting on my 30 years of teaching experience, as a pre-service teacher, classroom teacher, school administrator, curriculum writer, and now a teacher educator. As I looked back on and analyzed my growth, I came to understand that before pre-service teachers could provide an "education for life" for others—an education, that is, that included sociopolitical knowledge, ethical commitment, courage, solidarity, and dedication to democracy—they needed to develop a sense of themselves as individuals and teachers in a democratic society. This is perhaps especially true when teachers face a diverse population consisting largely of minority students.

In all, I strongly believe that schools of education are responsible for preparing teachers with processes and goals that promote academic, social, ethical, *and* civic learning—and to do this, as Dewey writes, through the "real life experience of the learner." To achieve this goal requires both the ability and the sincere commitment to facilitating dialogue and reflection that elicits the voices, ideas, and dispositions of the students. When this is done, all individuals are heard and all lived experiences are respected.

A Deliberative Pedagogy for Teachers

To recast my methods course in history and social science for pre-service K-6 teachers, I developed a course that is shaped by a deliberative pedagogy. My aim was to challenge prospective and practicing teachers to develop for themselves a deliberative pedagogy that they could take with them to their K-6 classrooms.

The deliberative process of teaching and learning, as I see it, introduces students to a diversity of perspectives in explaining and understanding events and experiences. Thus, it develops in students the habits of listening and carefully weighing the trade-offs that accompany every choice, the discipline to keep an open mind, the willingness to stand in someone else's shoes, the capacity to change, and the ability to work with others to make decisions for the common good. The deliberative pedagogy process acknowledges but does not accentuate differences and creates bridges between opposing positions. It also meets the four major learning goals of civic education identified by Thomas Ehrlich (1999). Ehrlich describes their basic components as follows:

1. *Academic learning*—introduces students to terms, concepts, theories, and practices.

2. *Social learning*—entails developing interpersonal skills and personal traits such as careful listening, empathy, and the ability to lead and compromise.

3. *Moral learning*—depends on students thinking about themselves and their beliefs in relation to others; begins to take place when students start to ask questions like, what is my community and what are my obligations to that community?

4. *Civic learning*—involves the students coming to understand the democratic processes of community, its diversity, the problems it faces, the need for individual commitment, and the importance of working collaboratively.

In structuring my course, I was strongly influenced by my involvement with the Kettering Foundation and its Public Scholars Program, where for the first time I had direct and extensive experience with deliberative forums, and by my participation in deliberations of the National Issues Forums (NIF). The primary features of my course are deliberative forums and issue framing, whereby people learn to present the different ways an issue is seen. Framing assumes there are legitimate different ways to see an issue and that they rarely fall into an either/or, this-or-that duality.

Along with teaching and modeling the aspects of critical literacy and concepts of social justice and democracy, I teach the theory and practice of deliberation and the process of framing an issue. One issue my students framed was the Latino academic achievement gap, important not only in California but to the country as a whole. First, we worked through several NIF issue books that dealt with education and race and ethnic issues. Next, we went through the process of identifying and framing the most salient approaches to closing this gap. We identified four such approaches,[1] which included actions to implement them and the trade-offs associated with each.

In identifying the approaches to closing the Latino achievement gap, I explicitly and deliberately drew on the experiences and opinions of my quite diverse teacher candidates. In school curriculums that deal with social problems—indeed, in much public discussion about social problems—entire realms of pertinent experience and many relevant perspectives often remain unacknowledged. In calling on the voices of my students, I aimed to correct that imbalance. In some instances, this was quite simple to do. When talking about immigration, for example, I had students from immigrant families share their experiences. In this and other

---

[1] The four approaches are: balancing standardized assessments (which usually are used to determine the adequacy of the teaching that students receive) with alternative assessments (which focus on the learning taking place among students); using "biliteracy" to teach—that is, teaching in the primary language along with meaningful opportunities to learn and use English; coordinating every stage of education with programs that make higher education both accessible and desirable to Latino students; and using a culturally relevant pedagogy.

ways, I regularly model the teaching I advocate, which includes students as participants in their own learning.

Another important component in my approach is what I call community building, by which I mean building a communal experience within my classroom. Everyone must feel safe to voice their opinions and know that they will be respected and valued. Thus, I initiate my course by engaging students in team-building activities to develop a new way of learning together.

For example, I ask the teacher candidates to look at their "world vision" first as individuals and then as a community of learners. I ask each teacher to write his or her name on an 8x10-inch card and in the four corners of the card respond to the following questions:

1. What brought you to teaching?
2. What are your personal and professional goals?
3. What is your level of engagement with the political world?
4. How do you want to influence the world you live in?

The teachers then assemble the cards into a quilt. At a glance, then, they can see their individual visions and the collective vision of the whole group. Then, we map out the work they need to do to accomplish their personal goals and the course objectives.

I always infuse an openly political flavor to these community-building activities. One aim is to bring out the surface similarities in the attitudes and views of the students, similarities that mask important distinctions that make the continual rebuilding of a sense of community essential. For example, my class has a large percentage of Latino students, in the activities I ask them to engage in highlighting the similarities in their Latino upbringings. At the same time, because my students include Cubans, Colombians, Mexicans, and Panamanians, as well as other Latinos, the activities are quick to show clear differences in the students' traditions, beliefs, values, and dialects.

By its very nature, a deliberative pedagogy is constructivist in the sense that it makes learning a student-centered process and thus is something that the students help construct. Students learn not by receiving information from an authority at the head of a class but through critical dialogue and self-reflection. I regularly ask my students to analyze their activities, their thinking, and their thinking about their thinking. For example, I ask, "How did you feel about voicing your opinion during our class deliberation?" One student wrote the following in her reflective journal:

> Because I am not accustomed to voicing my opinions, I became extremely nervous and had to hold back my tears during our class deliberation.... I can only imagine how my 4th graders feel when they are put on the spot.... Due to this experience, I see it is my responsibility to develop my own sense of voice to become an example for my students. I have come to understand the urgency of providing my students with the necessary skills and knowledge to ensure that by the time they get to the next grade level, and ultimately college, they will develop their own sense of voice, as it relates to other people's voices, and feel comfortable with the deliberation process.

Thus, instead of technically and mechanically following the designated history and social science grade-level textbook, I have teachers engage in the creation of a relevant and purposeful curriculum. This curriculum goes beyond (presumably) neutral knowledge. Rather, it presents points that are the result of complex dialogues, power relations, and struggles among different classes, races, genders, and religions.

A Space for Democracy

Before I could move forward to redesign my methods course, however, I first needed to determine whether the approach I had in mind was in accord with what the California History and Social Science Framework identifies as the "goals and strands" of the curriculum. Because these goals and strands determine the existing conditions and possibilities for K-6 education, I needed to know whether they allowed the kind of bottom-up, civic-oriented learning that I sought to develop, when learners and their activities, rather than fixed lesson plans, are the center of the process. In a word, they did. I found that while the section on grade-level standards does not explicitly address the democratic aspects of the curriculum, the goals and strands that are set out in the introduction to the History and Social Science Framework—the "prescriptions" that are meant to drive the content of the curriculum—are in fact perfectly aligned with the deliberative pedagogy and democratic education I intended.

Traditionally, teachers are trained to focus on the grade-level standards identified in a "prepackaged" curriculum. In most cases, however, the curriculum does not address the prescribed goals and strands, which are far from advocating a one-size-fits-all approach. Indeed, the goals and strands of the framework maintain that elementary school students should understand current conditions in their community, state, country, and the world. Further, they should comprehend the ideas central to liberty, responsible citizenship, and representative government and how these ideas have evolved into institutions and practices, which will be the students' responsibility to sustain as future voters and leaders. The California Framework for K–6 specifically lists the following goals and curriculum strands:

- Historical Literacy
- Ethical Literacy
- Participatory Literacy
- Cultural Literacy
- Geographical Literacy
- Economic Literacy
- Sociopolitical Literacy
- National Identity
- Constitutional Heritage
- Civic Values, Rights, and Responsibility
- Basic Skills Literacy

Given these goals and strands, I was able to receive the support of my department in reinventing my course around a deliberative pedagogy and was able later to assure my teacher candidates that such a course would meet teaching credential guidelines.

I then set about reinventing the curriculum for my two-semester methods course. I had three concerns. First, in introducing my students to the practice of deliberation, could I provide them with enough knowledge and experience to implement a deliberative pedagogy in their classrooms? Second, in their efforts to implement a deliberative pedagogy, what would be their major challenges and successes? Finally, would they be able to sustain the use of deliberation?

These concerns were built into the expectations I set out for my students in the class syllabus. By the end of my two-semester methods course, I expected them to be able to do the following:

- articulate the theory of deliberative pedagogy
- participate in deliberation in class
- reflect on their own deliberative experience in the class
- frame alternative approaches to the issue of teaching language-minority and other minority student groups
- analyze the state's curriculum standards, particularly for the grades they taught, and align the standards with a deliberative pedagogy, to allow for recasting their social studies curriculum in a deliberative framework
- develop and implement issue framing and deliberation in their classrooms
- reflect on their classroom implementation of deliberation, both the challenges and successes
- organize and participate in a countywide forum, which included community members, on closing the Latino achievement gap

Twenty-five teacher interns enrolled in the course. The teachers had diverse ethnic backgrounds (a majority were of Latino descent), and 70 percent came from low-income backgrounds. They all taught ethnolinguistically diverse students in urban settings with large, immigrant, non-English-speaking communities.

The first exposure to deliberative pedagogy for these teacher candidates came in a presentation I offered on deliberation and the need for them to pursue a practice of civic engagement by becoming what the educator James Banks (Banks and Banks 1998) calls "citizen actors." We examined the theory and practice of deliberation and the differences between belief and action and between intellectual and experiential knowledge. Next, to put these new perspectives into practice, we devised four alternative views of how people could work together to build a democratic society. View One was to start with society as it is now and to identify the changes we wanted to bring out. View Two was to analyze the forces that shape society and to identify the obstacles that limit the ability to bring about change. View Three was to focus on the particular aspects of society we want to change. View Four was to concentrate on deliberative pedagogy as a pathway to bringing about change. Finally, I introduced the class to the work of NIF, as an important tool for teachers in addressing the challenge of strengthening the citizen's role in a democratic society and helping to build a bridge that would link the concerns and values of citizens with the sphere of policymaking.

The teacher interns then analyzed, first in small groups and later as a whole class, the importance of democratic theory, the role of citizens, and the willingness of teachers to work towards civic engagement. They also examined California's K-6 class standards and the overall goals and strands for the history and social science curriculum, and quickly grasped the hand-and-glove relationship between deliberative pedagogy and both civic engagement and the state's history and social science curriculum goals and strands.

Next, the students engaged in deliberations in which I served as moderator, always modeling and explaining the purpose of my role as moderator and explaining their roles as deliberators. The issue books we used as the basis for the deliberations dealt with public education, racial and ethnic tensions, and immigration. These deliberations were by far the most rewarding part of the course for the students, and the one that aroused the most enthusiasm, for they were provided the opportunity to engage in a process that treated students as intelligent decision-making citizens and created a space where their voices were heard and respected.

After each deliberation, the students engaged in a debriefing that focused on what they had learned about themselves as deliberators and decision makers. Every debriefing session ended with a discussion of how the deliberative process could be implemented in their particular K-6 classrooms. With each such discussion, the teacher candidates increasingly saw the real possibility of creating and implementing a deliberative pedagogy curriculum in their classrooms.

With this experience, the students went on to organize a community forum on the topic of the Latino achievement gap. The planning began in the first semester, and the forum was held during the second semester. The attendance was modest—about 30 community members. But the students felt that they had passed a hurdle.

By the middle of the first semester, the students were ready to develop forums that would be appropriate for their respective grade levels—and to gain support from their supervisors and "cooperating teachers" (credentialed teachers who support teacher candidates in the classroom), to implement the dramatic, deliberative change in their classrooms.

The first step was to select topics that could serve as the basis for issue books appropriate to the particular grade levels they taught. Working in groups of four or five, according to grade levels, they researched the sociopolitical, economic, and racial/ethnic conditions in their community and then used the history and social science grade-level standards to determine appropriate topics for their respective grades.[2] The framework goals and curriculum strands they drew on in developing their deliberations were geographic literacy, historical literacy, sociopolitical literacy, and national identity.

Working in groups according to grade levels, they prepared one issue book per grade level. They then prepared lesson plans to fit

---

[2] The full state list of appropriate subjects for K-6 is as follows: kindergarten— My Community and Me; first grade—A Child's Place in Space and Time; second grade—People Who Make a Difference; third grade—Continuity and Change; fourth grade—California: A Changing State; fifth grade—United States History and Geography: Making a New Nation; sixth grade—World History and Geography: Ancient Civilization.

the level of their particular student population, listing activities that were appropriate to the age of the students and that also aligned with the state's requirements.

For example, in kindergarten, where My Community and Me was the grade-level standard, the interns took their cue from the framework goals and strands of geographic literacy and cultural literacy. Students went through the process of identifying where the immigrant populations in their community came from and the cultural and linguistic values and struggles they encountered in getting used to the American way of living, thinking, and speaking. Teachers reported that an overriding concern for these kindergarten students was speaking English as a second language. The children felt a little afraid of encountering people who spoke only English and not being able to communicate with them effectively. While the students needed to develop their English-speaking skills so that they could participate comfortably in U.S. society, with the guidance of the teacher they also were able to continue to appreciate and maintain their native language and cultural values.

Another example: In the fifth grade, the grade standard was "United States History and Geography: Making a New Nation;" the teachers focused on the goals and strands of national identity and sociopolitical literacy and developed a deliberation on the issue of gangs in the community. Interestingly, these gangs were multiethnic. Typically, gangs are composed of single ethnic groups. But in this instance, gang members came from different backgrounds and had different national identities. What brought them together was the desire to belong to something, the desire for a feeling of connectedness, which was one of the themes of the deliberation.[3]

---

[3] The full grade-level topics chosen by the teachers were as follows: kindergarten—Community of Immigrants: Where Do We Come From?; first grade—A Child's Place: Doing What You Can on Your Own—Becoming Your Own Advocate! second grade—Making a Difference in Our World; third grade—Working to Make Change at Your School; fourth grade—How to Prepare for Entry to California Universities; fifth grade—National Identity: Choosing What We Want to Belong to and Why; sixth grade—Learning to Read the World and the Word—Creating the Road to Higher Education.

All the teachers planned to take their students through the process of framing the issues and choices for the chosen deliberation topic and identifying trade-offs for each choice. Through this process, teachers sought always to reaffirm that life comes down to making decisions for the greater good, that in order to choose there has to be a chooser, in order to act there has to be a citizen actor, and in order to deliberate you must be open to multiple points of view.

With this structure in hand, the 25 teacher interns were ready to meet with their principals and their cooperating teachers to explain how the new approach would satisfy the grade-level standards and goals and strands of the curriculum framework. At this point, as a model for seeking permission to implement a deliberative pedagogy in the classroom, I shared the process I went through with my supervisors. After some difficulty—more on this in the next section—all the interns received the support of both principals and cooperating teachers and were allowed to develop and implement in their classrooms a deliberative pedagogy for the history and social science content area.

Obviously, it was much easier to implement a full deliberative process in the upper grades. In some upper grades, teachers were even able to use NIF books to conduct their forums. In the lower grades, teachers focused more on the process of teaching children to examine their reality (for example, guiding them to examine their living surroundings and how the surroundings compared with the conditions of the community and the world-at-large), to give voice to their opinions, and to begin to listen to the points of view of others in order to make the best choices. Children in kindergarten deliberated at a very basic level about issues that were meaningful to them—for example, their unequal access to playing sports, since the economic situation of many students prevented them from participating. In many cases, the problem extended to not having the necessary recreational facilities in their immediate community. The children discussed how their access might be increased. The process taught the students the value of weighing options and trade-offs to make decisions, an experience that conceivably planted a seed, which would further their development as citizen actors.

While implementing their deliberative programs, the teacher candidates regularly exchanged comments through written and oral reflections on the sometimes difficult challenges they faced in engaging their students. They found that the exchanges were most useful in addressing how to overcome the challenges. By helping them develop more clarity with respect to their vision and mission, the critical reflections, they explained, encouraged them to stay the course when they faced seemingly intractable problems.

One common struggle, found across all grade levels, was propelling students to develop their "voice"—providing the kind of space in which students felt comfortable talking about their experiences and giving their opinions. The teacher interns concluded that they had to bring about a paradigm shift in the standard power dynamics of classrooms, where students are normally treated as empty vessels to be filled by the teacher. Now, students had to be treated as contributors to their own learning. This meant the teacher needed to take on the role of a facilitator of teaching and learning and could no longer be the only person that imparts knowledge. This, indeed, is what happened.

At the end of the semester, the graduating teacher interns spoke to the incoming class of pre-service teachers, reporting on both their personal growth and their experiences in bringing a deliberative pedagogy to their classrooms.

Assessing Their Experiences

During the second semester, before the interns received their teaching credentials, I interviewed them in focus groups about their ongoing experiences with deliberative pedagogy in their classrooms and communities. For me, this was the best way to learn about the impact of my course and to learn about the challenges and resistance the interns faced in their schools. They spoke about these issues in our focus groups and also in their reflective journals as well.

Many of the teacher interns spoke of their earlier frustration with the one-size-fits-all curriculum of the prescribed textbook.

But they had not known what to do about it. They reported that the activities of our methods course, particularly the discussions about deliberative pedagogy and the collaborative examination of the standard academic goals of the curriculum, prepared them to take action to change the traditional curriculum. The first steps in doing this consisted of strategizing on how to develop grade-appropriate deliberations and how to persuade administrators to allow them to use deliberations. How to take deliberative pedagogy into their respective classrooms proved to be the most serious challenge they faced because it involved a paradigm shift in the traditional methods of teaching elementary school students, with teachers taking on the role of facilitators, allowing the views and thoughts of the students to form the basis for discussions. It often took much preparation by the teacher interns and much convincing of their administrators and the cooperating teachers at their schools to receive permission to pursue the deliberative way of teaching and learning. The primary worry was the length of time that seemed to be needed to teach this approach. A second concern was that the history and social science grade-level standards would not be met. The teacher interns resolved these issues with fully detailed lesson plans outlining the standards and goals and strands of the curriculum. The resistance had one good effect: it induced the teacher interns to be clear about why they wanted to implement a deliberative pedagogy in their classrooms. This clarity sustained them during difficult times.

For most teachers, the benefits to students were notable. The teachers especially spoke of their students' gains in cognitive skills. For example, the teachers regularly reported that after several sessions of engaging in deliberation, students encountering a new problem or issue in other content areas would be able to go through the process of identifying and analyzing "best alternatives" on their own.

Relevant here is the work of James Banks (Banks and Banks 1998), a specialist in multicultural and social studies education, who has developed a highly regarded social science curriculum to teach students how to make reflective and informed decisions as a basis for their becoming citizen actors. We discussed Banks' work in class. He maintains that many cognitive skills are involved in the higher-level thinking that is necessary for reflective and informed decisions: thinking strategies—problem solving, decision making, and conceptualizing; critical-thinking strategies—distinguishing between verifiable facts and value claims, recognizing logical inconsistencies in a line of reasoning, and identifying unstated assumptions; and microthinking strategies—reasoning, analysis (compare, contrast, and classify), and evaluation. Looking back on their experiences, a majority of the teachers believed that both they and their students came to develop and expand these higher-level thinking skills through their participation in deliberation.

In teacher education, conversations often revolve around strategies to develop critical-thinking skills as an end in itself. The comments of the methods class teacher candidates about themselves and about their students suggest that deliberative pedagogy is one pathway to developing the higher-level thinking skills that Banks argues are necessary to form critical-thinking citizen actors.

The following comments provide snapshots of the shifts in focus and the growth and insights that deliberative work brought to many of my teacher interns and (if their comments are accurate) their students.

> Without deliberative pedagogy, my lens would have continued to only have one monocultural window. I am now able to teach beyond the prescribed text and standardized tests to focus on knowledge that will develop critical and even global thinkers and productive decision-making citizens.

> My students will not have to wait until they attend college to learn about the benefits, techniques, and process of deliberation. This process has begun now, in my kindergarten classroom. My students are rising to the expectation of becoming smart decision makers. They love discussing the trade-offs to daily decisions we make as a class. I see the next United States President coming from this class.

When I started this course, I had no idea that it would be such a powerful tool for me both personally and professionally. Learning how to deliberate myself has been a catalyst for implementing the process of deliberation in my sixth-grade classroom. My students love it!

The process of deliberation helped me to move beyond my habits of thought, perception, and closedmindedness. Deliberative pedagogy is not about being taught but about waking up.

After engaging in and analyzing deliberative work through forums, I have been able to create curriculum units for my third-graders that have at their core the process of deliberative pedagogy. The cognitive operations my students utilize in this process directly develop "high level" thinking skills. This new way of viewing through "multiple windows," as my students say, carries over to the literature they are reading during our "literacy" block. Whatever they read, they now always ask, "Whose perspective is included in this?"

I have become active in working with the parents of my community. In addition to implementing deliberation in my fourth-grade classroom, I am now working with parents to frame issues that concern them about their child's education. It is an extremely satisfying experience to know that I can assist my community in this manner.

We can see from these comments and their between-the-lines implications that the process the teacher interns underwent in learning how to frame issues and deliberate was a strong force in propelling them to develop and implement an elementary school curriculum based on decision making and citizen action.

Concluding Observations

When I set about reinventing the curriculum for my teacher education methods course, a major concern was, can teachers who learn how to deliberate about public issues develop the necessary knowledge, skills, and confidence to implement a deliberative pedagogy in their classrooms? Pablo Picasso once said something like, "Anything new is hard to do the first time." But as tall an order as this project seemed at the outset, the end result has made more than worthwhile all the effort, hard work, and determination, particularly of the teacher interns, who went off a cliff of sorts when they enrolled in my methods course. Despite all the difficulties, teacher interns enlisted the support of their administrators and succeeded in navigating their way toward a curriculum based on deliberative pedagogy. What is more, they have found in this pedagogy a new way of teaching and learning.

As I type these words, I am happy to report that of the 25 graduates of my course, 15 continue to practice deliberative pedagogy in their classrooms. Some of them have become leaders in their schools, and some have succeeded in introducing deliberation into their communities. In particular, four of the program graduates have continued to advance their civic engagement work beyond the classroom and are currently involved in leading community forums, including a forum on the Latino achievement gap. Further, these teachers have agreed to participate in an in-depth study to determine how teachers can continue to support deliberative pedagogy in elementary classrooms and withstand bureaucratic and sometimes political pressures.

Such pressures have been at work on a number of the course graduates. Several teachers have reported that the pressure they are under to produce high test scores has pulled them away from a deliberative pedagogy and the authentic and powerful way of teaching they found in it. For an advocate like myself, the issue might be put this way: what is more important—higher test scores or higher thinking levels? On some days, I am harsher. "What is more important," I ask myself, "memory work or democratic work?"

One lesson here is that teachers need the support of their school districts, administrators, and teacher education institutions to implement deliberative pedagogy effectively and consistently. Based on conversations with these teachers, it is quite clear that for this way of teaching to penetrate the state department of education, schools of education and school districts need to value it and support it.

Today, more than ever, teacher preparation and professional development should never be reduced to a traditional form of training. In some situations, it may be that we need to exercise courage to go beyond it. As Freire (1998a, 1998b) argues (writing, as he did, about situations of oppression), teachers must be equipped with the knowledge of what it means to teach with courage. But whatever the resistance, teacher preparation should go beyond the technical preparation of teachers and be rooted in the ethical formation of democratic education and civic engagement.

Our increasingly globalized and diverse society demands it. Today, this society is marked by sweeping and unprecedented changes. As of 2007, for example, 60 percent—*60 percent!*—of the students in Southern California are Latino and 1.5 million are English language learners. Additionally, recent state anti-immigrant laws have begun to spark the political awareness in the heretofore, sleeping giant of the Latino community. In my view, such changes are not fleeting but rather are a sign that we are entering a new society and age that, through population changes, will challenge many of our traditional values, assumptions, and behaviors, including our traditional ways of teaching. We must think freshly not just about the general goals of education but also about the methods of teaching and what we want to educate our children for.

I think it is fair to say that helping students become effective citizen actors in today's world is a tremendous challenge.

I want to close with an anecdote about an effect of the methods course that I never expected—an effect on my own work. At this writing, I am preparing a master's level course for practicing teachers called Foundations of Democratic Education. Many of the teachers enrolled in this graduate-level course are graduates of my reinvented methods course, which of course is gratifying. However, these teachers were looking to deepen their understanding of deliberation and were dismayed to discover that I would not in fact be discussing how to develop a more advanced practice of deliberative pedagogy. Extremely disappointed, they insisted that I also reinvent this course, to which, finally, I agreed and, with their help, did. How could I say no to teachers who wanted to learn more about deliberation?

My effort to promote the use of a deliberative pedagogy in the classroom has now come full circle, as the teachers I have taught have taught me to expand the use of a deliberative pedagogy into graduate courses of education that I teach! I like to see this as a sign of the power of deliberation.

Cristina Alfaro is assistant professor in the Department of Policy Studies in Language and Cross-Cultural Education at San Diego State University. The majority of students in her classes in teacher preparation and professional development are immigrants or children of immigrants, speak English as a second language, and are first-generation college students. She is also the California State University chairperson for the International Teacher Education Consortium and directs the university's International Teacher Professional Development Program in which California teachers earn their certification in Bilingual Cross-Cultural and Language Academic Development.

References

Banks, James and Cherry A. McGee-Banks. *Teaching Strategies for the Social Studies: Decision-Making and Citizen Action*. Fifth edition. Boston, MA: Allyn & Bacon, 1998.

Dewey, John. *Human Nature and Conduct: An Introduction to Social Psychology*. New York: Modern Library, 1957 (originally published in 1922).

Ehrlich, Thomas. "Civic Education: Lessons Learned." *Political Science & Politics* 32 (June 1999): 245-250.

Freire, Paulo. *Pedagogy of Freedom: Ethics, Democracy, and Civic Discourse*. New York: Rowan & Littlefield Publishers, 1998a.

Freire, Paulo. *Teachers as Cultural Workers: Letters to Those Who Dare Teach.* Boulder, CO: Westview, 1998b.

Freire, Paulo. *The Politics of Education: Culture: Power, and Liberation.* South Hadley, MA: Bergin & Garvey, 1984.

Nieto, Sonia. *What Keeps Teachers Going?* New York: Teachers College Press, 2003.

Nieto, Sonia. *Language, Culture, and Teaching: Critical Perspectives for a New Century.* Mahwah, NJ: Lawrence Erlbaum Associates Publishers, 2002.

Noddings, Nel. "Renewing Democracy in Schools." *Phi Delta Kappan* (April 1999): 579-583.

Troyna, Barry and Fazal Rivzi. "Racialization of Difference and the Cultural Politics of Teaching." In B. J. Biddle, T. L. Good, and I. F. Goodson, eds. *International Handbook of Teachers and Teaching.* Boston: Kluwer Academic Publishers, 1998.

Chapter Seven

Learning about Deliberative Democracy in Public Affairs Programs

Larkin S. Dudley and Ricardo S. Morse

Public affairs practitioners are increasingly being asked to engage citizens in deliberative practices. Professional public affairs training needs to reflect this reality and teach the skills of deliberative democracy. This essay reports on a variety of efforts to teach deliberative democracy to graduate students through coursework and extracurricular experience. We describe how public affairs programs may include deliberative democracy in the curriculum through teaching basic participation models, the art of reasoned judgment, moderator skills, issue framing, and the crafting of research agendas from practice in real-world situations. Developing these democratic competencies will benefit students as future citizens and possible public officials.

Today, the *public nature of a career* in public affairs requires that graduate students develop competencies to teach citizens how to engage in the democratic processes of resolving common concerns. There are more than 250 graduate programs in public affairs in the United States. These programs—in public administration, public affairs, public management, and public policy—prepare students for public service careers, provide continuing education and advancement opportunities for current practitioners, and prepare doctoral students for teaching and research in academia, think tanks, and other organizations. We maintain that these graduate programs can play a critical role in advancing civic engagement in our society.

It is no longer enough for public service practitioners to be effective managers or policy experts; the current environment of public service demands practitioners who work collaboratively with citizens for the public good. John Nalbandian has found that the "contemporary roles, responsibilities, and values of city managers" include being "community builders and enablers of democracy"

(1999, 187). This finding is consonant with the many calls within public administration for a more participatory (or deliberative) practice (see, for example, Box 1998; Cooper 1991; Denhardt and Denhardt 2003; King and Stivers 1998; Wamsley and Wolf 1996), and also with the remarkable consistency of the codes of professional public affairs organizations in stressing the need for skills in deliberative engagement.[1] These skills go well beyond the "civic" component of a liberal education (see, for example, Anderson 1993 and Colby et al. 2003). Whereas all students need to develop general skills in deliberative participation, public professionals need to be able to organize and lead deliberative processes and contribute to research to improve such practice. We focus here on developing such *professional* competencies for the promotion of deliberative democracy.

While there are a variety of interpretations of deliberative democracy, most share the same basic meaning of deliberation: "to weigh carefully both the consequences of various options for action and the views of others" (Mathews 1999, 111). We concur with Wayne Ross, who recently wrote that deliberation is the "heart not only of education for democratic citizenship, but also of democracy itself" (2004). Indeed, for many, deliberative listening and speaking is essential to any concept of democracy (Barber 1984; Fishkin 1995; Gastil 1993; Mathews 1999; Pateman 1970). A subset of the civic skills of deliberative democracy deals with civic engagement. Civic

---

[1] For example, the first tenet of the Code of Ethics of the American Society for Public Administration is "serve the public interest," and it speaks directly about involving citizens in decision-making policy (http://www.aspanet.org/scriptcontent/ index_codeofethics.cfm). Similarly, the "Practices for Effective Local Government Management" of the International City/County Management Association includes elements like "policy facilitation" and "democratic advocacy and citizen participation" (http://www.icma.org). The Code of Ethics and Professional Conduct of the Institute of Certified Planners speaks of "the planner's responsibility to the public" (http://www.planning.org/ethics/conduct.html).

engagement refers to how citizens become engaged in the public sphere and how public professionals contribute to this process.

This chapter explores a variety of ways to teach the knowledge and skills of deliberative democracy to engage citizens. We also report on the application of such knowledge and skills in the field and the research questions this field research prompted. The first section of this paper, the teaching section, briefly outlines the kinds of knowledge and skills involved in teaching deliberative democracy and the variety of contexts in which this teaching can occur. Of particular interest is the suggestive research on whether deliberation can take place on the Internet. We then move to application and report on our experiences in the classroom and beyond.

Knowledge of Deliberative Democracy Needed in the Public Affairs Curriculum

Our argument begins with the conviction that civic education, the education that develops competencies for deliberative democracy, is a specific need of professional graduate education in public affairs. These competencies include the knowledge and skills needed for the effective organizing and facilitating of deliberative processes. This is a complex task, as a partial listing of the needed competencies indicates:

- Understanding public participation and the principles of deliberative democracy
  - Theories of participatory democracy and related conceptual components, such as social capital and civil society
  - Knowledge of different models/processes of deliberation and when to use them
  - Understanding of group processes and principles of conflict resolution
  - Reflection on the relationship between the role of the expert and the role of the citizen
- Appreciating reasoned argument and diverse perspectives
  - Understanding and appreciating diversity
  - Ability to cope with conflict

- Gaining moderator/facilitator skills
  - General facilitation skills, including techniques for different circumstances (for example, nominal group process and fish bowl)
  - Finding common ground among participants
- Framing issues for discussion
  - Identifying and convening stakeholders to learn their views
  - Relaying citizen/stakeholder concerns to appropriate outlets for action
- Conducting research on deliberation and contributing scholarship

Of course, this list can be expanded. The main point is that there is a wide range of knowledge and skills relative to deliberative democracy that current and future public servants need to be effective in engaging citizens and advancing deliberative democracy in society.

The question for public affairs education, then, is how to teach these competencies, the subject to which we turn next.

Building an Understanding of Deliberative Democracy and Public Participation in a Stand-Alone Course

At present, very few Master of Public Affairs programs offer stand-alone courses in the area of citizen engagement and participation, and of those that do, most tend to focus on developing knowledge rather than skills (Schachter and Aliaga 2003). Virginia Tech and Iowa State University are exceptions. Iowa State has piloted an intensive one-week summer course, "Community Participation and Conflict Resolution," which emphasizes both theory and practice. Virginia Tech also regularly offers an upper-division undergraduate course on "Community Involvement," which is available as an elective for graduate students.

Here we draw on our experience in developing and teaching both courses. In assembling the literature for the courses, we found many useful "how-to" texts from which to choose, including *The Public*

Participation Handbook: Making Better Decisions through Citizen Involvement (Creighton 2005), *How to Make Collaboration Work* (Straus 2002), *Public Participation in Public Decisions* (Thomas 1995), and *The Collaborative Leadership Fieldbook* (Chrislip 2002). These nuts-and-bolts, toolbox-oriented texts can be supplemented by theoretical texts that express strong democratic perspectives; examples include *Government Is Us* (King and Stivers 1998), *The New Public Service* (Denhardt and Denhardt 2003), and *Citizen Governance* (Box 1998).

The recently published *Deliberative Democracy Handbook* (Gastil and Levine 2005), a mix of theory, case studies, and process descriptions, would make an excellent textbook for a stand-alone course. For more theoretical background, there are many excellent readers (see, for example, Bohman and Rehg 1997).

To deliberate is to deal with conflict. Here, one book stands out—the classic *Getting to Yes* by Fisher and Ury (1991), which provides foundational instruction on conflict management skills that students can connect with and quickly grasp. There are also a variety of useful books and articles about group processes and facilitation skills as well as helpful case studies.[2]

Among the many topics that were covered in both courses, a highlight was the incorporation of materials from the National Issues Forum Institute. In two iterations of the Iowa State course, students participated in a forum on immigration using a National Issues Forums (NIF) book and then discussed the techniques used

---

[2] Rich material on group process and facilitator skills can be found in *The Skilled Facilitator* (Schwarz 2002), *Facilitator's Guide to Participatory Decision-Making* (Kaner 2007), and the excellent collection of articles in *The Consensus Building Handbook* (Susskind, McKearnan, and Thomas-Larmer 1999). Helpful case studies are found in *Government Is Us* (King and Stivers 1998), *The Collaborative Leadership Fieldbook* (Chrislip 2002), and the *Deliberative Democracy Handbook* (Gastil and Levine 2005). The Electronic Hallway (www.hallway.org) is an excellent source of material case studies and role plays with many cases focusing explicitly on citizen participation. One very helpful (and free) resource that includes cases and role plays is *Turning Lemons into Lemonade*, a training packet developed by the Southern Rural Development Center (http://srdc.msstate.edu/training/trainingcurricula.htm).

by the moderator and recorder. The mixture of participating in a forum, discussing the forum skills and techniques, and exploring how they might be applied in practice was an excellent learning experience. In small groups, the students also framed an issue using an NIF guide (Kettering Foundation 2001), and afterwards stepped back and discussed how to apply the process to professional settings in which they might find themselves.

Other experiential exercises, such as observing participation events outside of class and writing reviews of the events, were also beneficial. Another useful teaching method is to have students select a specific participation method, such as nominal group technique or fish bowl, and teach it to the class. Afterward, the class can consider the merits of the method, how deliberative it was or was not, and in what conditions it would be appropriate.

Some of the assignments and in-class activities can focus specifically on developing deliberative skills. In one such assignment, students, using a guidebook developed by the Public Conversations Project (available at http://www.publicconversations.org), organized and facilitated a deliberative dialogue of their own. The students turned in a portfolio chronicling the experience, including an essay reflecting on what they learned. A good culminating assignment for such a course might be a "professional practice" essay, which encourages students to link the theory and practice they acquire over the semester with their future careers. Students must learn to think holistically about the interrelationships between their future professional lives and concepts like democracy, community, and deliberation. Other experiential, skills-developing activities include in-class simulations and role plays.

In summary, the stand-alone course attempts to focus equally on the development of both knowledge and skill through a mixture of readings and class discussion coupled with simulations, role plays, and case studies. The experiential elements of stand-alone courses engage the students and help them connect the theory of deliberative democracy to the practice of deliberative democracy. Our students frequently told us they appreciated the exercises, which gave them experience and showed them the "practicality" of theory. In the end, the goal is to develop practitioners with both a deliberative sensibility and the relevant skills needed to express that sensibility in their professional roles.[3]

Preparing Graduate Students to Use Deliberative Techniques in the Classroom and Online

We have also worked with graduate students in a variety of courses to develop the students' capacity to mentor undergraduates in the methods of deliberation and the process of reaching public judgment in the course of weighing alternative compelling cases (Anderson 1990, 201). The two examples below respectively cover deliberation in a leadership course and an extension of deliberation to an online format.

Deliberation in a Leadership Course

In this example, faculty and PhD students from the Center for Public Administration and Policy at Virginia Tech taught undergraduates in the school's honors program to be forum facilitators for students in the Residential Leadership Community (RLC), an undergraduate program in which students live together and take common leadership courses. In effect, the RLC group serves as a stand-in for a group of citizens who are trained in deliberation to resolve a common problem.

The faculty and graduate students taught the honors students a variation of the forum approach pioneered by Kettering Foundation and the National Issues Forums Institute. To explain briefly, this approach features a nonpartisan overview of three or more ap-

---

[3]Many other related topics make sense for such a stand-alone graduate course, including, to list only a few, theories of social capital, civic society, citizenship, diversity and cultural competence, and some of the classic writings on participation, such as Arnstein's "A Ladder of Citizen Participation" (1969) and, more recently, King, Feltey, and Susel's "The Questions of Participation" (1998).

proaches to an issue and identifies the arguments for and criticisms of each approach. The forums are different from adversarial debates because they encourage participants to analyze each response, the arguments for and against it, and the trade-offs, costs, and consequences for each. We found this deliberative model appealing because it encourages the teaching of a cluster of important skills, among them: understanding how values influence the framing of an issue; identifying the complexity of an issue in terms of costs and trade-offs; and the inclusion of the voices of people who are not in the room. We also valued this approach because it helped the graduate students who were training the undergraduate facilitators to apply and consider some of the theoretical issues of deliberative democracy in a real case.

According to observations of the RLC forums by multiple instructors over time, the deliberative format does indeed encourage students to see the several dimensions of a policy issue and to appreciate the values behind the approaches to resolving it. Closed-ended evaluation questions indicated that the RLC student participants gained considerable knowledge of the several approaches, some of them diametrically opposed to their own. Comments from students included: "Hearing about other's experiences added to my own perception of problems/lacks in our society." "Being able to talk about these issues in this kind of setting is a good way for people to realize and understand why other people believe what they believe." "Yes, it was definitely a positive experience and worth doing again. It's important for students to see all sides of a subject."

The faculty of the Residential Leadership Community involved in this project were unaccustomed to the NIF deliberative approach. The following comments typify their responses.

> There is value in the forum process—how to dialogue—but there needs to be a better understanding of how we should facilitate. Perhaps have all the faculty and student moderators go through a forum together and see how we should facilitate.

> We like the forum and would like to see it continue. I like the developmental idea of moving from debate to delibera-

tion—of seeing more than one or two perspectives. First-year students need this. We also found this experience to be a community-building activity for our class.

Among the facilitators, debate and dialogue broke out around a variety of issues: How would we know that deliberation had occurred? What techniques worked better to get students involved? Would this type of learning enhance otherwise traditional approaches? Graduate students and faculty began to examine the ways in which they were teaching deliberation and what facilitation means.

In all, these results were evidence to the faculty and graduate students that the forum technique could be taught to citizens and could be a useful tool in helping people with differing views resolve a problem of common concern. Needless to say, one forum will not produce major intellectual or behavioral change in a student or a citizen, as Daniel O'Connell (1997) has noted, but a forum can help students and citizens become more accepting of others' viewpoints and move beyond their preconceived ideas on topics. For major intellectual or behavioral change, we would suspect that a more intensive and integrated approach to citizen participation and deliberative democracy would be needed.[4]

Conducting Research on Deliberative Forums: Face-to-Face Groups versus Online Forums

Prompted by the increased interactions between government and citizens in virtual space, we worked with one of our PhD students, an instructor in political science, to extend the NIF model to an online format. This time the topic was campaign financing. We were able to design a research project to compare the outcomes of a traditional NIF presentation of campaign financing among undergraduates in a single, face-to-face forum of 40 students with the outcomes of online threaded discussions in a large class of 120 students over the course of several weeks. In threaded discussions,

---

[4] See the discussion of McMillan and Harriger (2002) for an explanation of the need for a more intensive format to produce change.

online participants post their initial comments, which then serve as the basis for another round of comments. One set of comments is thus "threaded" onto another set. In both situations, we again wanted to see whether groups who had been taught deliberation could teach it to others who then could use it to address common concerns.

In the face-to-face forum, undergraduate students served as moderators just as they had in the RLC forums. For the online forum, the instructor randomly assigned every student to 1 of the 5 discussion groups of approximately 24 members each. Each group participated in an online threaded discussion (also referred to as a bulletin board) maintained on a class Web site, developed using CourseInfo software (now known as Blackboard) licensed to Virginia Tech.

The online discussions occurred during two sessions. After reading the issue book *Money and Politics* (National Issues Forums Institute 2000), students entered at least one comment to the campaign financing alternatives presented in the NIF publication. During the next week, a volunteer from each discussion group prepared and posted a summary paragraph, which tried to capture a preliminary consensus of the participants. During the third week, every group member made at least one further comment responding to the summary posted for his or her group. Thus, the only facilitation that occurred in the online forums was the review and summary prepared by a volunteer group member.

The members of the research project compared outcomes in two ways: from the pre- and postsurveys of students in both groups and through a content analysis of the transcripts of the face-to-face forums and the text of posted messages in threaded discussions. From the pre- and postsurveys, we found that discourse in both settings produced changes in students' positions around the topic, most notably in acknowledging a deeper understanding of the questions surrounding campaign financing and a fuller appreciation of the multiple ways to view the issue. Again, students saw the value of teaching deliberation that others could use to discuss and understand difficult issues.

However, the transcriptions of face-to-face forums and messages posted to threaded discussions pointed to differences between the two formats and to the usefulness of the virtual format. Among deliberators, both personal risk taking, measured by the frequency of *I* statements, and identification with the group, measured by the frequency of *we* words, were greater in the threaded discussion. These results give support to the view that online media can be a valuable aid to deliberation and that a deliberative format can be part of an online approach for a larger class.

Because the two kinds of forums were organized somewhat differently in order to meet each instructor's needs, our findings are only suggestive. Even so, they are intriguing. We may be observing a generational development, with virtual deliberation being seen and accepted as an extension of all the forms of virtual communication to which those under 25 are accustomed. The experiment also prompted questions among faculty and graduate students. In what places and with what policy issues could online forums be valuable? How much difference in forum outcomes can be related to the medium? Thus, this comparison of traditional and online forums not only involved students in deliberation but also involved researchers in an experimental process, which led to further reflection on the role of technology in civic engagement.

"Real-World" Issues and New Research Agendas

In this section, we discuss three community projects in which our students dealt with concerns that had "real-world" consequences, some quite serious. One notable aspect of these experiences is that they inspired our students to pose new issues for research. Another aspect is the tension between citizens and experts that frequently emerges in real-world issues and that were part of the three deliberative projects we describe. This can be a thorny problem, especially today, when the supporters of citizens and the supporters of experts often approach the work of government from very different perspectives.

A recent article by John Nalbandian (2005) argues that many local government officials find themselves in the middle of two opposing forces, the drive for administrative modernization and the drive for civic engagement. Modernization creates an administrative culture driven by efficiency and technique and encourages more and more players from the private sector and nonprofit organizations to become stakeholders in public decisions. Thus, one of the effects of a more complex network of specific stakeholders involved in public decisions is that citizens who lack expertise or vested interest in these decisions may well have less opportunity to be involved.

According to Nalbandian, the characteristics of local government modernization include a basic idea that citizens are customers to be served. The problem is that the idea of "customer" does not include an emphasis on citizens' responsibility. When a citizen is a customer, then the government is seen as a provider of services. While citizens as individual consumers can vote with their feet or complain individually if they are unhappy, this perspective does not encourage citizens to engage issues actively, find common ground for action with other citizens, or take a sustained interest in governing.

The forces of civic engagement see citizens quite differently. According to Nalbandian (2005) and many others, some of the characteristics associated with civic engagement are: engaging citizens in administrative processes, acknowledging expression of direct democracy, enabling more transparency, ensuring two-way communication with citizens about policy and service delivery, and creating a social fabric through partnerships with other nongovernmental sectors. Citizens can be respected as "experiential experts" in that they bring to the table the expertise of living in the situations others wish to fix.

Nalbandian points to the conflict between the forces of modernization, which homogenize our lives and erase community identity, and the need on the part of citizens for identity and for connection to civic culture and communities that create "anchors and resting points" (Nalbandian 2005, 313). Through most of the 20th century and now into the 21st, we have seen the growing prominence of the expert in government as the one who advises and is the decision maker because of the person's access to a body of established and presumably value-free knowledge. What is more, this knowledge is often unavailable to citizens—for example, in the case of a very technical knowledge—even when experts would like to invite the citizens into decision making.

Thus, one of the most important tensions facing students aiming toward a profession in public affairs is the need to recognize the importance of contributions from both experts and citizens and the need to balance them. The efforts of many in public administration have shown that there is no one method to resolve this tension. This said, we have found that a deliberative democracy approach is, indeed, one way to integrate the expertise of knowledge with the right of citizens to express what they value and why. The following three projects provide examples.[5]

A Divided Highway

The problem facing a nearby small town, Wytheville, Virginia, had the potential for major community disruption, including a significant loss of local revenue. The issue was whether to divide and relocate two major highways. A team from Virginia Tech was asked to manage what would be the lengthy community process of identifying the highway locations that the community preferred and to be the focal point for a community "visioning" effort to help the community develop a better sense of its future. In all, the project would take some three years. In describing the project, our

---

[5] The research report here is based on the team efforts of many faculty and students now or formerly at Virginia Tech. We wish to recognize the contributions of our colleagues: James Armstrong, James Bohland, Kim Chiapeto, Mary Beth Dunkenberger, Muxian Fang, Joseph Freeman (Lynchburg College), Erin Hofberg, Jeff Janosko, Sally Johnson, Dong Won Kim, Soo Young Park, Ray Pethtel, James Phillips (VCU), Andy Sorrell, Max Stephenson, Bethany Stich, Ann Wolford, Kathryn Young, and Diane Zahm. Some of the material appears in an article by Morse et al. (2005).

prime emphasis will be on the lessons learned by the managing team of faculty and five graduate students, essentially a research team, which was led by a graduate student.

To serve as the basis for forums, the team needed to construct an issue book on the fundamental issue that the community had to decide: "What do we want our community to be in the future?" To determine the alternative views that would be the heart of the issue book, the team adopted the issue-framing technique developed by the Kettering Foundation (2001). Statements reflecting alternative responses were gathered from a variety of sources: through research on such pertinent factors as the effects of population growth and possible economic scenarios, from sessions with groups of stakeholders, and from interviews with townspeople.

The team involved the community in the process. Graduate students conducted 50 local interviews; developed a profile of the community's demographic, economic, and educational trends to inform citizens of Wytheville's relative position compared to other communities in Virginia; and assembled a stakeholder committee in preparation for issue-framing sessions. The team then facilitated four sessions of issue framing with the stakeholder group over a six-week time period. In the initial meeting, participants reviewed the profile of the community and the stakeholder interview data, then brainstormed issues and concerns related to the question of what the community's vision for the future should be. In subsequent meetings, the group clustered concerns, developed themes, and eventually fleshed out four distinct approaches for a community vision. Between meetings, the graduate students typed up and clarified the knowledge being generated by the group. During meetings, the students facilitated the deliberative process and otherwise moved the issue framing along.

From this process, an issue book, titled *Shaping Our Community's Future: Which Way Do We Go?* was developed. A local printer produced hundreds of copies at cost. Over the next several months, dozens of community forums were facilitated by the research team in churches, civic clubs, industrial plants, town hall, hospitals, and the local community college. Town and county officials were also involved. After almost a year of community forums, the stakeholder group reconvened and, through a process of deliberation, synthesized the results into a community vision statement. The research team again facilitated the process.

The enthusiasm of the citizens enhanced the team's belief that deliberative democracy could make a difference in real-world settings. Incredible to watch in this setting was the evolution and broadening of the community's focus from a narrow immediate question of road relocation to a larger question of the future of the community. The research team also observed the value of the process of deliberation as a way of building civic infrastructure. An example from one forum is representative. A forum of approximately one dozen community members seemed to devolve into an "us versus them" discussion, emphasizing what "they" (local government) were or were not doing about perceived community needs. Midway through this conversation, one of the participants asked the group, in effect, "What are we doing?" At that point:

> There was a noticeable shift in how an issue was framed from "what they can do for us" to "what can we do for ourselves?" The shift in the conversation allowed the group to open the door to new lines of thinking, including how they can develop leadership in a broad sense. This turned the discussion toward what could be done in the schools and how the community could create a climate of active citizenship (Morse 2004, 175).

Such examples of community learning (see Morse 2006a and 2006b) were evident throughout the process and illustrated for the research team how deliberative practice helps develop the sense of citizen responsibility (we) in contrast to the customer mentality that only considers what "they" can do for "me."

The three-year effort produced important community outcomes and, for the research team, many rich discoveries regarding civic engagement and deliberation. For the five graduate students, the experience served as valuable in-service education in deliberative engagement. The process of the community issue framing and the deliberations that followed prompted the graduate students to dig deeper into the effects and value of forums. They asked such questions as: What relationships do forums have to the development of civic culture? Can a deliberative habit be formed across a diverse citizenry? How would it be institutionalized? What relationship does citizen deliberation have to the decision-making process of local officials?

The work became the basis of one dissertation (Morse 2004) and a critical source of real-world experience for several other graduate students (MPA and PhD) who worked with the community. Issue framing is a critical component of the deliberative process, and this experience proved especially rich in showing how citizens think about public issues and the value of a structured way of collectively framing them.

Planning for Virginia's Transportation Needs

As the previous example shows, fieldwork with citizens and public agencies presents challenges of practice that can spark research agendas for graduate students. Another such field opportunity arose around the framing of issues and deliberations about the future of transportation in the state of Virginia. The issue framing necessarily involved officials—that is, experts—from the Virginia Department of Transportation (VDOT) and other transportation agencies.

The research team first analyzed comments from 12 earlier public hearings on the future of transportation. The team then conducted two issue-framing sessions, one with transportation agency professionals representing all transportation modes, such as highways, rails, and ports; and one with transportation stakeholders, such as local planning officials, those involved in transporting the handicapped, and associations of cyclists and environmentalists. In this process, the research team faced the challenge of convincing the transportation officials that issues could be stated in terms that would make sense to citizens. For example, many of the transportation officials said the technical information surrounding budget allocations to the different transportation modes would be difficult for citizens to understand. However, when the officials actually sat in on citizen forums, what surprised them was that citizens were willing to discuss priorities in spending, considered different allocations of funding, and expressed a desire to see funding increased for transportation, even if it meant taxes were raised. Further, while many of the transportation officials had discussed the budget only in terms of allocation, citizens tended to relate the budget allocation questions to broader concerns, such as the need to understand the justification for some of the large-scale projects, the timeliness of project completion, and the need to balance environment, access, and the conflicts in local land-use laws and state transportation planning.

Through a presentation to, discussions with, and feedback from the several teams representing Virginia's transportation agencies, the themes that emerged from the issue-framing sessions were combined into three basic approaches to the future of transportation in Virginia: (1) build and maintain roads; (2) preserve and protect the cultural and natural environment; and (3) improve mobility and access for people and goods.

With the approaches in place and expressed in the form of a discussion book, forums were held around the state. In an effort to make sure that all voices were heard, students debated the virtues of random versus purposive sampling of stakeholders, regions, and citizens. Then, in the forums, citizens made it clear that they wanted to know what happened to their opinions after the forums—which meant that the research team needed to find ways to inform citizens of the effects of the deliberations. This was not a simple matter. First, the students and faculty involved had to explain how results were reported to the Department of Transportation. Then they had to learn whether the results were passed on to the state legislature or the governor's office, and if they were, in what form and with what effects. And all this had to be transmitted back to the forum participants! Which, to make a long story short, it was.

Important research questions arose from this project. First, a deeper reflection on the effects of forums came about when we moved away from simply asking whether people had changed their opinions to the realization that the most common scenario of change in the forums was one in which extreme views became modified, with forum participants generally moving away from "strongly agree" or "strongly disagree" toward the middle in their answers to various opinion questions (Park 2004). This indeed is an important effect of forums that requires further investigation.

Second, we pondered how to respect the holistic integrity of an individual regional forum and yet represent some of the areas of consensus across the state, a similar dilemma to representing views across the nation. While there seemed to be some statewide consensus as to the importance of planning and mobility, there also were differing issues of concern by locality.

A third question was how the insights from forums related to the mandates of agencies, in this case the Virginia Department of Transportation. In the law, VDOT is required to carry on citizen involvement that is "reasonable and meaningful" (Stich 2006). These mandates required that the process offer citizens the widest possible participation, be democratic in the search of disparate opinions, directly involve a cross-section of constituents, look for common ground, include quality-of-life issues, and help formulate policy direction. In terms of these requirements, how would forums compare to other forms of understanding citizens' viewpoints? As a result of involvement in the project, Bethany Stich (2006), PhD student in Virginia Tech's Center for Public Administration, explored comparisons among the forums, focus groups with city officials, and citizen surveys as part of her dissertation.

Fourth, the contrast between citizens and technical experts led us to raise the question of what happens to deliberative materials from ordinary citizens in the process of agency decision making. Much of the literature neglects to explain how public participation activities relate to actual state visions or whether community visions can be implemented under current state policies. What are the relationships between the outcomes of citizen forum involvement and the political reality of solutions beyond the authority of the state agency sponsoring the forums? For example, in regard to transportation, the solution of better coordination between local land-use laws and state transportation planning would be beyond the reach of VDOT.

In analyzing the project within a larger framework of evaluation of state visioning, Stich (2006) traced the recommendations made by ordinary citizens, traditional interest groups, and other consultants to see how the citizen's ideas were or were not considered by the transportation agency. Although she found that Virginia's transportation vision overall was heavily influenced by the citizen participation activities, including the deliberation of the forums, the VDOT comprehensive plan does not tell the citizens how the transportation agencies intend to get there. This finding raises even more questions about the relationship of deliberation and institutional action. Stich (2006) found that many of the citizens' concerns go well beyond the responsibility of the transportation agencies involved in the long-range plan's creation. Instead, they would require intergovernmental cooperation at a much higher level than is traditional in Virginia, the action of the state legislature, and better measurement tools. Thus, the search to better understand deliberation and its relationship to public administration is not over. It will require further exploration into how the complexity of policy issues is complemented by the complexity of action in the political arena of federalism and separation of powers.

Developing Virginia's First Futures Forum

A third real-world research experience for our graduate students was the issue framing and preparation of an issue book on human capital development for the inaugural session of the Virginia Futures Forum conducted before an audience of 150 of Virginia's top leaders in the state capital, including the outgoing and incoming governors. The theme for the first forum was "Competing in the 21st Century: Moving Virginia's Human Capital Meter." To frame the issue with officials and citizens in Virginia, produce an issue book (Dudley and DeRosear 2005), and facilitate deliberative groups in the inaugural policy forum, graduate students and faculty from Virginia Tech had collaborated with the Council on Virginia's Future, the Tobacco Indemnification and Community Revitalization Commission, the Virginia Workforce Council, and the Office of the Governor (Dudley and Nutter 2006).

Prior to the forum at which participants broke into small groups to deliberate on Virginia's human capital development, the issue framing for the forum book brought together representatives from business, education, and government (Dudley 2006). Graduate students learned how to combine an extensive review of the research literature with the framing from participants and to listen for the nuances of the particular case of Virginia human capital concerns alongside the universal research findings. Thus, an important part of the learning was extending our understanding of how to explain and implement the construction of an issue book and forum summaries within the framework of more familiar research traditions of brainstorming, representative sampling, random sampling, and content analysis. Further, we uncovered a tension between framing the deliberation for a broader question and the desires of some involved to have findings that could lead to immediate legislative or agency action. These are questions that we continue to pursue at the state level as we work to experiment with different models of bringing citizens' voices to the table.

Can Experts and Citizens Work Together?

In these projects, a dialogue regularly arose within the research team over the relationship between citizen participation and administrative expertise, the question with which we began this section of the paper. Throughout the project in Wytheville, the project with the Department of Transportation, and the first Virginia forum, we encountered the tension/complementarities of citizens/experts. Sometimes the interaction among our agency, citizens, and facilitators could best be described as the expression of a model that was consistent with the deliberative democracy movement, which emphasizes a long-term dialogue among all participants about both governance and specific issues (see Box 1998; Denhardt and Denhardt 2003; and Stivers and King 1998). For example, the first Virginia forum opened up concerns about the need to create additional mechanisms for citizens to be heard. At other times, we found our actions and the results of our forums were more consistent with a model of expertise, which is basically a management model in which the emphasis is on receiving comments from citizens through traditional channels, such as town council meetings or transportation hearings, and using those comments to inform administrative decisions on an issue-by-issue basis (see Creighton 2005 and Thomas 1995). It is exciting that ideas for combining the two are being considered in Virginia in further development of the state forums.

A final note: Project meetings, though an outside-the-classroom experience, were nevertheless important teaching and learning opportunities. Thus, we find that extracurricular learning opportunities in the field, such as our project meetings, truly brought theory and practice together for both the students and the faculty. Cultivating opportunities for this kind of learning in the field can be an important consideration in the overall pedagogical planning of a public affairs program.

Conclusion

In addition to the resounding recognition in the public affairs literature of a need for teaching competencies in deliberative democracy, there is a formal recognition of this need in the professional codes for public affairs. Thus, the theory-practice disconnect may not be as wide as assumed (Denhardt 2004). What is needed, however, is a professional curriculum that teaches competencies in deliberative democracy. While there are many different conceptual frameworks and methods to meet this need, all have advantages and disadvantages. Here, we have focused on one deliberative model of public participation and noted specific uses of the model for teaching deliberative skills, issue framing, and increasing the awareness of the research agenda associated with democratic deliberation.

The efforts described in our paper leave us with several questions about curriculum. Do the Masters in Public Affairs and other professional programs equip students with the competencies to use and teach the method of democratic deliberation? If so, how? If not, what kind of curricular modifications may be necessary? We further note that public affairs programs can make a significant contribution toward developing needed deliberative competencies in undergraduates. To what extent are these contributions being made? Finally, are we encouraging our PhD students to participate in research in this area?

Some answers to these questions may be stimulated by the deliberative experiences we have discussed. For us, an evolution in learning, teaching, and conceptual questions arose in practicing democratic deliberation in the graduate classroom, in preparing undergraduate facilitators, in comparing virtual and face-to-face deliberation, and in conducting forums with citizens and practitioners in the field. We found that a synergetic combination of incorporating the concepts and skills of deliberation in the classroom with experience in the field is an exciting and useful way to develop these competencies in our students. As public affairs scholars and students engaged in action research around the problems of deliberative democracy, teaching and research agendas are fulfilled simultaneously; and perhaps more important, students graduating with professional degrees are better prepared to lead deliberative processes in their professional realms of responsibility.

Larkin S. Dudley is an associate professor and former program chair of the Center for Public Administration and Policy at Virginia Tech, Blacksburg, Virginia. Her areas of teaching and research include public participation, organizational theory, and public policy processes. She has been involved in practice and research in deliberation for the last seven years and during that time has worked closely with the Kettering Foundation.

Ricardo S. Morse is an assistant professor at the University of North Carolina's School of Government, where he works with local government officials and citizens around issues of community and regional collaboration. He also teaches in the school's MPA program. He previously was on the faculty of the Public Policy and Administration Program at Iowa State University.

References

Anderson, Charles W. *Prescribing the Life of the Mind.* Madison, WI: University of Wisconsin Press, 1993.

Anderson, Charles W. *Pragmatic Liberalism.* Chicago: University of Chicago Press, 1990.

Arnstein, Sherry R. "A Ladder of Citizen Participation." *Journal of the American Institute of Planners,* 35(4) (1969): 216-224.

Barber, Benjamin. *Strong Democracy: Participatory Politics for a New Age.* Berkeley: University of California Press, 1984.

Bohman, James, and William Rehg, eds. *Deliberative Democracy: Essays on Reason and Politics.* Cambridge, MA: MIT Press, 1997.

Box, Richard C. *Citizen Governance: Leading American Communities into the 21st Century.* Thousand Oaks, CA: Sage, 1998.

Chrislip, David D. *The Collaborative Leadership Fieldbook: A Guide for Citizens and Civic Leaders.* San Francisco: Jossey-Bass, 2002.

Colby, Anne, Thomas Ehrlich, Elizabeth Beaumont, and Jason Stephens. *Educating Citizens: Preparing America's Undergraduates for Lives of Moral and Civic Responsibility.* San Francisco: Jossey-Bass, 2003.

Cooper, Terry L. *An Ethic of Citizenship for Public Administration.* Englewood Cliffs, NJ: Prentice Hall, 1991.

Creighton, James L. *The Public Participation Handbook: Making Better Decisions through Citizen Involvement*. San Francisco: Jossey-Bass, 2005.

Denhardt, Janet V. and Robert B. Denhardt. *The New Public Service: Serving, Not Steering*. Armonk, NY: M. E. Sharpe, 2003.

Denhardt, Robert B. *Theories of Public Organization*. 4th ed. Belmont, CA: Wadsworth, 2004.

Dudley, Larkin S. "Doing Deliberation: Government, Business, And Education—Three Way Collaboration." Presentation, American Society for Public Administration. Denver, CO. March 2006.

Dudley, Larkin S. and Katherine DeRosear. *Competing in the 21st Century: Moving Virginia's Human Capital Meter*, Virginia Futures Forum and Virginia Tech. Blacksburg, VA: Virginia Tech, 2005.

Dudley, Larkin S. and Dave Nutter. Preparing Virginia's Human Capital for the Future, *Virginia Issues and Answers*. Vol. 12, No. 2 (Summer 2006).

Fisher, Roger, William Ury, and Bruce Patton. *Getting to Yes: Negotiating Agreement without Giving In*. 2nd ed. New York: Penguin Books, 1991.

Fishkin, James S. *The Voice of the People: Public Opinion and Democracy*. New Haven, CT: Yale University Press, 1995.

Gastil, John. *Democracy in Small Groups: Participation, Decision Making and Communication*. Philadelphia: New Society, 1993.

Gastil, John and Peter Levine, eds. *The Deliberative Democracy Handbook: Strategies for Effective Civic Engagement in the Twenty-first Century*. San Francisco: Jossey-Bass, 2005.

Hughes, Owen E. *Public Management and Administration*. 3rd ed. New York: Palgrave, 2003.

Kaner, Sam. *Facilitator's Guide to Participatory Decision-Making*. 2nd ed. San Francisco: Jossey-Bass, 2007.

Kettering Foundation. *Framing Issues for Public Deliberation: A Curriculum Guide for Workshops*. Dayton, OH: Charles F. Kettering Foundation, 2001.

King, Cheryl Simrell and Camilla Stivers, eds. *Government Is Us: Public Administration in an Anti-Government Era*. Thousand Oaks, CA: Sage, 1998.

King, Cheryl Simrell, Kathryn M. Feltey, and Bridget O'Neill Susel. "The Question of Participation: Toward Authentic Public Participation in Public Administration." *Public Administration Review*, 58(4) (1998): 317-326.

Mathews, David. *Politics for People: Finding a Responsible Public Voice*. 2nd ed. Chicago: University of Illinois Press, 1999.

McMillan, Jill J. and Katy J. Harriger. "College Students and Deliberation: A Benchmark Study." *Communication Education*, 51(3) (2002): 237-253.

Morse, Ricardo S. "Community Learning: The Process and Structure of Collaborative Engagement." In *Modernizing Democracy: Innovations in Citizen Participation*, ed. Terry F. Buss, F. Stevens Redburn, and Kristina Guo, 49-77. Armonk, NY: M.E. Sharpe, 2006a.

Morse, Ricardo S. "Community Learning in Practice: Insights from an Action Research Project in Southwest Virginia." In *Modernizing Democracy: Innovations in Citizen Participation*, ed. by Terry F. Buss, F. Stevens Redburn, and Kristina Guo, 78-103. Armonk, NY: M.E. Sharpe, 2006b.

Morse, Ricardo S. "Community Learning: Process, Structure, and Renewal." Ph.D. diss. Virginia Polytechnic Institute and State University, 2004.

Morse, Ricardo S., Larkin S. Dudley, James Armstrong, and Dong Won Kim. "Learning and Teaching about Deliberative Democracy: On Campus and in the Field." *Journal of Public Affairs Education*, 11(4) (2005): 325-336.

Nalbandian, John. "Professionals and the Conflicting Forces of Administrative Modernization and Civic Engagement." *American Review of Public Administration*, 35(4) (2005): 311-326.

Nalbandian, John. "Facilitating Community, Enabling Democracy: New Roles for Local Government Managers." *Public Administration Review*, 59(3) (1999): 187-196.

National Issues Forums Institute. *Money and Politics: Who Owns Democracy?* Dayton, OH: National Issues Forums Institute, 2000.

O'Connell, Daniel W. "Teaching the Art of Public Deliberation: National Issues Forums on Campus." In *Education for Citizenship*, eds. G. Reeher and J. Cammarano, 135-152. Lanham, MA: Rowman and Littlefield, 1997.

Park, Soo Young. "Report on Transportation Forums." Unpublished report. Blacksburg, VA: Virginia Tech Transportation Institute, 2004.

Pateman, Carole. *Participation and Democratic Theory*. Cambridge, UK: Cambridge University Press, 1970.

Ross, F. Wayne. "Negotiating the Politics of Citizenship Education." *PS: Political Science and Politics*, 37(2) (1999): 249-251.

Schachter, Hindy L. and Manuel Aliaga. "Educating Administrators to Interact with Citizens: A Research Note." *Public Organization Review*, 3(2) (2003): 191-200.

Schwarz, Roger. *The Skilled Facilitator*. Revised edition. San Francisco: Jossey-Bass, 2002.

Stich, Bethany Marie. *Community Visioning in Long-Range Transportation Planning: A Case Study of Virginia*, May 05, Center for Public Administration and Policy. Blacksburg, VA: Virginia Tech, 2006.

Straus, David. *How to Make Collaboration Work*. San Francisco: Berrett-Koehler, 2003.

Susskind, Lawrence, Sarah McKearnan, and Jennifer Thomas-Larmer, eds. *The Consensus Building Handbook*. Thousand Oaks, CA: Sage, 1999.

Thomas, John Clayton. *Public Participation in Public Decisions: New Skills and Strategies for Public Managers*. San Francisco: Jossey-Bass, 1995.

Wamsley, Gary L. and James F. Wolf, eds. *Refounding Democratic Public Administration: Modern Paradoxes, Postmodern Challenges*. Thousand Oaks, CA: Sage, 1996.

SECTION IV

Deliberation and the Campus Community

Chapter Eight

Deliberation, Civic Discourse, and Democratic Dialogue in the Context of Academic Change[1]

Douglas J. Walters

Against the background of an eight-year process in which a four-year private university tackled academic transformation on a universitywide basis, this essay examines how deliberation, civic discourse, and democratic dialogue in the classroom and the cocurriculum became important elements in the school's transformation. The author gives special attention to the first-year program.

When I arrived on the University of Charleston campus during the fall semester of 1998, the university was in the third year of an academic transformation that reflected a basic shift in the institutional learning paradigm. As the new dean of students, I found myself in the middle of tumult and apprehension. The entire university had made a commitment to transforming the way students were taught as well as what they were learning.

As a public school educator and administrator for over 30 years with no experience in higher-education administration, I was placed in a very interesting situation. Professionally, I believed that learning needed to be holistic and that traditional learning pedagogy needed to adjust to meet the needs of the Generation X'ers and the new Millennial students who were attending college. The Millennial

---

[1] In this chapter, I often use *deliberation, civic discourse,* and *democratic dialogue* interchangeably. At UC, people in political science tend to speak of *democratic dialogue*; in public policy, people often speak of *civic discourse*. People versed in National Issues Forums speak of *deliberation*. Distinctions could be made, but in this context, they are not needed for the broad picture. Of course, any reference to a forum indicates the kind of deliberation promoted by the National Issues Forums.

students are generally said to have more surface information than any generation of students entering college but little skill in analyzing anything in depth; thus, they need a pedagogy that, in effect, pulls them below surface information.

But whatever my views of learning and the needs of today's students, given my newness on campus, I felt that I was not in a position to influence the direction or plans already in place or evolving at the University of Charleston. Therefore, I spent the first academic year (1998-1999) developing an understanding of the institutional culture and mores; listening to the many voices of the campus community; observing students, faculty, and administration; and reading, reading, reading! It was an immense learning curve for a seasoned public educator who thought that he was fully aware of how education and learning should take place.

By the time I was in my second semester on campus, it became evident that the academic transformation the university had undertaken was traumatic for many and refreshing and invigorating for many others. As I established my personal creditability with the UC family, I began to ask questions and make comments that reflected my views about learning and the constructs that I believed needed to be in place for learning to be maximized as the university expanded both the curricular and cocurricular programs of the college. One of the constructs was campuswide venues for civic discourse and democratic dialogue through activities and programs traditionally found in the cocurricular experience.

I believed this was one area in which I could make a difference. By focusing on deliberation, our cocurricular team could shoulder some of the burden of moving forward on proposed changes in instruction-based traditional pedagogies. As I saw it, UC's college students needed a variety of learning experiences and venues that make room for different learning styles. This was one feature of civic discourse and democratic dialogue experiences. They also enhanced the students' exposure to other views about important community issues. Further, I believed they offered a perfect opportunity for Millennial learners to remove themselves from the isolation of a high level of interaction with learning technologies.

What follows is the story of a four-year private university that integrated deliberative opportunities into the whole first-year experience and sought to introduce deliberation into the academic and cocurricular experiences of other students as well. This infusion was possible because the entire campus had agreed to and was making the switch to a new learning paradigm. This paper will describe the broad process of the academic transformation and focus in particular on the first year of the college experience in both the curricular and the cocurricular realms.

Extraordinary Transformation: From Teaching to Learning

The transformation that the University of Charleston underwent is grounded in a profound shift in the philosophy of the relationship between student and teacher. Put simply, this is a shift from an institution organized around the *instructional paradigm* to one organized around a *learning paradigm*. A clear exposition of the differences between the two paradigms is found in Robert Barr and John Tagg's "From Teaching to Learning—A New Paradigm for Undergraduate Education."[2] The instructional paradigm postulates that student learning occurs when students complete a required number of courses consisting of a set number of credit hours. Faculty deliver content, primarily through lectures, and use tests to determine how much a student remembers of that content. In contrast to the instructional mode of lecture and tests, the learning paradigm postulates that learning occurs when *students construct their own learning* through well designed, *active experiences* leading to a *desired goal or outcome*. The difference, to oversimplify, is between supplying students with a textbook versus having the students, in effect, create their own textbooks.

Full implementation of the learning paradigm requires an entire institution, for such a shift demands fundamental changes not only

---

[2] R. Barr and J. Tagg, "From Teaching to Learning: A New Paradigm for Undergraduate Education," *Changes*, (November/December, 1995): 13-25.

in the classroom but also in an institution's structures and in the way the institution defines faculty and student relationships. Further, in an institution built on the learning paradigm, nonfaculty personnel—and the whole cocurricular realm—become increasingly important to student learning.

The university had recognized as early as 1991 that it would have to change to survive. At first, the primary driver for change was the economic pressure resulting from changes in technology (for example, distance learning and information technology), fewer West Virginia high-school graduates, and increased competition from low-cost public institutions. The university's leadership also recognized that society itself was changing, with new demands for greater accountability in higher education. Students and parents wanted assurances that their investment in higher education was worthwhile. Comparing the price of a low-cost degree from a public institution to that of the same credential from a private institution, they began asking for reasons why they should pay the higher price. At the same time, business and industry leaders began to grumble about employees who could not write, could not read, could not calculate, and could not think or participate in discussions about important community issues.

Here are some of the high points of the university's response to the challenges it faced.

A full institutional planning process began in 1995. The university family (including community leaders, employers of graduates, and alumni) considered such questions as: How do we position ourselves to be unique in the competitive small, private university market? What knowledge and skill set would service students 10 years after graduation? In the next two years, the university decided to transform itself by undertaking the vast task of moving from an instructional paradigm, the standard educational method of imparting knowledge, to a learning paradigm, the full dimensions of which had yet to be completed.

As an initial step, the faculty's Curriculum Committee convened a series of subcommittees to meet the following needs: define and articulate the level of skill and/or knowledge required of students for the university to fulfill the transformation from teaching to learning; design a plan for helping students achieve the desired competencies that were part of the new paradigm; and develop the guidelines to identify effective nontraditional pedagogies and the accompanying methods by which students could demonstrate their achievement.

The university quickly saw that a commitment to move from the instructional paradigm required changes on an enormous scale, and in May 1995, it applied for a grant of one million dollars from the Claude Worthington Benedum Foundation to provide the financial resources for the needed faculty development and for a new administrative position to spearhead the initiative. In the fall, the foundation approved a $600,000 grant over three years to support the transformation.

By 1997, the university, influenced by the desire of its stakeholders to broaden and enrich the learning experience of all UC students, had settled on the goal of integrating liberal learning—loosely speaking, the skills and knowledge that are the foundation of a responsible and productive citizen in the modern world—throughout its college curriculum, a concept scarcely heard of at the time. The key to this integration was the identification of six areas in which students had to demonstrate core competencies: citizenship, communication, creativity, critical thinking, ethical practice, and understanding scientific principles. Competencies were to be shown by what the university called Liberal Learning Outcomes.

In conjunction with these goals, starting in 1997 and continuing through the summer of 1998, select faculty members worked to develop a new model program for the first year of college. Called Initial College Experience—or ICE—it consisted of three freshman "learning communities," each designed to explore one of three areas: social science, the humanities, or science. In addition, all three communities would integrate freshman English composition, speech, and the development of required computer skills into their content instruction.

While ICE was evolving, work continued on developing disciplinary and program outcomes, learning activities that would meet these outcomes, and assessment procedures to measure them.

By August 2000, two years after I had arrived, the faculty had approved outcomes and agreed to continue to refine them and to begin to integrate them into each major. It was agreed that Liberal Learning Outcomes would be integrated into all first-year courses by fall 2001, intermediate-level courses by 2002, and the full curriculum by fall 2003.

Today, all academic programs and courses have articulated outcomes, the levels of achievement that must be met by the student, and methods for assessing that achievement. Liberal Learning Outcomes have been tightly woven into the curriculum and course outcomes in all academic programs. This integration serves to emphasize the importance of liberal learning, making it clear that no matter what the academic major, the ability to think, to write, to read, to calculate, to act ethically, and to participate as a citizen are essential.

Additionally, Liberal Learning Outcomes and program outcomes have been combined with community-involvement/service-learning requirements, thereby comprising an integrated educational experience. Thus, successful achievement of the outcomes provides validation that each student leaves the university prepared, in the words of its mission statement, "for a life of productive work, enlightened living, and community involvement."[3]

The Seeds of Deliberation and the Birth of a Partnership

Needless to say, as an educator and teacher, it was extremely exciting to witness this transformation firsthand, and, soon after I arrived, to begin to bring civic discourse and democratic dialogue to the fore. To add to my initial excitement, I was fortunate to discover a campus resource that had been in place four years prior

---

[3] I note that the university is the only institution of higher education in West Virginia listed in the annual editions of *Great Colleges for the Real World*.

to my arrival and that would help the Division of Student Affairs become more closely involved with the new learning paradigm evolving on the UC campus.

This part of the story begins well before my arrival, in the 1990s when a small group of community volunteers working with adult literacy programs in underserved populations throughout West Virginia discovered National Issues Forums (NIF) and saw that its abridged versions for new readers might be just what the group needed to help promote literacy. With a small grant from the West Virginia Humanities Council to pay for NIF guides, the literacy group went to work. Its clear success led the council to the idea that *public deliberation* might be a compelling way to reach West Virginians who were not being served by more traditional humanities programming. Deliberation, it saw, could serve the needs of all citizens to engage in productive, nonpartisan dialogue about common problems and issues and could perhaps help democratically formed public judgment influence the decisions of state and local agencies.

The council soon developed a full fledged program in which it used NIF issue books to complement its existing historical and literacy programs with public discussions of related current issues. A key strategy of its work was to form partnerships with diverse organizations that shared the council's goals. Among these partnerships was one with the University of Charleston, which had long been seen by local residents as a community resource, as well as a private institution of higher education.

By the mid-1990s, then, the university was regularly hosting community forums on its campus on a wide range of public issues, an activity that proved beneficial to both its student body and to the surrounding community. The need for and value of this kind of work was epitomized by an exchange that took place in a public forum the university hosted in 1995. The topic of the forum was "Governing America," and it was attended by approximately 40 community residents and about a dozen UC students. The students interacted fully with the community members, especially one young student who appeared visibly energized by the discussion. At the end of the forum, however, she expressed dismay. "I'm frustrated," she said. "I'm a political science major. I've been to tons of debates, but I've never been in a discussion like this before, and I'm 19 years old!" From across the room a woman chuckled as she responded, "Don't feel bad, honey. I'm 80 and it's my first time too." Powerful testimony to the process of civic discourse.

By the late 1990s, after developing partnerships throughout the states, the Council established a permanent presence for public deliberation in West Virginia. It formed a nonprofit 501(c)(3) organization, and the University of Charleston opened its arms to the new organization—The West Virginia Center for Civic Life—providing office space, equipment, and public space for community discussions.

Thus, deliberation was a familiar presence on the UC campus. In effect, the stage was set for me to help bring deliberation to the cocurricular area. I had the thought that once this happened it could serve as a catalyst for bringing deliberation into the first-year curricular program.

The Flowering of Deliberation

This is where I stood after my first 10 months on campus: I had completed the cultural and learning audit that I believed necessary for me to make a meaningful contribution to the school's extraordinary program of transformation, I had an awareness of the changes that were set in motion to shift from the instructional to the learning paradigm, I understood the core values and mores of the institution, I knew the faculty and staff reasonably well, and I was beginning to understand that many of the principles of leadership I had practiced for many years in public education were relevant in higher education.

The basic principles that guided me for many years focused on what I have called the four P's of leadership:

1. *Plant* the idea (seed). Tend to it and nurture it as needed.

2. Work the *process* of the idea, giving it time.

3. Temper your leadership with *patience* as the idea/seed takes root and develops.

4. Model a *personal* relationship with those responsible for developing and implementing the new idea/seed.[4]

At UC, I took these basic principles and employed them as the cornerstones for developing a strategy for making the curricular and cocurricular experience at UC as seamless as possible for our students.

In my heart of hearts, I have always felt that learning takes place in a variety of settings. It does not have to occur in the traditional walls of a classroom at any level of education. As dean of students at a transformed UC, I was in a position of influence to take my theory of learning to the level of creating scenarios for learning outside the traditional classroom setting with the full support of a faculty that had committed the entire university to changing its educational paradigm from teaching to learning. After almost 35 years in education, I had an opportunity to construct, within the perimeters of the cocurricular realm, an academic credit experience that would be embraced by *academia*.

I naturally began with the West Virginia Center for Civic Life, deeply involved as it was with deliberative education and civic discourse through the National Issues Forums. The center had *planted* the idea/seed and now it was time to work the *process*.

In my second year as dean of students, I began to talk with a variety of student groups to ascertain their interest in deliberation. Fortunately, I found a small group of students who were strongly interested, and I developed a close relationship with them. Then, with the assistance and guidance of Betty Knighton, executive director of the West Virginia Center for Civic Life, we began to work with these students, mostly history and political science majors, to sponsor a series of workshops on deliberation and civic discourse. The process was one of exploration and discovery as we uncovered

---

[4] Copyright Douglas Walters. Walters, *Academic Change,* 14.

a number of issues that resonated with our students. By the end of the fall semester, this small cadre of students had been trained as moderators and had conducted two deliberative forums for the campus community, using NIF issue books.

In the 2000 spring semester, the process expanded. The students we were working with requested the opportunity to develop *their own* issue book for an NIF forum. This was a big step forward. Again, Betty Knighton came to the rescue and trained, as well as led, the small core group through the process of developing, framing, researching, and writing their own issue book, which dealt with child care for young parents. This experience certainly reinforced my personal belief that some of the most significant learning for a student—an understanding of personal insight, respect for others' thoughts, and an understanding of the oral process—can take place outside the traditional learning setting of the classroom.

The students promoted the child-care forum and raised the money to pay for both the costs of publishing the issue book and the refreshments for the forum. The forum was held in the evening and was attended by over 100 students and community members. It was a big success, and, as I originally had hoped might happen, came to serve as the catalyst for integrating civic discourse and deliberation into the fiber of the UC learning experience.

The forum had an especially strong impact on the ICE social science faculty. It demonstrated to them that UC students were socially aware and willing to work outside the framework of the traditional academic setting. Drawing on this experience, the social science faculty made deliberation a regular part of its classroom program. About the same time, deliberation skills became part of each learning community, new students were introduced to deliberation in their orientation to the campus, and a series of NIF campus forums was proposed. Thus, the UC model of integrating civic discourse and deliberation into the academic and cocurricular programs began to develop.

The model went to other West Virginia campuses too.

At the end of my second year, the Division of Student Affairs in collaboration with the Center for Civic Life submitted a successful proposal to the West Virginia Commission on National and Community Service for a VISTA/Americorps volunteer position to manage the proposed series of NIF forums and related democratic dialogue programs that would be conducted on the campus. With the coming of the VISTA/ Americorps volunteer, the flexibility to grow the concept of the NIF on campus for both the curricular and cocurricular venues especially in the first-year experience was in place. Further, the volunteer (and his several successors) not only developed the concept on the UC campus but also worked with other campuses throughout the state. Deliberative programs based on the UC model are now established on nine other West Virginia campuses.

Civic Discourse, Public Deliberation, and Democratic Dialogue on the UC Campus

Today, the concept of civic discourse, public deliberation, and democratic dialogue are embedded into the academic fiber of the first-year experience of all UC students and are woven throughout the rest of their college experience. Our students have come to accept that dialogue and discourse are basic to learning in or out of the classroom. In 2005, UC completed its first four-year cycle of students who have had this learning experience; it graduated the second group in 2006. Data from surveys conducted by the National Study of Student Engagement indicate a higher level of civic engagement among UC students than among students on almost all other American college campuses.

Here are key elements of how deliberation, civic discourse, and democratic dialogue have become part of UC's college experience:

- Students are exposed to civic discourse from their first weekend on campus. It is part of the orientation process for transfer students as well as first-year students, thus demonstrating university support for dialogue as a necessary component of community involvement.

- National Issue Forums is embedded into a variety of first-year ICE courses, including humanities, social science, and communication, as well as university courses that are designed to help first-year students master the complexities of university life. All first-year and transfer students are required to participate in a forum as part of their educational experience. This involvement can consist of participating in a forum followed by a written reflection on the experience, framing a forum issue, or moderating a forum.

- All residential first-year students are part of a Living Learning Community that has the support of an upper-class student—called a First-Year Peer Educator—who is trained to moderate civic discourse/democratic dialogue and who works with the students to conduct a program of ongoing, small group forums. The forums take place in the residence halls. They may involve a specific learning community, all of whose members live on the same floor, or the entire building, all of whose residents are first-year students. Students select the topics of the forums based on the content of the First-Year ICE courses.

- Several upper division courses in arts and sciences require participation in a minimum of one deliberative forum per semester. In fall 2006, the Department of Social Science began offering a course in Civic Discourse for three hours of academic credit for students at all class levels.

- Students use participation in forums and training in moderating forums for academic credit in the areas of persuasive speech, citizenship, teamwork, and leadership—all Liberal Learning Outcomes. In the area of citizenship, students also receive academic credit and obtain a Liberal Learning Outcome in Citizenship for completing beginning, intermediate, and advanced levels of understanding democratic dialogue.

- In the cocurricular area, chartered student organizations of all types—service, Greek, honor, and so on—vie to sponsor one of six annual forums on topics of their choice. The forums are evening events, open to students, faculty, and community members. The application process is rigorous, and the organizations are chosen on the basis of the topic they each propose. Each group receives a small stipend and community service or service-learning credit for serving as forum moderators and sponsors. This process has allowed students from various academic disciplines to see that deliberation is vital to rounding out their collegiate learning and can be embedded into a variety of settings. Additionally, it allows UC students opportunities to enhance their understanding and practice of citizenship, ethical practice, oral communication, and critical thinking.

- The VISTA/Americorps volunteer who serves as the program advisor for civic discourse and democratic deliberation on campus, also serves as a resource expert for faculty in helping design courses that include civic discourse and democratic dialogue. Further, to repeat an earlier point, through the help of the VISTA/Americorps volunteer, the UC model of embedding civic discourse and democratic deliberation into the classroom is now used on nine other West Virginia college and university campuses.

- The program advisor for the NIF deliberation-oriented Center for Civic Life has been integrated into the staff of the Division of Student Affairs.

- In the 2006-2007 public school year, UC students worked to train and assist local high-school students to present forums in the communities surrounding UC. This effort is part of a larger development. When I left the university in 2006, active learning was far more prevalent that it was when I first arrived, in 1998. At UC, active learning has been defined as encompassing those activities that engage the learner outside such traditional "receiver" modes as lectures. Active learning, then, would include group work, experiential learning, internships, community service, and civic discourse. The greater prevalence of active learning is in part a direct result of using deliberation as a focal point for introducing students to better and broader communication strategies.

Does It Matter?

While these changes took place, many positive changes in enrollment and public recognition also took place. Of course, there is no easy way to parse the specific elements that have led to such results. The university has transformed itself, and part of this transformation involves a widespread emphasis on deliberation, civic discourse, and democratic dialogue both in the classroom and the cocurricular realm. Speaking broadly, it seems clear to me that the UC enhanced-learning environment led to the increased enrollment and public recognition and that deliberation and dialogue, which served to strengthen UC's newly expanded learning environment, are an important part of the story.

The following facts and assessments outline, if I may say so, a profile in success:

- Since 1999, the residential population has increased 268 percent.
- Freshmen who took the Academic Profile in fall 2001 and took it again at the end of the sophomore year in late spring 2003 showed a net gain score of 11 points, 2 points above the 9-point national average for sophomores at liberal arts colleges.
- University retention rose from 64 percent in 2001-2002 to 87 percent in fall 2006.
- In 2005, 98 percent of the graduating class was employed or enrolled in a graduate program.
- As of 2005, the five-year graduation rate had increased 9 percent.
- From fall 2005 to fall semester 2006, enrollment increased 19 percent.
- In 2006, *US News and World Report* listed UC as the best "comprehensive" four-year college in West Virginia (meaning a school that grants degrees at several levels and has both liberal arts and professional programs) and the 21st best small college in the South.
- Given the flexibility students have gained through the academic transformation from teaching to learning, they are now designing their own majors.

To this basically quantitative list, I would add the following qualitative points:

- There is a new understanding of learning in the "public space" of the campus and the surrounding community. Student deliberation is more welcome within the traditional classroom setting as well as outside it.

- While the basic revised curriculum in all academic majors has been completed, continuing curricular change to meet the learning needs of today's student is still seen as a necessity, especially if UC is to keep students actively involved in public dialogue.
- Learning is active, both inside and outside the traditional classroom walls. The UC faculty has learned that the student voice should be encouraged as part of the learning process.
- UC's students are more likely to challenge the construct of their learning with greater articulation than previous students could muster because today's students are better communicators and understand that they can make a difference through democratic dialogue.
- Given UC's paradigm shift in learning and pedagogy, the faculty is more likely to relinquish control of how they teach, manage their classrooms differently, and listen to the student voice, which has become more active and passionate as a result of more public conversations.

I end on a personal note.

As I stated at the beginning of the chapter, I was a novice dean of students with no higher-education administrative experience when I came to the University of Charleston. The road that I traveled the eight years with my UC colleagues was exciting, exhilarating, and challenging, and despite the frustrations and self-doubts that many of us suffered, I would not trade one moment of it as the UC community drastically changed the way students were taught and what they learned and completed the transformation that allowed and encouraged student deliberation at multiple levels.

How refreshing it was to be part of a learning community of faculty and administration who saw the university as a dynamic entity that needs to continue to grow, to be receptive to the change process, and to nurture the many phases of learning that are necessary for the student!

Douglas J. Walters, *now a consultant in organizational leadership, was dean of students at the University of Charleston in Charleston, West Virginia, from 1998 to 2006. He had been a public-school educator in the largest school district in West Virginia, serving as a classroom teacher, high-school administrator, central-office director, and administrative assistant for professional development and communications for Kanawha County Schools. For more than 20 years, he was an adjunct professor in educational leadership and secondary instruction and curriculum at Marshall University. He has degrees from Morris Harvey College (University of Charleston) and Indiana University, where he was a Ford Foundation Fellow. Walters has received a number of state, regional, national, and international awards for his work in education, community development, leadership development, and international community service. He is the father of two sons and has three grandchildren.*

Chapter Nine

Deliberation and the Fraternal Futures Initiative

Dennis C. Roberts and Matthew R. Johnson

Many campus fraternal organizations have struggled, in recent years, with declining membership, lack of fraternal chapter accountability, and poor academic performance of members. In efforts to address these problems, college administrators and international headquarters of these organizations have tended to impose administratively determined policies and procedures and to implement values-based programs calling for a return to fraternal organizations' founding principles. These top-down strategies attempt to force fraternal members into a "one-size-fits-all" approach that ignores students' voices and neglects the importance of taking campus history and culture into account in creating change. This essay describes a new approach—the Fraternal Futures Initiative, started at Miami University in 2002. The program utilizes National Issues Forums to foster dialogue within fraternal organizations as an alternative to using imposed rules and past expectations to meet current problems.

M any campus administrations and fraternal governing bodies have been struggling unsuccessfully to find a remedy for persistent problems of social fraternal organizations—problems that range from hazing to alcohol abuse to anti-intellectualism. In this paper, we describe a new approach to resolving such problems —the Fraternal Futures Initiative, an approach rooted in deliberation—and report on the promising results of its use on 10 campuses of different sizes and characters.[1]

---

[1] A note on terminology: The term *fraternal organizations*, which we use frequently, and the synonymous *Greeks*, which we use less often, generically refer to both sororities and fraternities. In this time of increased gender awareness, to say that sororities are included in the term *fraternal* may seem out of date, if not sexist. But that is the standard terminology in this area, and in this discussion, in which what is said about fraternal organizations is meant to apply equally to sororities and fraternities. We have made no effort to construct a new, more neutral term.

Starting a Conversation about Fraternal Organizations

Fraternal organizations have been on college campuses for almost 200 years and have gone through periods of prosperity, notoriety, and disdain. At their founding, they had lofty purposes—enhancing students' scholarship, building character, and serving as ideal communities that drew the best from all their members. Today, when fraternal organizations get in trouble for hazing, alcohol abuse, exclusionary membership practices, and anti-intellectualism, they reflect anything but such lofty purposes. Although the evidence indicates that problems occur most frequently with men's groups, women's groups are not free of criticism, nor are culturally-based groups such as the historically African American groups or the newer Latina/Latino or Asian groups. Those in higher education and in the umbrella inter/national organizations that oversee fraternal groups are ever more frequently convened in hand-wringing conversations about what to do.

One particularly catalytic moment occurred in spring 1997 when the lead author, along with another campus administrator and an officer from the National Panhellenic Conference, an umbrella organization of 26 inter/national women's fraternal groups, rode down an escalator together after a disturbing conference presentation. Two lawyers had talked about the many reasons why campuses and headquarters should be cautious about pursuing any kind of mutual or orchestrated work to improve the disturbing problems of fraternal organizations. Among the major concerns was that working together might jeopardize the autonomy of fraternal organizations. Another was that a closer working relationship might invite potentially greater liability for both campuses that host fraternal organizations and the inter/national oversight bodies. Dejection filled the room, but no one spoke for change—until the trio on the escalator owned that they were intensely frustrated with the situation.

How, they asked each other, could otherwise reasonable people, holders of influential leadership positions, be compromised by fears

that a close working relationship might result in legal entanglements, which none of them could tolerate? Both campuses and
headquarters serve the same students. Why shouldn't they work
to get on the same page in supporting each other?

These three individuals went back to their colleagues to insist
that a new kind of conversation be undertaken, one that recognized
that both campuses and inter/national headquarters have mutual
challenges and goals and that, in fact, neither can be successful
without the support of the other. The result of the discussion that
followed was the first Greek Summit, convened in fall 1997 under
the joint auspices of the National Association of Student Personnel
Administrators, the National Interfraternity Conference, and the
National Panhellenic Conference. The gathering included approximately 40 people—campus administrators, inter/national head-
quarter representatives, along with legal counsel and a facilitator.

The discussion started cautiously. Wary of one another's purposes, the participants needed to learn a new kind of language, one
that assumed trustworthiness and a willingness to work toward
shared goals. The facilitator guided the group through the exploration of their biases and concerns and progressively helped them
to move to a problem-solving perspective. The participants began
to place issues on the table and then to identify clusters of concerns.
The first Greek Summit was off and running, and by the end of
the meeting, the participants had made a commitment to explore
the mutual work of improving campus fraternal organizations.
Only in hindsight did it become clear that the group lacked key
players—students and alumni.

The Conversation Opens Up

Further Greek Summits were held in 1998 and 1999. One of the
more profound and persistent themes in these meetings was the
critical importance of engaging alumni and students in the changes
that both campuses and headquarters sought. Even as this theme
kept reappearing, campuses and headquarters were investing
resources in conferences, programs, publications, models, and

interventions, all designed to turn around the fraternal negatives. International headquarters began to provide their personnel with risk-management training and tested new alcohol-abuse prevention models, while campuses drafted new policies, models, and agreements. Despite all this effort, the problems persisted. Even when initiatives showed initial signs of success, all too often the tide was reversed before positive conditions could be stabilized. As the participants of the 1999 Greek Summit saw the situation, the basic problem was one of leadership—or, more accurately, the lack of a shared leadership that included alumni and students in taking on the tough issues that had to be addressed to transform the fraternal experience on college campuses for today's young men and women. Put another way, change and improvement would not come just because administrators wanted it. It would only come if members of fraternal organizations wanted it and were involved in shaping it.

The energizing awareness that a lack of shared leadership was at the core of the inability to reform and improve fraternal organizations led to a commitment to stage a meeting that differed from the planned 2000 Greek Summit. This meeting would include undergraduate students from fraternal organizations along with campus administrators and headquarters officials. The purpose of the meeting was to provide an opportunity for a more open and honest conversation at which the active presence of students would validate the relevance of their "stakeholder" perspectives.

Miami University (in Oxford, Ohio) hosted the meeting. Known as "the mother of fraternities" because five fraternal organizations established their first chapters there, the campus now boasted more than 50 fraternal organizations of every type, size, and focus. The meeting consisted of campus representatives, personnel from fraternal headquarters, and student members of fraternal organizations.

The honesty and candor at the core of this meeting resulted in a proposal to establish an initiative aimed at creating a new kind of fraternal leadership. The initiative, "Transforming Fraternal Leadership," sought to influence campuses, chapters, and individual members of fraternal organizations throughout the country. It would focus on creating an educational Web site about the progressive stages of fraternal membership, from recruitment through the education of new members to the full cycle of member participation. Cultivating leadership was to be at the core of this Web-based curriculum. Presumably, by disseminating information broadly and engaging multiple stakeholders, new understandings of fraternal leadership and its dynamics could be fostered.

Hard necessity brought this plan to a halt. While initial reactions to the idea of the Web site were positive, the request for funding met with a cool response. As a result, the Transforming Fraternal Leadership proposal was abandoned.

Not long after this happened, the lead author of this paper began to explore the possibility of creating a deliberative discussion process in which fraternal members could consider different approaches to improving their organizations and so become more fully aware of fraternal problems and their own responsibility in resolving them. Not only is this approach to improvement in accord with the majority of evidence about organizational change, it is consistent with the founding purposes of fraternal organizations as democratic and participatory organizations. We hoped that involving students in identifying fraternal problems and empowering them to resolve these issues would result in their taking action to protect the future of their organizations.

We saw one problem. The usual site for deliberative dialogue in higher education is inside the classroom. But the deliberations we planned would take place outside the classroom. What would bring fraternity members to engage in a deliberative discussion that might take several hours? The answer seemed clear. The deliberation needed to focus on something of high personal value to the participants. In this case, the value was obvious—the participants' affiliation with their fraternal organizations.

The deliberative model we used was drawn from the Kettering Foundation's research on "choice work." In this model, discussion is framed around three or four approaches to an issue of common concern, and each approach is accompanied by the pros and cons of advocates and critics. This framework allowed participants to discuss what was important to them and to discover ways to act collectively.

Before describing how we developed a deliberative discussion guide for the program we call Fraternal Futures, we outline several theoretical perspectives that helped us understand how to involve students in the kind of deliberation we were proposing—one that dealt not with abstract problems but with the places where students live and learn.

Willing to Take Responsibility—Ready or Not?

Foremost among the perspectives on which we drew is Marcia Baxter Magolda's Learning Partnership Model (2004), which aims to help educators interact with students in ways that promote the students' learning, their ability to determine their own beliefs and values, and their relations with other people. The model rests on three assumptions and three principles. The three assumptions are portraying knowledge as complex and socially constructed, showing that the self is central to knowledge, and sharing authority and expertise. The three principles are validating students as knowers, situating learning in students' experiences, and defining learning as "mutually constructing meaning."

From these assumptions and principles, we identified four key aspects of the model that provide a base for Fraternal Futures and the renewal of civic engagement in fraternal organizations. The first aspect is the need to begin with students' interests, a proposition that had shaped our thinking from the outset. Second is the need to start with local issues in small groups to foster a sense of empowerment among students. Third is to be strongly committed to allowing students to participate in cocreating their future, a commitment that requires that administration and headquarters personnel relinquish control, share authority, validate students as learners, and understand that students' perspectives derive from their own experiences (put more formally, that knowledge is socially constructed). The last aspect is the need to enrich students' understanding of deep and complex issues, which has the further effect of helping students to develop critical-thinking skills.

Three additional models helped us understand how to motivate students to become involved and to take responsibility for their experience. One comes from the Wingspread Summit on Civic Engagement, where, in March 2001, 33 undergraduate students met to explore their views of civic engagement. Sarah Long (2002), a student participant, documented these views in *The New Student Politics*. For the Wingspread students, involvement in civic affairs meant transcending the conventional view that political involvement involved only voting and petitioning. The three key tenets of involvement for Wingspread are having access to collective decision making, possessing a personal interest, and pursuing one's involvement through small, local efforts. These conditions are directly aligned with basic notions of deliberative democracy and are also consistent with Baxter Magolda's Learning Partnerships Model.

The two additional perspectives that helped us understand the conditions that discourage or support serious student involvement in campus issues come from Richard Keeling (1998) and Alan Berkowitz (1998). Keeling proposed new ways of addressing HIV/AIDS on campus. His essential concept is that homophobia is partially responsible for perpetuating risky sexual practices by making it uncomfortable for gay, lesbian, and bisexual students to be open about their sexual orientation. This veil of secrecy results in poor information about and reluctance to adopt healthy sexual practices. Berkowitz studied the accuracy of students' perceptions about the drinking behaviors of others, concluding that the belief of students that there was a high use of alcohol on campus encouraged individual personal abuse, while the belief that there was low use reduced personal abuse. For both Keeling and Berkowitz, prevention depends on honesty, accuracy, involvement of a broad number of students, and attention to the campus environmental conditions that have perpetuated risky sexual and alcohol-use practices.

Baxter Magolda, Wingspread, Keeling, and Berkowitz have four themes in common: to encourage honest and realistic analyses of shared problems, to foster a personal commitment to change, to encourage a more complex understanding of the issues, and to empower citizens to be involved in civic issues (Roberts and Huffman 2005). The NIF forums that have been used in numerous other areas and on varying topics achieve essentially the same goals that these other models propose.

Engaging Students in Taking Charge of Their Responsibility

As we indicated, Miami University has a long and rich history related to fraternal organizations, whose members currently number a third of the university's undergraduates. These organizations rarely display the problems and behavior that concern critics of fraternal organizations. On the other hand, the prominence given to fraternal organizations at Miami sometimes contributes to complacency and smugness. The perpetuation of some traditions is assumed and seldom examined for purpose and rationality. As a result, these organizations are not the shining example to others that they should be. With this in mind, staff and administration at Miami University challenged students to help devise a choice-model discussion guide to engage their peers in serious conversations about the viability of fraternal organizations in today's society, first at Miami and then in other campus communities.

We focused our efforts on the Greek Values Society, formed several years before at Miami University as a way to encourage Miami fraternity members to promulgate the founding and shared ideals of all the fraternal organizations in which they were involved.[2] The members of the society come from many Miami University fraternities and sororities. A very strong group in its first few years,

---

[2] For those who study the purposes of fraternal organizations, it is easy to conclude that they contain a common thread or purpose. In fact, many of these groups were based on Masonic organizations and show a particular commitment to the protection of democratic ideals that was central to the Masonic movement in the United States in the 19th century.

the society became less active and less effective as original members graduated and new members lost their commitment to the core purposes on which the group was founded. We saw the Fraternal Futures Initiative as an ideal vehicle for renewing the society, giving it an invigorated and fresh purpose.

In spring 2002, with the upcoming fall as the official starting point of the Fraternal Futures Initiative, we used the documents and reports from the 2000 meeting of headquarters, campuses, and students, to draft a discussion guide with several approaches for shaping the future of fraternal life. Once this was done, the draft had to be redesigned with student participation. This deeper process of creating a choice model with and through students would result in the kind of student "buy-in" that was essential to the future of the project.

Several issue-framing meetings took place during fall 2002 and spring 2003. As might have been expected, the members of the Greek Values Society, who initially were filled with energy, became impatient with the laborious process of refining approaches and coming to a conclusion on the model. Some of the resistance might also have been ambivalence in facing up to the problems that were part of their organizations. There were frequent assertions, for example, that the real problem was that others just did not understand and did not especially appreciate the many positive things that fraternal organizations did. A signal moment occurred when we informed the students who were present that many folks in the administration would prefer that fraternal organizations just go away. The room fell silent at this suggestion—then the group went back to work!

Ultimately, the students' willingness to persevere in the process demonstrated the kind of commitment to the model that we sought. The result was an issue book with three approaches to the future of fraternities—increasing the range of people who could become members, focusing on values and accountability, and working together to address fraternal health and safety concerns—with the trade-offs that accompanied each approach.

With the issue book completed, the first pilot efforts to test its usefulness began. The question was, would the Fraternal Futures issue book provide a good basis for fraternal groups to confront the problems of fraternal life and to examine how to move into a healthier, more productive future? Once the initial pilots demonstrated both the usefulness of the choice model and the fact that students were quite capable of moderating their own deliberations, the serious testing of the model began at Miami and elsewhere.

Where and How Can Fraternal Futures Be Used?

As of spring 2006, some 1,200 students and 10 different institutions have utilized Fraternal Futures: Miami University, Kutztown University, Jacksonville State University, Westminster College, Franklin & Marshall University, Drake University, Florida State University, Eastern Michigan University, Northwestern University, and Simpson College. They range from large, public institutions with large fraternal populations, to small, private schools with small fraternal populations. The outcomes—different in each situation—demonstrate varying degrees of success.

Not everything has gone as we had hoped. At the outset, we operated on the belief that the transformation from "positional" to shared leadership required the collaboration of campuses, inter/national fraternal organizations, and individual members. Only such a collaboration we believed, would create fraternal communities where a substantial portion of the membership would engage in these organizations to help them improve. Unfortunately for our purposes, we discovered that the leadership programs of inter/national fraternal organizations focused on emerging and positional leadership, as opposed to centering on shared leadership for all members. Perhaps it is not surprising, then, that our effort to partner with national organization leadership schools and conferences has brought minimal response.

Working with campuses has been easier and more successful. Ultimately, the key variable was finding a way to maximize the potential of Fraternal Futures in individual campus settings. For instance, at one campus, Fraternal Futures was part of Greek Week, when students from different fraternal organizations engaged in various deliberations with the aim of promoting a communal value of leadership. In another instance, Fraternal Futures was a stand-alone program that brought students together on a Saturday afternoon specifically to deliberate about their future. In each case, we had extensive conversations with an administrator at the university (usually the fraternal affairs professional) to discern what might work best in the respective situations.

Our guiding principle is that each campus has unique dynamics that a single one-size-fits-all program could not fully address. For example, after extensive conversations with a particular campus, we decided that deliberations that included both women and men would not initially lend itself to robust conversations, given the strong polarity on that campus between sororities and fraternities. Mixed-gender conversations ensued down the line, but only after the initial, single-gender conversations.

Our work has brought us to a number of conclusions about partnering with campuses and organizations. Most important is to find administrative partners who are willing to take the risk of engaging students in the resolution of their own problems and who are committed to student involvement. Finding such partners requires a great deal of clarity on our part, because we have to convince others of the value of engaging students in authentic dialogue. Some potential partners have been apprehensive about the practicality of recruiting undergraduates to two-hour conversations that do not culminate in a tangible action plan. To this concern, we responded that it was not possible to construct an action plan that led to lasting change in a single two-hour deliberation. The explanation did not always suffice.

It seemed to us that some administrators were apprehensive about relinquishing control to students to dictate what should be done to improve their organizations. Possibly, they were hesitant about what issues students might unearth in their discussions with one another—the need for greater institutional support and resources, for example, or inconsistency in messages between campuses and headquarters.

What We Learned from the Deliberations

Given the intricacy of deliberations, we used a number of ways to gain a better understanding of what happened in them, with the hope that we could glean the difference they made with students. We used surveys, pre- and postforum questionnaires, and conversations with moderators as our three main sources of data.

Several prominent findings emerged from our data.

Broader Perspectives

Comments from nearly half of the students indicate that the forums have given them a better understanding of both the need for group efforts among fraternal organizations (or, put another way, that fraternal organizations share common problems) and the issues that face fraternal organizations, a change that involves a broadening of perspectives.

The shift to a more community-focused effort or to a realization that other chapters have the same problems is expressed in the following comments. "I'm glad to know how much we really all have in common." "If we're all fighting the same battle, how come we don't work together?" "We have a lot of work to do, and it's going to take everyone firing on the same cylinders to make it work."

For many who expressed this sentiment, the forums had brought to light a multitude of common problems associated with fraternal organizations, an insight that sparked excitement and at least the willingness to become more involved in dealing with the problems. The comment of one woman epitomized the view of many who expressed this theme: "I've realized that coming together and talking about these things is really the only way that we are going to change. Without it, we're simply going to maintain." As this last comment indicates, a better understanding and a broadening of perspectives also often reveal a similar action-oriented outlook. As one woman said, "I've seen that there are a lot of different perspectives and that there is so much that could be done to help better the future of Greeks. We just need to take action now." One student similarly remarked, "This really helped lay out the bigger picture of Greek life, and, most importantly, what we can do about it." These and comparable responses indicate that, after their deliberations, many participants were able to see things on a larger scale and begin to think about how individual actions affected the greater fraternal community.

For the first time, many students were able to step outside of their own fraternal experience and reflect upon the broader community as a whole. "I think I'm just in such a bubble in my chapter. I never even thought about the Greek community as whole," said one sorority member. Another woman said, "I guess I've never really thought of myself as a 'Greek' but more of a [sorority name]." The deliberations push students from thinking about their experience simply in terms of their own chapter to thinking about how their experience relates to a larger context.[3]

A great advantage of the deliberative approach of the Fraternal Futures Initiative is that even if students lack maturity and experience, they come to understand that they are "stakeholders." They come to see that *this* is their experience and that they are invested in the preservation of their fraternal organizations, for their own time in college if not for future generations. Further, they see not only that they have a role in the future of their organizations but also that any action to secure the future of these organizations must be collective.

Deciding Among Choices

At the end of the deliberations, students are asked to select the approach or combination of approaches they most favor among the three approaches they have examined together:

---

[3] These sentiments exemplify Robert Kegan's theory of subject/object relationships. By *subject*, Kegan means those elements of our meaning-making in which we are so deeply enmeshed that, as a rule, we can rarely reflect and act upon them. Conversely, *object* refers to those parts of our meaning-making that "we are able to reflect on, handle, look at, be responsible for, relate to each other, take control of, internalize, assimilate, or otherwise act upon" (Kegan 1994, as cited in Love and Guthrie 2000, 66). Deliberation seems to help people gain an object-like relation to what formerly had been subject.

- changing recruitment procedures, strengthening diversity, and targeting a wider array of individuals for membership;
- holding members more accountable, developing and enforcing membership standards, and becoming more values focused in programming; and
- addressing health and safety concerns by partnering with other organizations and administrators.

Students found utility in all three choices, indicating that each choice mattered to some students.

We also asked the students to choose which among 11 potential trade-offs they are most willing to accept with each approach. Time and again, the most prevalent response, at each campus, was that students are least willing to accept potential trade-offs that could decrease the bonds of sisterhood/brotherhood. They are most willing to accept the trade-off that a change toward values-based recruitment would force recruitment to become more exclusive. This view was endorsed by roughly 20 percent of the respondents.

Anecdotal Outcomes

Several other outcomes deserve mention.

Through informal conversations after deliberations, we received many comments indicating that the Fraternal Futures experience was the first time that anyone had ever asked students what they thought about the future of their organizations. "If you would have told me that I would have spent my Saturday talking with members of [several fraternities] about problems we're having, I would have told you that you were crazy.... But it was awesome," commented one fraternity president. Students often struck this note as they reflected on their deliberation experiences. Expressions of appreciation were frequently followed by calls for further discussion. As one student put it, "It was really great to come together with everyone and talk about our issues. I've always thought there's so much going on in Greek life aimed at solving problems, but I guess I just never thought to try to sort them all out. After this, I've realized we need to talk about this stuff more." She continued,

"[The deliberation] was cool because it wasn't like everyone was debating or trying to prove something. We're all in this together, and that's how we approached this." One Greek professional told us that he could not believe the interaction among the groups, especially between groups that historically have been at "sword points."

We also found that the reactions of moderators to deliberations they conduct on campuses other than their own proved valuable. We actively recruit and train Miami students to moderate deliberations, and they routinely travel to other campuses to be moderators. They are always apprehensive prior to their visit, mostly because they feel they must possess "all the answers," but also because they are nervous that the students in their deliberations will not engage in the conversations. With a little coaching and encouragement, the moderators set out on their travels—and return to report that they had a wonderful and meaningful learning experience. The comment of one moderator is typical:

> I had so much fun and learned a great amount about myself as an individual, the campus/Greek system of Westminster College [where the person moderated the deliberation], and also the Greek community as a whole.... It was so interesting to note the differences in the systems of our two schools, but the sharing of these differences caused all of us to truly benefit from the experience.... It was so much fun and the amount that I learned from the experience was immeasurable!

Moderators told us that they planned to use what they learned from the deliberative approach in their respective fraternal organizations, as well as in other student organizations in which they were involved. We can only speculate on how such experiences may affect the engagement of these moderators in their respective fraternal organizations.

Westminster Case Study

In closing this section on what we learned, we describe an outcome that, in its own way, reveals the strength of deliberation.

Fraternal Futures was fortunate enough to partner for two years with Westminster College in Fulton, Missouri. Westminster is home to roughly 900 students, approximately 60 percent of whom belong to fraternal organizations. Roughly a third of this group, 219 students, participated in the deliberations.

Westminster's fraternity system began in the 1800s and is rich with tradition. Yet the fraternal community has longstanding and seemingly intractable problems—a state of affairs reflected in the forum results. The number of students who came out of the deliberations with a greater awareness of the problems that exist and a desire to begin to address them was much smaller than on any other campus we visited. In addition, we saw a much smaller increase in concern about the future of fraternal life, both in the feeling that students had a role to play and had the ability to make a difference in the future of their fraternal organizations and in their commitment to action.

This may seem discouraging, but it is not the whole story. Before the deliberations began, students expressed considerable cynicism about their usefulness. But as the process unfolded, students quickly warmed up to the idea of gaining a better understanding of the problems within their fraternal community and the roles they might play in fixing them. Initially, many students talked about their belief that Westminster's administrators wanted to close fraternal organizations and that any effort on their part to stop the administrators would be futile. More knowledgeable students, however, dispelled these rumors. As one of the forum moderators said, "It wasn't until [the students] knew that they weren't on the verge of being closed down that they started really talking about their problems." A number of students indicated that, to an extent, the comments transformed their own views of what was possible. As one student said, "It's good to know that we have support. We now have an idea of how to move forward."

We believe the Westminster experience illustrates an important point: the deliberations of Fraternal Futures have the potential to take on a life of their own. While moderators ask questions aimed at prompting students to consider different viewpoints and different courses of action, what follows—the dialogue and the commitments, if any—is almost entirely created by the participants. Which is why it is essential that students have the opportunity to voice their views.

Notes on Bringing About Change

Anyone who lives in, works with, or studies complex organizations knows that change does not come easily. In the case of fraternal organizations, we would argue that three conditions make it even more difficult. First, while fraternal organizations are coordinated through their purpose and mission, and through administrative oversight, undergraduate chapters are broadly dispersed over more than 1,000 campuses, each of which follows its own guidelines in hosting these chapters. Second, most fraternal organizations were founded with secret rituals and symbols that continue to serve as mystical barriers to those who are not part of the organization. Finally, there is no one institution or organization or group to which fraternal organizations are accountable; accountability may be variously claimed by the campus, inter/national headquarters, alumni, peers, and/or others.

While the response to Fraternal Futures has been gratifying, we are still baffled that more campuses have not requested it. Indeed, several campuses that initially expressed interest did not, for whatever reason, follow through on implementing the program. The strongest positive responses have come from campuses where trusted professional acquaintances were available to us.

One of the questions we have explored is whether the change strategy we are pursuing has been too dependent on administrative staff rather than on students themselves. Since Fraternal Futures is explicitly designed to foster student engagement, shouldn't students be the ones deciding whether to try it? As we reflected on our experience, we concluded that in the ideal situation, Fraternal Futures would be requested, coordinated, and run by students. However, we also believe that the headquarters and campus professionals who are committed to enhancing fraternalism are critical partners in restoring healthful vigor to fraternal organizations, if for no other reason than the fact that they provide continuity in contrast to the students who turn over every few years. A balance of staff and student commitment is likely to be the most successful strategy. In all cases where it is possible, students should be informed about and involved in decisions related to the use of Fraternal Futures as a catalyst for change.

Another nagging question for us is how fraternal organizations are seen in the context of the higher-education learning community. If they are regarded as contributing constructively to learning, then educators are likely to invest resources in improving them. On the other hand, if they are seen as nothing more than tangential to education and the campus community—unrelated private entities over which an institution has little to no influence—there is little or no reason to provide such support.

From a student perspective, the place of fraternal organizations in higher education largely depends on a student's particular educational aims. The range of views on this matter runs the gamut. Some students see their fraternal involvement as augmenting the university's mission, while others fail to see any connection or, even worse, may believe that fraternity life undermines the university's educational goals.

From the perspective of college and university administrators, the place of fraternal organizations in higher education is primarily a matter of whether they reinforce and support the educational purposes of the institution. This said, it should be noted that from campus to campus the educational aims of fraternal organizations vary as much as, or more than, the educational aims of individual students. With regard to the affiliations that result from the fraternal experience, administrators may place some value on these relationships, but primarily they are seen in terms of student involvement with and alumni loyalty to the college or university.

Finally, inter/national headquarters personnel generally maintain that fraternal organizations should enhance the collegiate educational experience. However, many of the headquarters are avid in protecting the autonomy of their organizations, and they resist with surprising assertiveness any encroachment on this autonomy, even when the proposed change would advance the educational purposefulness of fraternal life. This attitude seems to be softening. With recent pressures from families, the public, and institutional staff, more headquarters are beginning to encourage tighter educational alignment of fraternal organizations with their host campuses.

After the Forums

While deliberation does not necessarily require action, and while the deliberations of Fraternal Futures do not aim for specific action but rather for a new level of active awareness, it is natural to expect that deliberating groups and communities will want to consider taking or encouraging actions that they conclude are important to their future. Needless to say, courage and confidence are essential if change is to be embraced as natural and necessary rather than disruptive.

A key text here is Rosabeth Moss Kanter's *Confidence: How Winning Streaks and Losing Streaks Begin and End* (2004). According to Moss Kanter, nine organizational characteristics signal the onset of a losing streak: communication decreases, criticism and blame increase, respect decreases, isolation increases, focus turns inward, rifts widen and inequities grow, initiative decreases, aspirations diminish, and negativity spreads. How might Fraternal Futures speak to these difficulties?

Decreased communication makes for a downward slide because it reflects an unwillingness to have tough conversations and address fundamental issues. Fraternal Futures moves in the opposite direction. Its deliberations attempt to provide a forum for candid conversations where students know their voices are heard and the tendency to blame is avoided. Increased isolation contributes to decline by creating barriers to fresh ideas. Deliberations can expose such isolation. Recall the remark of a junior sorority woman in the course of a deliberation: "It's like we live in a bubble here.

I barely even know other Greek members outside of my chapter." Such comments indicate that fraternal organizations are headed for a "losing streak" unless they increase communication among organizations and begin to take responsibility for resolving their problems.

Moss Kanter offers three cornerstones for rebuilding confidence —restoring accountability, cultivating collaboration, and inspiring initiative. Restoring accountability requires facing facts and reinforcing responsibility, which is at the core of the Fraternal Futures Initiative. She contends that organizations need to talk frankly about problems and expectations, admit responsibility for problems, have open dialogue and widespread communication, set clear priorities, and pay attention to detail. Her research indicates that despite popular views to the contrary, people do in fact enjoy having open and honest dialogue about real issues and believe that it is needed for meaningful change. With regard to straight talk, open dialogue, and establishing priorities, the value of Fraternal Futures is obvious.

To cultivate collaboration, Moss Kanter (2004) advocates promoting a team atmosphere, demonstrating respect for internal and individual talent, creating an informed and accountable team, and structuring new conversations that deal with important, meaningful work. Fraternal Futures seeks to meet these needs as it asks students to examine fundamental questions that deal with the essential nature of fraternal organizations. It also seeks to create an atmosphere that enables students to consider the views of others and build on them.

About inspiring initiative and innovation, Moss Kanter writes: "Of all the pathologies that accumulate in a losing streak, one of the most damaging to individuals, and eventually to the place they work and live, is passivity and learned helplessness" (Moss Kanter 2004, 256). To inspire initiative and innovation, she suggests departing from tradition, innovating through collaboration, and considering "surprising successes." Through the authentic dialogue that emerges from a Fraternal Futures deliberation, students address the issues arising from unhealthy traditions and seek ways to turn negative energy into a positive force. Moderators prompt students to consider "sacred cows," those untouchable practices and ideas that are so carefully avoided in many conversations about the state of fraternities and sororities on college campuses.

It is our hope that Fraternal Futures deliberations will begin a conversation that will reverse losing trends in fraternal groups, much as losing streaks have been broken elsewhere. Then and only then can winning organizations, perhaps even champions, emerge among fraternal organizations on college campuses.

Conclusion/Summary

Fraternal Futures arose from frustration about how to deal with the problems posed by organizations that have been present on college campuses for 200 years, touching the lives of hundreds of thousands of students. It built on numerous conversations and encounters that occurred over almost a decade, work that we hope will pay off in more educationally purposeful, viable organizations that will be part of the higher education landscape for many years to come. We feel strongly that fraternal organizations will not survive unless they pursue deep and sustained conversations that renew them as an integral part of the campuses on which they exist.

The initial efforts of Fraternal Futures have created momentum for change on the several campuses where the model has been used. Students have spoken and continue to speak through their participation. They have told us that they appreciate being heard and that they are willing to put forth the effort to be part of positive change. Their responses to postparticipation questionnaires indicate that, at least as far as fraternal organizations are concerned, they see the potential, the benefit, and the importance of becoming civically engaged in matters that are important to them.

Our work with Fraternal Futures shows us that if we seek to renew civic engagement in general, or in fraternal organizations in particular, we must: (1) begin with students' interests; (2) start with local issues in small groups; (3) allow students to cocreate their future; and (4) enrich students' understanding of the issues

(Roberts and Huffman 2005). Ultimately, this approach will allow fraternal organizations to remain on campuses throughout the nation and to fulfill the promise that many of their founders saw in them—the promise of fostering responsibility, leadership, and character in their members.

Dennis C. Roberts, PhD, is assistant vice president for faculty and Student Services at Qatar Foundation, where his responsibilities include working with staff who coordinate recruitment/admission, financial assistance, and campus and residence life. Prior to arriving in Qatar in November 2007, Roberts served as associate vice president for student affairs at Miami University in Oxford, Ohio. He is a former president of the American College Personnel Association and hass been a member of the international Leadership Association and hasfounding. He currently serves as a senior scholar of the American College personnel association, since its college Personnel Association, and is a member of the Board of Trustees of the LeaderShape Institute.

Matthew R. Johnson is currently a research assistant at the Kettering Foundation. He is a former graduate assistant in the Office of Student Leadership at Miami University. He holds a master's degree in College Student Personnel and a bachelor's degree in marketing. His studies in the College Student Personnel Program and work with the Fraternal Futures Initiative have led him to pursue a career in organizational leadership in higher education.

References

Baxter Magolda, M. B. "Learning Partnerships Model: A Framework for Promoting Self-Authorship. In *Learning Partnerships: Theory and Models of Practice to Educate for Self-Authorship,* eds. M. B. Baxter Magolda and P. M. King. Sterling, VA: Stylus, 2004.

Berkowitz, A. D. The Proactive Prevention Model: Helping Students Translate Healthy Beliefs into Healthy Actions. *About Campus,* 3 (4) (1998): 26-27.

Keeling, R. P. "HIV/AIDS in the Academy: Engagement and Learning in a Context of Change." *NASPA Leadership for a Healthy Campus Newsletter* 1 (1998).

Long, S. E. *The New Student Politics: The Wingspread Statement on Student Civic Engagement.* 2nd ed. Providence, RI: Campus Compact, 2002.

Love, P. G. and V. L. Guthrie. "Kegan's Orders of Consciousness." In *Understanding and Applying Cognitive Development Theory. New Directions for Student Services,* No. 88. San Francisco, CA: Jossey-Bass, 1999, 65-76.

Moss Kanter, R. *Confidence: How Winning Streaks and Losing Streaks Begin and End.* New York: Crown Business, 2004.

Roberts, D. C. and E. A. Huffman. "Learning Citizenship: Campus-Based Initiatives for Developing Student Change Agents. *About Campus* 10(4) (2005): 17-22.

SECTION V

Deliberation and Civic Education:
A Four-Year Study

Chapter Ten

Contexts for Deliberation: Experimenting with Democracy in the Classroom, on Campus, and in the Community

Katy J. Harriger and Jill J. McMillan

This study explored the possible impact of providing college students with a civil way to "speak politics" through learning deliberation. The authors worked with a group of students, called "Democracy Fellows," throughout their four-year career at Wake Forest and compared them to a class cohort each year. The study reveals that context makes a difference in the effectiveness of deliberation as a tool of civic pedagogy. The classroom was a hospitable environment for acquiring knowledge, linking theory and practice, and honing deliberative skills that could be transferred to other environments. On the other hand, it is ill designed to be an authentic democratic site, to connect the academic and the "real world," and to move easily from talk to action. The campus venue offered wider exposure to and appreciation of the deliberative model, relative ease in planning and logistics, and a general increase in students' political efficacy. The disadvantages are the limited issues for student action, variable administrative interest and response, and the retention of a safe haven for political talk that fails to parallel political reality. The community context proved to be the most authentic deliberative environment by fostering appreciation of a serious local problem, providing an opportunity for community organizing, and bridging the town/gown divide. These assets were counterbalanced by difficulties with recruitment and diversity, issue selection, limited student efficacy, and role tensions for the professors/researchers. The authors conclude that the ideal civic education program would utilize all three contexts, being mindful of the strengths and weaknesses of each.

In response to the well-documented issues of political alienation among America's youth, many have argued that higher education should reconsider its commitment to civic education. Spurred by this concern, we have been engaged in a project that considers how teaching the process of deliberation and then practicing it by engaging in and conducting deliberative forums in increasingly "real-world" settings might contribute to students' interest in civic life and to their participation in it. To explore this, we worked with a group of students, gradually expanding their forum experiences over the four years of their college experience.

We framed our study using the notion of context, which in this case, meant the different settings that college students could develop the democratic skills of deliberative talk—the classroom, the campus, and the larger community. Our project was intentionally developmental. We wanted to know whether the deliberative skills of the students expanded as they moved from the classroom to the larger community. We also sought to take into account the maturing of the students, both educational and political.

To compare the benefits and limitations of each context, we drew on the work of John J. Patrick (2000), who offered a multitiered, developmental approach to understanding the goals of civic engagement work. Patrick maintained that colleges and universities who wanted to develop programs to nurture the citizenship of their students should consider four key components: *acquisition of knowledge* about the concepts, principles, and history of democracy and the role of citizens in a democracy; *development of the cognitive skills* of thinking critically and constructively about what this substantive knowledge means for the way democracy works and for the role of citizens; *development of the participatory skills* for civic involvement, which include interacting with others, deliberating about public policy, and influencing policy decisions; and *encouragement of dispositions of citizenship*, which include promoting the general welfare, recognizing the common humanity of each person, respecting and protecting rights, taking responsibility for one's participation, and supporting democratic principles and practices. Patrick's categories enabled us to track whether students' views of citizenship deepened through increasingly real-world exposure to deliberation.

When we examined the benefits and limitations of each context, in large part through Patrick's components, we found, first, that the different contexts do make a difference in what students learn and, second, that each context contains particular benefits and limitations in teaching and preparing students to become active citizens.

The Democracy Fellows Project

In 2001, we began our longitudinal research project into deliberation and civic engagement, examining the experiences of a group of students as they made their way through four years of education at Wake Forest University, a private, liberal arts college in North Carolina where we teach. We were interested in exploring several interrelated questions. First, and most generally, we wanted to know how the college experience shapes students' attitudes and behavior toward civic engagement. Second, we wanted to know whether students who learn how to deliberate about public issues develop different attitudes and behaviors about civic engagement from their peers who have not had this experience. Finally, as we have said, we were interested in understanding the effects of context on the experience of deliberative forums. We pursued these questions by focusing on three sets of students.

The Participants

The first group consisted of 30 students who were recruited from the entering class in fall 2001 to participate in what we titled the Democracy Fellows program. We selected these students to reflect the general demographic makeup of the entering class, and over the students' four-year career they participated in various activities, which together provided them the opportunity to experiment with democratic decision making. During the first semester, we conducted entry interviews with each Democratic Fellow to establish a baseline of the students' political views. In subsequent years, we interviewed the students in focus groups, to explore their ongoing experiences with deliberation and campus life. Finally, in the senior year, we conducted individual exit interviews. All of these sessions were audiotaped and transcribed.

We compared the Democratic Fellows to a different set of 25 students, who served as a control group and whom we randomly selected from a list of the 2001 entering class, minus the 30 Democracy Fellows. This control group, which we examined in focus groups each year, [1] was not exposed to the deliberative experiences provided the fellows. In the first year, we compared the baseline views of politics of both groups by using the focus groups of control students to ask them the same questions that we asked the Democracy Fellows in individual interviews. In subsequent years, while the Democracy Fellows and their class cohort were asked some of the same questions, only the Democracy Fellows were probed about their experiences with deliberative activities, because the class cohort did not engage in such activities.

During the second year of the study, we talked with a third group of students who were neither in the Democracy Fellows program nor part of the class cohort. Instead, they were 25 students from all classes who participated in a campuswide deliberative forum planned and hosted by the Democracy Fellows in October 2002. Put broadly, we wanted to see the effects of a single deliberative experience. In this report, the third group is identified as Deliberation Participants.

The Chronology

As we have noted, we exposed our Democracy Fellows to increasingly complex, increasingly real-world deliberative experiences. In year one, the fellows' initial exposure to deliberation

---

[1] The original cohort served as the core each year but was supplemented, when necessary, to maintain a critical mass of nonfellow respondents from the class of 2001.

came through their first-year seminar, "Deliberative Democracy," held during the fall of 2001. All first-year students at the university must enroll in a semester-long seminar that promotes critical thinking through experiences in group discussion and regular writing assignments. Subjects vary widely. Our seminar focused on the theory and practice of public deliberation. Each seminar is capped at 15 students, so the Democracy Fellows were divided into two sections, and we team-taught each one.

We began the seminar by exploring democratic theory about the citizen's role in a democracy and about the importance of public talk. In the second part of the seminar, we taught the students how to deliberate by having them participate in three classroom deliberations in which we served as moderators. For these deliberations, we followed the National Issues Forums (NIF) choice-work approach, using three NIF issue books (produced by the Kettering Foundation), which focused respectively on public education, race and ethnic tensions, and the role of the university in promoting civic engagement. After each deliberation, we spent time "debriefing," talking through what went well, what went less well, why problems developed, and how they might be overcome.

In the last third of the seminar, we taught the students how to frame an issue for public deliberation, using a campus issue of their own choice. The fellows first formed small groups to investigate current campus concerns that would lend themselves to deliberative discussion, then worked through the process of selecting an issue, and chose "Building Community at Wake Forest." The next step was to frame the issue—which in this case consisted of identifying three approaches to building community (improving campus social life, building a stronger intellectual climate, engaging with the local community)—so that it could be the basis of an issue book, which they would write during the next semester.

To end the seminar, we asked the students to write an essay that examined their experience with deliberation, the extent to which it corresponded with the theoretical literature they had examined at the start of the seminar, and the prospects for deliberation as a method of developing citizenship both on college campuses and in the larger society. Our assessment of the impact of the seminar is based in part on these essays, our own observations, and the comments offered about the seminar in subsequent interviews with the fellows.

In the second year of the project, the Democracy Fellows left the classroom for the larger campus. In the months prior to fall 2002, the fellows prepared for their campus deliberation on "Building Community at Wake Forest." In addition to the extensive work they did researching, writing, editing, and publishing the issue book, approximately half the fellows engaged in a moderator training workshop, and others worked on publicity, recruitment, and logistical issues around the event itself. On October 8, 2002, the big night finally arrived. Some 120 people—from the 4 constituencies of students, faculty, administration, and townspeople—gathered in the Student Center for the deliberation. Following a plenary session in which three fellows introduced the issue, the large group broke up into smaller groups where each of the four constituencies was represented. Democracy Fellows moderated the groups.

We asked all the participants to fill out pre- and postdeliberation surveys assessing their attitudes about the issue of building the campus community and their preferences for the various choices that had been identified in the issue book as possible ways of building this community. Some time after the deliberation, we conducted 9 focus groups, 3 with Democracy Fellows, 3 with Deliberation Participants (the 25 students from all classes), and 3 with the class cohort. With the fellows and Deliberation Participants, we probed their experience with the campus deliberation itself, which had led to changes to the first-year orientation and to the creation of a new coffee house on campus (a response to improving campus social life).

In year three, the Democracy Fellows went beyond the campus into the local community. On October 2, 2003, the Democracy Fellows hosted a deliberation on the topic of urban sprawl in the Winston-Salem community. The event was held at a community science museum, and was attended by approximately 50 people, a notable falling off from the 120 who attended the campus deliberation.

As with the campus deliberation, the community event was re-searched and planned by the Democracy Fellows during the spring semester preceding the fall deliberation. Students chose the topic of urban sprawl because it had become an issue in the Winston-Salem community and because they had received permission to adapt an existing NIF issue book on the topic to fit the local situation. Once again, Democracy Fellows formed subgroups to work on the issue book, recruitment, publicity, and logistics. Over the summer, the issue book was completed, edited, and published. In early fall, participants were recruited, and the issue book was distributed to them.

While we had access to the participants in the campus deliberation, this time we lacked access to the community participants, but we did conduct focus groups with the Democracy Fellows to probe their attitudes about the experience, and we similarly conducted focus groups with the class cohort of the fellows.

This community deliberation concluded the scheduled deliberative agenda for the Democracy Fellows. During their final year and a half, no deliberative activities were scheduled; however, a number of fellows participated in two other events—one on campus and one off—that made use of their deliberative skills and training and that came about by invitation. In the second semester of the senior year, we concluded our data gathering by conducting exit interviews with each of the fellows and three focus groups with a senior class cohort.

The Basic Findings

We engaged in this study, first and foremost, to learn whether sustained exposure to deliberation as an alternative method of public talk would encourage a disposition toward democratic engagement. On this issue, the findings are clear, and the following three outcomes are illustrative of the enhanced propensity toward engagement that the fellows exhibited.

At the outset, we found that students said they lacked the knowl-edge to engage in politics, a problem that abated with the fellows.

They reported that because of their first-year seminar on democracy and deliberation, they had a notion of citizenship and a rough understanding of democracy and how the American political process worked, information that most students in the control group (with the exception of the few who took political science courses) continued to lack.

A parallel finding has to do with the generalizability of political knowledge. Over time, the students in the control group continued to think that political knowledge was a specialized knowledge needed by students who wanted to major in politics. In contrast, Democracy Fellows, only a few of whom ended up being political science majors, all quickly came to think of citizenship and politics as part of their ongoing work. Citizenship and politics were simply part of who they were and part of what they did.

The last finding we note comes from a comparison of political efficiency among the Democracy Fellows and among the senior class as a whole. From the senior survey data, we found that the Democracy Fellows ended up with a much stronger sense of efficacy on campus than did the senior class. Put another way, their sense of having a voice on campus was substantially stronger than the sense the senior class had of its voice. The difference between the fellows and their classmates first emerged after the campus deliberation, an event that turned out to have real-world consequences. Further, even though the community deliberation in Winston-Salem was far less successful by almost any measure, the fellows' sense of efficacy was not lost. It appears that once one has a clear experience of efficacy, it can withstand at least some experiences of failure. If this is so, it seems a good lesson for those of us who are interested in fostering a sense of citizenship among our students.

For readers who want to explore these and other relevant findings about the differences between the Democracy Fellows and their fellow students, we refer them to our book documenting the project (Harriger and McMillan 2007). In the rest of the paper, however, we concentrate on the contexts of deliberation, to examine with more detail how students learn to become citizens through deliberation.

The Classroom Context

It may go without saying that the classroom is an obvious context for teaching college students deliberation. At most institutions, the classroom and the curriculum, representing the domain in which the faculty exercises primary control, offer the potential for accomplishing each of the four educational components of effective civic education that Patrick identifies. However, we found the classroom to be a stronger venue for teaching knowledge and critical thinking than for simulating an actual political environment or for appreciating the dispositions of citizenship that reveal themselves when discussants are directly affected by the issue-at-hand. We consider the positives of the classroom venue first.

Classroom Advantages

Acquiring knowledge.

As we noted above, we found in our early interviews with fellows and the class cohort that one of the significant and self-identified barriers to civic participation was a lack of knowledge about the political system, how it operates, and how to become involved in it—and a lack of confidence in the knowledge they did have. We found in later interviews that a strong predictor of student confidence in becoming engaged in politics, whether in the form of discussion with others, joining a campaign, or being part of a group working on some social issue, was the classroom experience of learning about the political system and how it operates. Both notions are consistent with Patrick's notion of the importance of political knowledge.

We also found that whether students had acquired that knowledge often depended on whether they deliberately sought it out in their course selection. Even with a broad, two-year liberal arts divisional curriculum, it was possible for students to avoid spending any time learning about politics. In all, students who were not in the Democracy

Fellows program were less likely to have had classroom exposure to discussions of democracy and citizenship, even after four years of college.

Democracy Fellows, who went on to have a variety of majors, most of which were not political science or communication (our individual fields), nonetheless all shared at least the exposure obtained in the first-year seminar. One fellow wrote in his final first-year essay, "I have found in this short time span of the Deliberative Democracy class … that I learned more about the history of basic ideas about democracy than I have in the rest of my life." The fellows' enhanced confidence in their role as active citizens and their ability to talk knowledgably and critically about deliberation, democracy, and citizenship were evident in each of the subsequent years of interviews following the first-year experience.

Linking theory and practice.

Classroom deliberation enables students to "enact" both the knowledge about political and deliberative theory they have learned and to practice it in ways that reinforce the cognitive skills and the political dispositions that Patrick recommends. Furthermore, the classroom offers a "safe" environment where the consequences of stumbling or erring are far less than they are in the real world. Practicing democratic skills, such as deliberation, in the classroom also allows students to become more analytical about the functions of public talk, for example by engaging in it themselves and then stepping back and assessing what they have just experienced. The debriefing exercises that followed each of our classroom deliberations, in which we asked the students to apply our theoretical discussions about the benefits and challenges of deliberation to the experience they had just had, were always the most insightful discussions of the class.

One debriefing session in particular stands out. Our deliberation on race and ethnic tensions had been a difficult and often painful two days, and the fellows showed little ability at the end to find common ground for agreement or for action. Our debriefing of that experience—Why was it so hard? What does that tell us about deliberation on difficult issues?—was one of the most powerful learning experiences of the class. Not only did the debriefing require keen and honest description, explanation, and evaluation of what had occurred, it brought students face to face with their own personal discomfort in discussions regarding race.

Democracy Fellows talked about this deliberation quite a bit in their final essays as they processed what that experience might mean for the usefulness of deliberation. For example, one student left the class somewhat skeptical about such utility: "In our class with race and ethnic tensions," she wrote, "we were not able to talk through the issue. If only fourteen people of limited diversity of perspectives cannot talk through an issue and find common judgment, then I am skeptical of the ability of a larger group of people to deliberate." She noted the dispositional flaw that she had witnessed: "instead of meeting together at a common point, we went away from each other."

When reflecting on their deliberative experience as a whole, many students talked more generally about how much they had learned from hearing the perspectives of others who were different from them. Discussing the way group knowledge emerged through the deliberation, one student wrote, "When I entered a deliberation, I possessed a personal knowledge of the issue, yet by temporarily putting aside my view and listening to others' stories, I gained a public knowledge about 'Race and Ethnic Tensions' and 'Public Education' that I would never have had alone."

Transferring skills to other settings.

While Patrick's four key components specifically refer to civic education, our students were eager to extend the influence of their deliberative training. The deliberative practice, critical thinking, and democratic dispositions learned through the seminar had particular staying power for the students once they left the seminar and encountered challenging discussions in other classes and in other settings.

In our senior exit interviews, for example, the fellows talked about how learning the deliberative model for talk and embracing the democratic theory ideals underlying it (equality of participants, considering the experiences and underlying values of others, looking for common ground, considering whose voices were missing and what the missing might say, taking seriously the benefits and trade-offs of each approach to a policy question) had influenced the way they developed as students and as campus citizens.

One student said, "I think the [skills of deliberation] will always be a consideration when I'm ever in a group.... I think that if I'm remotely in charge or have the ability to contribute to the manner in which ... things are going, I would encourage [deliberation] because it's applicable to everything. Fraternity stuff, definitely. In the business world, yeah." This same student described his use of deliberative skills in leading his fraternity during the senior year. Another student talked about using these skills while serving as a resident advisor in the dormitory. Others even spoke about using them in their personal relationships with friends. Perhaps most significant in terms of the impact on how we talk about and practice politics, students identified their experience with deliberation as having a current and future impact on "speaking with and listening to others," being "open-minded," and "taking seriously the other's point of view." While we made no specific attempt to tie the foundational knowledge, practice, cognitive development, and keener dispositions of the first-year seminar to their wider lives and practices, our students, almost to the last one, insisted on making that link, and they did so independently.

Classroom deliberation, then, yielded all of the civic education components emphasized by Patrick: knowledge of democratic theory and deliberation as a model of public talk, cognitive development in assessing the deliberation as it progresses and in evaluating its outcome, participatory skills that were beginning to be developed, and the perspective taking necessary for building political dispositions. However, as we show in the next section, we regard knowledge acquisition and cognitive development as the classroom's greatest victories. Participation and development of political dispositions gained traction in the more democratically authentic venues that the students would experience later on, when we were to see the fellows adapt and fine tune the skills they had learned.

Classroom Limitations

Despite the obvious learning advantages of the classroom setting, we found that while the classroom is essential to reaching students "where they are," it cannot simulate an authentic democratic environment and discussion. Thus, Patrick's components must of necessity be attenuated when: the classroom is more like a lab, not the real world; student "citizens" are not really in charge of their own destinies; and student deliberators have little power to move from talk to action. It is especially difficult to cultivate in student deliberators the political dispositions that come from deliberating alongside citizens personally affected by an issue.

The undemocratic characteristics of the classroom.

The classroom, with its teacher-student relationship, presents obvious challenges to the democratic ideals of deliberation. The reality is that the classroom context necessitates that students must be evaluated and graded, and the persons responsible for that assessment are the professors. Thus, despite the effort to make the classroom as democratic as possible, in the end the power imbalance remains. Even if some educators believe that grades are counterproductive, most of us are not in settings in which we are at liberty to abandon them.

The conditions of the classroom bring a degree of artificiality to the exercise of practicing democracy, and it is very difficult to overcome. In our own case, with so much class time given over to discussion, deliberation, and other forms of participation, we did not feel free to eliminate from these practices some kind of evaluation. Admittedly, we gave students frequent feedback and encouragement in one-on-one encounters to make that evaluation as educationally valuable as possible, but in the end, they were all aware that for the purposes of the class we as instructors were not their "fellow citizens." Classrooms are great settings for exposure to and experimentation with democratic ideals, but in the end, they are not great models of democratic communities.

Further, the classroom is not immune from the recurring democratic problem of individual dominance, especially if grade-motivated students worry unduly about the assessment of their individual contributions. While we succeeded in moderating the problems of power and dominance—in the first-year seminar, for example, we did a workshop that focused on practicing in a very intentional way the skills of listening and of identifying the values underlying the policy positions of others—we did not succeed in eliminating these problems. Some students saw in the classroom experience the same unequal power dynamics at work that they saw in the larger political realm. One young woman noted that in the class this power dynamic "was fairly evident—at times only a few people talked, and while the others may have had comments to make, the floor was controlled by a select few."

There was a perception over time, however, that the group had improved. "Our third deliberation," wrote one young man, "was marked by students engaging other students, and more participation by more people." A rather quiet young woman became a believer in deliberation because, despite some ongoing power differential, she thought all voices had been valued and "everyone is allowed to participate." She wrote, "We see that deliberation does more than tolerate differences; it uses them."

Disconnect between the classroom and the real world.

The "nonworldly" character of the classroom also seemed to undercut the possibility of transferring deliberation out into the world. Despite the classroom opportunities to link theory and practice, which appeared to teach that democratic citizenship was important and that deliberation could work to reduce polarization and conflict by talking through difficult public issues, the students encountered substantial counterevidence in their interactions with the campus and the larger political community.

In their final freshman essays evaluating the deliberative model, the fellows talked with optimism about the potential of deliberation in some essentially educational settings but with pessimism about the barriers to making it work in the larger political world. They recognized that citizens would have to be trained, as they had been, to think about politics differently, and they wondered about the willingness and the ability of people to take the time to learn to deliberate. For some of the students, the necessity of learning to "do deliberation" was an obstacle to its success in the broader community.

In later years, their earlier optimism tempered somewhat, the Democracy Fellows even expressed skepticism about the prospects for a more democratic campus, pointing to the clash they identified between the ideals of democracy they had been exposed to in our class and the reality of what they encountered in other classrooms, in campus life, and in the broader political world. In their senior interviews, they still held on to both the notions learned in the "Deliberative Democracy" seminar about what citizenship *could* be and the value of deliberative talk in their *own lives*, but they were also very much aware of the countercultural nature of the model and the challenges of implementing it in the real world. Clearly, the classroom setting cannot adequately simulate the challenges of implementing democratic practice in the world beyond it.

The difficulty of moving from talk to action.

Finally, the deliberative model we employed in this project has an end point in which the group participants seek to identify common ground for action. The moderator encourages them to think about when they have found common ground in their discussion and what concrete actions they might take as individuals and as a group to bring about change in the policy area they have been discussing. Students in the seminar found this to be the most difficult part of the classroom deliberations, largely because they felt they had no power to influence policy outcomes regarding the issues we discussed. They were occasionally able to identify individual actions they could take—tutor a child in the local schools, try to get to know someone of a different race or ethnic background—but they were unable to think of themselves in a collective sense as having power to influence education policy or race and ethnic tensions.

In sum, the classroom provides an excellent venue—and a familiar and comfortable one—to impart foundational knowledge; to provide an opportunity for supervised practice; and to allow students to experiment with interactive skills that have wide, even lifelong, utility. As a democratic archetype, however, the classroom has some limitations: a teacher is still "the boss," and institutional rules, such as grades and attendance, prevail, thereby straining the argument that students are involved in a real-world democratic

exercise in which they will be able to move their classroom
talk to meaningful political action.

The Campus Context

When we use Patrick's civic education model to consider the
effect on our students of moving their deliberative activities from
the classroom to the campus, it seems clear that while students
continued to advance in the civic knowledge that they had begun
to gain in the classroom, the migration into the public arena put an
increased focus on and tested various elements of their practical
civic skills. On campus it would be necessary to grapple with and
weigh the alternative ways of approaching a substantive issue, one,
in this case, they had some power to affect; participate with their
peers and with those in positions of authority above them to influence their collective culture; and hone their civic dispositions by
considering, and even being persuaded by, the diverse perspectives
of other campus citizens. In other words, the campus context not
only posed a challenge that basically did not exist in the classroom,
it also presented opportunities to fine tune learning and skills
initiated in the safer environment of the classroom.

Campus Advantages

Wider exposure to and appreciation for the deliberative model.

As we reported earlier, the campus deliberation enabled
the Democracy Fellows to tackle a relevant campus issue
and to showcase a viable model for addressing it. Overall,
it is clear that both the Democracy Fellows and the Deliberation Participants (who attended the campus deliberation
but lacked the other deliberative experiences of the fellows)
felt positively about the process they experienced. Deliberation Participants were particularly enthusiastic and identified
in their enthusiasm many of the characteristics of deliberation
that its supporters hold up as desirable democratic talk.

They recognized and appreciated the value of diverse voices being heard, the equality given the participants' voices despite their status differences on campus, the ground rules that encouraged listening and taking seriously the views of others rather than promoting polarized debate, and the structure and common knowledge provided by the issue book. Indeed, the Deliberation Participants had a kind of wide-eyed wonder about the potential for a process that was largely very new to them and that they enjoyed being part of.

The Democracy Fellows too were genuinely pleased and excited with their accomplishment in pulling off the event, but they cast a more critical eye on the deliberative process of which they were already aware. They were more willing to identify possible problems and were more cautious about what the outcomes might be and how and where the process would work on campus and in the community. It seems clear that their more extensive experience with and critical examination of deliberation and democratic theory was in play in their assessment of the deliberation's success.

Especially encouraging to the Democracy Fellows and to all of us who wondered about the utility of deliberation as a campuswide decision-making tool were the pre- and postdeliberation results, which showed that the deliberation did indeed alter the participants' attitudes, in some instances fairly substantially. As a result of the deliberation, agreement increased on each of the four formulations characterizing the lack of community on campus—the isolation of students from the larger community, the lack of school spirit, the separation of groups, and the lack of intellectual community. For example, the percent of respondents who were "very concerned" about students being isolated from the larger community had increased from 31 to 44 percent at the conclusion of the discussion. Concern about the lack of school spirit increased from 43 to 57 percent, and concern about the lack of an intellectual climate increased from 39 to 47 percent.

In answering open-ended questions, the majority of participants agreed that the deliberation had had an effect on their
attitudes about the issue, and most said that there were
things they would do about it. The kinds of likely actions
that were identified included working to motivate others
toward more campus involvement, building relationships
with people and groups otherwise overlooked, and sponsoring activities that bring diverse groups together.

So, on balance, the students who attended the campus
deliberation declared it a rousing success, both in their
reported attitude change and later as they reflected upon
the experience in their focus groups. Perhaps most important
for this study, students explicitly articulated the potential
for using deliberation at future campus decision-making
junctures. They apparently reasoned that the political
exercise that had energized and encouraged them—even
changed their minds—could do the same for classmates
and other campus citizens.

Relative ease in planning and implementation.

Though the planning and implementation of the campus
deliberation stretched the fellows' time and resources, they
moved rather effortlessly and confidently through that
process. They personally knew many of the people—
students, faculty, and administration—whom they were
dealing with. Soliciting participation and help in implementation was relatively painless—an important point that
should not be overlooked by educators who seek to use the
deliberative process on campus. The ease of the process
would sharply fail to hold for the community deliberation
that was next on the fellows' schedule.

Political efficacy.

We noted the sense of efficacy that the Democracy Fellows
developed, starting with the success of the campus deliberation, about which the fellows felt a strong sense of pride.

The feeling of efficacy persisted, and perhaps grew stronger, as the campus came to recognize the deliberation as valuable and as other groups took up the issues raised there (Student Government, Division of Student Life, Board of Visitors, Board of Trustees). In the end, changes to the first-year orientation program and the development of more "public spaces" on campus (the new coffee shop) could be traced to the deliberation. One fellow said: "I loved our campus deliberation.... [Having] the opportunity to see where actually it went was actually very impressive." While we did not measure larger cultural shifts with regard to this event, it is possible that its success functioned to further "democratize the campus" (Morse 1992)—at least to improve the general climate of decision making on campus and the students' role in it.

Campus Limitations

Despite the positive benefits of the campus experience, there are limitations here too as to what such an experience can accomplish in developing engaged citizens. Some scholars (Allan 1997; Becker and Cuoto 1996) have noted that one of the drawbacks to teaching democracy on campus by modeling it institutionally is the limited power and influence that students are afforded. Our research suggests that this fact does not go unnoticed by students.

Limited issues for student action.

We were fortunate that the fellows selected as a subject of their campus deliberation one that students actually had some ability to impact. Some of the other topics that they considered—building a parking deck, converting a nearby upscale shopping center into a student hangout, replacing the current food service—offered little potential for student action.

Over the four years of our study, we repeatedly asked students what role the university should provide them for learning to engage in citizenship. Most echoed the opinion of one Wake Forest student (not a fellow) who believes that students lack the maturity, experience, and commitment to participate in governance: "I don't think students should be elevated to be making major administrative decisions when there are people who are there in those positions for a reason." Another nonfellow opined that she feared, if given equal authority for their own governance, students might show up to deliberate "only if there were free food."

This is not to say, however, that the scope of student involvement cannot be enlarged, as indeed it was in the campus deliberation. The challenge, as we have seen, is to find issues on which students have the possibility of creating action— that is, of actually contributing to an important outcome— lest the deliberation experience leave them further disillusioned about the promise of deliberative democracy.

Administrative interest and response.

Also consistent in the four years of the study is the unanimous sense of where power resides on campus. Repeatedly the students identified Reynolda Hall—the administrative building on campus—as the source of campus power. As with most top-down organizations, if administrators do not get on board with a student initiative, it is most likely doomed to fail. Fortunately, with the campus deliberation, key administrative figures attended the deliberation, and others were brought into the campuswide discourse after the fact. The issue book became the subject of more than one administrative retreat and, in addition, was used extensively to alter pre-school student orientation. While students could point to several past issues on campus when they felt disenfranchised (see McMillan 2004), the discussion on building the campus community was not one of them.

Maintaining the "bubble."

Wake Forest students characterize their existence on a somewhat homogeneous and insulated campus as living inside a bubble. The campus context basically reinforced this impression, and reminded us as instructors that the campus deliberation, as successful as it was, was still at least one step removed from a true experience in democratic decision making.

The fellows operated within their comfort zones as they made contacts, recruited, negotiated, and publicized. More important, the preponderance of the concerns deliberated that evening kept students firmly in the center of their own narrow, self-interested universe—a situation that was to change dramatically when they took their deliberative efforts out into the wider Winston-Salem community.

In sum, while the classroom venue introduced deliberative theory and skills, the campus forum allowed Democracy Fellows the chance to plan and execute an actual deliberation for a challenging outside audience of their professors, peers, and fellow campus and community citizens. By the measures presented here, the students succeeded in their goals; additionally they introduced a viable decision-making model and the potential for increased political power to those who would use it. From Patrick's perspective, they vastly increased their political knowledge about a campus issue; reinforced both their cognitive and participation skills; and strengthened political dispositions—at least local ones—as they heard the viewpoints of their fellow campus citizens. As a general exercise in democratic pedagogy, however, a campus deliberation can be hindered by the range of potential issues, administrative interest and sanctions, and the artificially "safe" political environment within the campus boundaries.

The Community Context

While the campus venue clearly raised the stakes for the Democracy Fellows' civic development, Patrick suggests that civic learning falls short if students do not ultimately test their knowledge and cognitive skills by participating and developing political dispositions in the real world with real issues experienced by real people. If the campus deliberation allowed the fellows to stay inside their bubble, the community deliberation—on the topic of urban sprawl—clearly burst it, forcing them beyond the protection of their teachers and friends into the local community that surrounded them. Here they had to participate face to face with people often very unlike themselves, concerning issues whose complexity and intractability stretched the fellows' minds and imaginations. Bursting the bubble was clearly this venue's greatest effect, with ambiguous results, but students were able to identify other, more specific outcomes that were clearly positive.

Community Advantages

The issue book and appreciation of local issues.

In creating the issue book on local urban sprawl, students interviewed city leaders from all sectors: the mayor's office, neighborhood associations, the Chamber of Commerce, environmental groups, and real estate interests. This research and the ultimate write-up taught them the unique problems that Winston-Salem faces and underscored the complexity of the issue for the average citizen. Thus, the more general political knowledge acquired in the classroom gave way to specific facts, figures, and opinions of Winston-Salem citizens as they encounter urban sprawl on a daily basis.

In terms of the deliberation itself, the fellows sensed that participants appreciated their efforts and demonstrated that appreciation by having read the issue book and being prepared to discuss it. For the students, this was a victory in and of itself. One student remarked:

> I think people that read the issue book were inspired by it because everyone that came, at least in my group, was very informed; you could tell that they had read the book. Every single one of them connected like every single point about every single issue, so like I was really impressed, and in general I think they were impressed with the book and very receptive to it.

While the fellows were initially somewhat disconnected from the subject of urban sprawl in their adopted city, the process of researching the topic and then, at the deliberation, engaging it with local citizens, broadened their awareness. One student noted, and others agreed, that "I learned a great deal from just hearing people from Winston-Salem who are not connected to Wake Forest … and just being able to get different people together and listen to them talk about an issue that the majority of them felt pretty passionate about" was worthwhile.

Exposure to community organizing.

While the process of planning and implementing the campus forum proceeded with relative ease, students found the process with the community forum daunting, dealing as they had to with people whom they did not know and whose particular constraints they were unable to appreciate. Most disappointing to the fellows was the response or lack of it from potential minority participants.

From our perspective as educators, however, we deemed the challenges of location, publicity, and transportation to be more realistic to actual civic engagement than were students' experiences in their own familiar environs. In fact, we regarded the obstacles as tacit education in Patrick's dispositions because the students were able to witness firsthand the practical difficulties of citizenship, such as coming out to a public meeting after a hard day's work or finding a babysitter. In retrospect, one Democracy Fellow suggested that the group might have taken "the wrong approach to the second deliberation. We kind of thought … since the first one went so well, it will be so easy, we don't have to worry about recruiting, it should be easier.…We didn't realize that it was going to be actually a lot harder." For students to truly learn about civic activism, the difficulty our students experienced in taking deliberation "on the road" may, in fact, have been a decided value.

Bridging the town/gown divide.

While the students were disappointed with the smaller and less diverse number of people who participated this time compared to the campus deliberation (50 participants rather than 120), they did feel that those who attended had a meaningful experience. One student said that the smaller-than-hoped-for turnout allowed for small deliberative groups, which he felt improved the quality of the discussion: "I don't think it would have been the same sort of dynamic within the group [if the group had been large] because the people who participated really enjoyed it.... I think we could see that afterwards, when people were actually talking and mingling and looking at sheets on the board [other groups' notes]."

In the same spirit, other students felt that participants left with more knowledge about the issue and about the views of people different from themselves. Some recounted anecdotes in which they observed a participant seeing things in a new light or acknowledging that someone they had disagreed with had a good idea. In other words, students not only felt their own dispositional ranges expanding, but witnessed that process happening with the community participants as well. In our debriefing, we all wondered whether the positive experience of participants might make them more appreciative of the college students in their midst and more sympathetic to the need to bridge the disconnect between the university and the community.

Community Limitations

There is little question that a considerable amount of civic learning took place in the community experience. But there were also challenges and limitations that, in retrospect, the group saw as being inherent in moving away from the campus and into the community. Overall, the fellows engaged in more negative talk about the experience of *organizing and conducting* the community deliberation than about the experience of *participating* in it.

Recruitment and diversity.

Clearly, the central criticism the Democracy Fellows had of their community deliberation experience was their lack of success in getting a large and representative sample of the community to participate in the deliberation. They had the least success in getting members of the minority community, as we have mentioned, but they also had little success in getting students from Wake Forest to attend. The people who did participate tended to be white, affluent, and highly educated.

While the fellows made some acknowledgement of their own inexperience at handling a sizeable event such as this, they primarily attributed the low turnout to external constraints. A number of fellows identified barriers that affect all kinds of political participation, at all levels of the electorate. One student noted, with considerable agreement from others, that "it was an uphill battle ... that we were losing from the very beginning because it's very difficult to get people ... involved in civil and government type issues.... It's like people just ... go home, they're tired and just want to watch TV, that's it." Another student acknowledged that the attendance "was partly our fault," but went on to say that "there was, like, no incentive for these people to come.... It is going to be hard to recruit people who just aren't interested and who don't have the time in their daily lives."

Issue selection.

Many of the Democracy Fellows talked about whether the issue itself contributed to low turnout. While there have been problems of urban sprawl in Winston-Salem and the region was recently identified in a national survey as one of the worst places for urban sprawl in the country, students felt that the issue may not have been sufficiently timely. Students also speculated that the public might simply feel that sprawl is an inevitable part of urban life and there was little to be done about it. Others mentioned the complexity of the issue and the knowledge required to understand it as factors that might limit broad-based participation in such a discussion.

Students also pointed out that the complexity of the issue made the traditional action discussion at the conclusion of the forum more challenging. For example, one student said, "It's such a monumental issue, it's almost like, what can you do? Like, what can one voice really change?"

In addition, the presence of a city councilman who effectively "hijacked" one group convinced students that while citizens may be heard in one evening's deliberation, real systemic change was more likely to happen at the higher reaches of government. Clearly, if students were right about the flexing of power that they witnessed and the resultant feeling of helplessness, efficacy could be diminished rather than enhanced by a community deliberation such as ours.

Limited student efficacy.

Particularly troubling to the Democracy Fellows was their widespread perception that despite the success of and appreciation for the issue book, the larger community did not take them seriously, which affected everything from the students' ability to recruit, to their comfort in even *trying* to recruit, to their credibility as moderators of the event. One student said, "I don't think people at Wake [the school] feel any connection to the town, and I think a lot of people feel that the town doesn't like them, you know, that we're kind of, like, a burden to the town." Another student said, "Especially maybe at Wake Forest, it is kind of hard to be taken seriously by the greater Winston-Salem community, maybe because most of us aren't from here, and we aren't really all that acclimated."

The community under a microscope.

The most serious philosophical challenge to our students and to us as teachers and researchers was the tension between the value of the community deliberation as a pedagogical exercise for the students and its civic value to the citizens and community of Winston-Salem (Harriger and McMillan 2005).

In our traditional faculty roles, we felt the obligation to make certain that our students came away from the experience having learned more about deliberation and about how it might work in a large, diverse, political community. Consequently, we felt it was important for them to be responsible for organizing the event, recruiting the participants, and preparing the materials to be used. Our role tension came into sharp relief, however, when we watched the students underestimate the timing and complexity of advertising and recruiting for this event. On the one hand, our teaching and research interests told us that if they did not do an effective job in these tasks, it was best to let them "fail," given our belief that most learning comes from trial and error, and often, failure. On the other hand, as citizens of the community, we felt an ethical obligation not to treat our neighbors as "subjects" to be experimented with for our pedagogical and research purposes.

We also believed it was important for the students to see that "detachment" on our part was inappropriate and civically irresponsible. It would be wrong to invite community members into a public dialogue about making Winston-Salem a better place to live without doing our best to make sure that the experience was a positive one, at least in its execution if not in its outcomes. In short, we came face to face with what it means when the community itself becomes the learning environment.

The community experience provided an appropriate capstone for the four years of deliberation training, because in many ways it was the most difficult and yet the most authentic venue. The event extended the pursuit of political knowledge to a critical local issue; exposed students to what it

means to activate not just friends but total strangers to
political discussion and responsibility; and afforded them
the opportunity to reach out beyond the campus gates to
address an interest and a need within our community. Those
same advantages also carried the seeds of dissatisfaction,
even failure: students bemoaned that they were unable to
recruit broadly and well; that the issue may have seemed
intractable; and that they themselves may have ultimately
lacked the credibility to pull off a fully successful community event. We as instructors worried about potential role
conflict as we guided the event. Ultimately, however, we
believe that the community deliberation, despite being
somewhat bittersweet, took each of Patrick's criteria of
civic education to a new level: knowledge acquisition
became up close and personal; cognitive skill building
happened ad hoc and onsite; participation required every
skill that had been learned in the classroom and on campus—
and then some; and dispositional challenges and learning
came at the students from all directions.

Conclusion

There is little question that the college experience itself is a
powerful force in shaping students' propensities toward civic engagement or detachment. Many important things that shape students'
development as citizens happen personally, educationally, and
politically. After four years of experimenting with teaching deliberative skills in different settings, we feel confident in saying that
this can be a powerful way of educating students about their role
as citizens. The Democracy Fellows did develop differently from
their class cohort as a result of their deliberative experiences. Each
of the settings we experimented with provided a layer of understanding and experience that helped our students grow into more
thoughtful, critical thinkers who appear committed to being
engaged citizens in their future communities. Most important, the
combination of this experience—the learning plus the practical

involvement—appears to have provided them with an alternative way of understanding what politics might be and with a skill set that they are using in their own encounters with others in group problem solving. We also learned, however, that no single setting provides adequate education for the learning model Patrick proposes for effective civic education: knowledge acquisition, cognitive skill building, participatory skill building, and the creation of democratic dispositions. The limitations of each setting are best corrected by the benefits that derive from other settings. The ideal university program for building civic engagement in its students would include exposure to democratic ideals and decision-making processes in the classroom, the campus, and the larger community.

Katy J. Harriger is professor of political science at Wake Forest University, where she teaches courses on American politics, constitutional law, and, of course, civic engagement. She first became involved with the Kettering Foundation in the 1980s as part of the Public Leadership Education project.

Jill J. McMillan is professor emerita of communication at Wake Forest. She studies organizational and institutional rhetoric and, in particular, how individuals and groups are denied or unwittingly relinquish their voices.

References

Allan, G. *Rethinking College Education*. Lawrence, KS: University Press of Kansas, 1997.

Becker, T. L. and R. A. Cuoto. Introduction. In *Teaching Democracy by Being Democratic*, eds. T. L. Becker and R. A. Cuoto, 1-22. Westport, CT: Praeger, 1996.

Harriger, K. and J. McMillan. *Speaking of Politics: Preparing College Students for Democratic Citizenship through Deliberative Dialogue*, Dayton, OH: Kettering Foundation Press, 2007.

Harriger, K. and J. McMillan. "Public Scholarship and Faculty Role Conflict." *Higher Education Exchange* (2005): 17-23.

McMillan, J. J. "The Potential for Civic Learning in Higher Education: "Teaching Democracy by Being Democratic." *Southern Communication Journal* 69(3) (2004): 188-205.

McMillan, J. J. and K. J. Harriger. "College Students and Deliberation: A Benchmark Study." *Communication Education* 51(3) (2002): 237-253.

Morse, S. W. *Politics for the Twenty-first Century*. Dubuque, IA: Kendall-Hunt Publishing Company, 1992.

Patrick, J. J. "Introduction to Education for Civic Engagement in Democracy. In *Education for Civic Engagement in Democracy*, eds. S. Mann and J. J. Patrick. Bloomington, IN: Educational Resources Information Center, 2000.

Chapter Eleven

Notes and Reflections on Being a Democracy Fellow at Wake Forest University

Allison N. Crawford

This personal reflection provides a student perspective on the four-year Democracy Fellows research study of college students exposed to deliberation, a project based on growing concerns about student political disengagement. The author offers a review of her undergraduate experiences, including deliberative dialogue in the classroom setting and how exposure to the program's themes affected choices and the development of ideas and values.

In fall 2001, I became 1 of 30 incoming freshmen selected to participate in the Democracy Fellows program, a 4-year, longitudinal study at Wake Forest University to explore whether exposure to the deliberative process would affect the political attitudes and civic engagement of college students. It was well known that studies had shown that the political and civic involvement of college students had been declining for many years. In 2001, for example, a survey of incoming freshmen found that only some 28 percent felt it was important to keep up with political affairs, down from 60 percent in 1966 (Bennett and Bennett 2001). A year later, a study found that since 1972, when 18- to 21-year-olds gained the right to vote, the number of Americans under 25 who voted had declined 13 to 15 percent (Levine and Lopez 2002, 1). One researcher, Diana Hess, had used the term *democracy dropouts* to describe many Americans, particularly college students (Hess 2000, 293).

It was in this context that two Wake Forest professors, Katy Harriger and Jill McMillan, created the Democracy Fellows study, to test whether deliberative experiences would increase the political and civic involvement of college students. In their article in this collection, "Contexts for Deliberation," Professors Harriger and McMillan describe the study and outline its results. Here, as a recent graduate of Wake Forest and the Democracy Fellows program, I offer my personal reflections on the program and its influences on my college experience and the development of my political and civic interests.

Why I Became a Democracy Fellow

As a high-school student and a future political science major, I applied for the Democracy Fellows program to learn more about political life generally and to participate in campus politics in an unconventional way. I did not have a complete understanding of the concept of deliberation or the term *deliberative democracy*, but I was interested in dialogue and in addressing the role of being a citizen in our democracy, and I looked forward to learning in a classroom that involved group discussion and offered opportunities for collaborative work. I also thought I would be participating in a project that could have a major impact on the campus political system. I viewed the $2,000 stipend that the project provided as a bonus, and I am sure I would have participated without any stipend at all.

Completing the application for the program led me to reflect on the factors that influenced my political involvement and interests. In high school, I was an active member of student government and a number of other student committees. Both of my parents were public administrators, and I knew from their work that politics and government were more than just the actions of elected officials. At the same time, although I was very much involved in my school and church communities, I was unable to sustain an interest in national political proceedings and elections. I volunteered for a local political party during high school, but my commitment and interest was minimum.

When I came to meet the other Democracy Fellows, I found that they were surprisingly diverse, with a wide range of backgrounds, experiences, and opinions. While many had been very active in local politics during high school, others seemed rather disinterested in politics. I think I was somewhere in the middle, not a democracy dropout, but maybe close. The class diversity made for thought-provoking discussions, which, without our quite knowing it, provided an opportunity to develop the democratic skills of seeing multiple perspectives and learning from conflict (Hurtado et al. 2002, 168).

Learning Deliberation in the First-Year Seminar

As Professors Harriger and McMillan explain in "Contexts of Deliberation," the first year of the project was devoted to a seminar on deliberative democracy. Because 30 students were too many for a class in which dialogue and discussion was central, we were divided into 2 sections of 15 each. The seminar began by focusing on both the democratic and communication theories of public deliberation in a democracy. After obtaining a strong theoretical foundation, we participated in three in-class deliberations—on public education, higher education and citizenship, and racial and ethnic tensions—using National Issues Forums (NIF) issue guides.

An important aspect of our in-class deliberations was the opportunity to talk about our personal lives. Many of our comments naturally drew on our hometown experiences. Talking about the familiar seemed to make people willing to share. Even now, more than four years later, I can recall much of the information I learned about my classmates from these discussions—where they grew up, how they participated in their communities, what they felt had influenced them. Learning about my classmates' backgrounds and experiences helped me better understand and appreciate their opinions.

With each of the three topics on which we held our in-class deliberations, we discussed our varied views on several possible approaches for dealing with the issue. As we did this, we came to understand the importance of "choice work," weighing the benefits and drawbacks of each choice in a way that would enable us to recognize that choosing one option might mean forgoing another. Our discussions were enriched by writing policy papers to improve our research skills, and the papers helped us to bring a range of ideas, including scholarly ones, to the deliberation table.

We spent a great deal of time discussing our conceptions of citizenship and identifying our civic duties. As is true of many students, our initial conceptions of citizenship involved voting and little more (The Harwood Group 1993). Because most of us had just turned 18, many fellows spoke bitterly about not being able to vote in the 2000 presidential election. I was almost embarrassed to find that I was one of the few who had still not registered. I did so soon after.

I also clearly remember my experiences as the only African American student in my section. Most of our class discussions and deliberations were a positive experience for me; I did not feel out of place or attacked by my classmates because of my racial background or views. One reason for my comfort, I came to see, was that while the topics of our first two deliberations, on public schools and on education for citizenship, were relevant to me, they were not issues that brought tension into my daily life. Even though we were always "wrestling with the choices," I could typically walk away with a good feeling. In fact, deliberation was just an in-class *exercise* to me until we deliberated using the *Racial and Ethnic Tensions* issue book.

In this deliberation, sharply unlike the other deliberations, I felt that there were very few people who shared my views. I also felt as if I were responsible for representing a number of voices instead of just my own. There were many comments I wanted to make, but could not see how to present them without dominating the conversation.

I was not the only person to feel uncomfortable with the subject matter. The whole class seemed reluctant to discuss the issue. I recall our discussion as very shallow and difficult. We talked about a lot of surface issues with some hesitation, and only a few of us seemed willing to bring up really controversial topics or opinions.

Even so, I believe the experience helped prepare me for the rest of my college career and for similar experiences in other classes. I continued to discover that it is difficult to be the only African American in a classroom, especially when race comes up. I learned early how to articulate my thoughts, even if I did not feel that anyone would listen to or appreciate them. Additionally, the experience helped underscore for me the importance of having a diversity of voices at a deliberation. This can be difficult to achieve in campus settings when student populations lack diversity. Just asking, "Who haven't we heard from?" as we often did in a class, is not an adequate replacement for having authentic voices at the table that would serve to help students hear and appreciate viewpoints other than their own.

Nonetheless, despite a few difficult times, I had very positive experiences in our classroom deliberations. While my core values and opinions rarely changed as a result of deliberating, I often came away with new insights into the problems we discussed and different ways to address and look at them. These experiences enabled me to put into practice the theory of deliberative dialogue that I had learned at the start of the semester.

In more personal terms, as a student who often had a unique perspective to contribute, I learned to step out of my comfort zone and articulate my thoughts and opinions. I also began learning to listen to others before I started to craft a response to what I was hearing. This may seem like a simple task, but I found it not so easy to do in practice. I have come to learn that people seem to acknowledge my point more if I take the time to acknowledge theirs. For example, I recently participated in a deliberative forum and heard myself say, "I can agree with what you are saying, however my experience...." Learning to listen more carefully led to many "Ah-ha" moments, and now I often say, "Thanks for sharing.... I hadn't thought of that one." It took me a long time to get to that point, just as it took me a while to listen to what is going on around me instead of waiting impatiently to be acknowledged by a moderator to make a comment. I think I can say now that I care less about being right and more about being a part of an exchange of ideas and opinions.

It may be that deliberating encourages this kind of growth. Repeated exposure to deliberative skills and the regular practice of deliberating seemed important to our group as a whole. In my experience, opportunities for misinterpretation abound in a deliberative setting; deliberators have the responsibility of making sure their points are heard and understood by fellow deliberators. I am sure I was not the only fellow who benefited from many opportunities to deliberate. For this reason, I am skeptical of the effectiveness of an isolated deliberation tossed into a semester of "real work." I feel that a successful deliberative experience should be treated as an integral and consistent part of a curriculum. Otherwise, one classroom deliberation will become just one event.

One singular experience is relevant here. On the morning of September 11, 2001, we were in our Democracy Fellows First-Year Seminar class. After learning of the events, we spent the class session talking about the terrorist attacks and how we felt about what had happened in our country. Unlike the situations in other classes, there was no real pressure to "get back to work"—we *were* working. Our work was always about discussing issues, and I think it helped many of us to talk about the events of September 11th within a setting devoted to deliberation and open dialogue. To discuss an issue so directly relevant to us, on both personal and public levels, in such a setting made our class more personal.

Deliberating Outside the Classroom

As Professors Harriger and McMillan explain in "Contexts of Deliberation," the Democracy Fellows organized and conducted two public deliberations. The first was an on-campus deliberation in our sophomore year, the second, an off-campus deliberation in our junior year.

For the on-campus deliberation, after a period of research and interviewing our peers and some school administrators, we chose the topic of "building the campus community." With the help of our professors, we worked through the issue-framing process and developed three approaches to building a campus community— (1) building social connections and school spirit, (2) strengthening relationships with the neighboring community, and (3) fostering the development of an intellectual community. Those of us who worked on the issue book researched the history of our campus traditions, investigated what other campuses were doing to build community, and interviewed students and various school administrators, including, for example, the school chaplain, an important figure on our campus. With the data, quotes, and research we collected, we were able to add flesh to the three approaches.

The topic and the process made sense to us. Building campus community was an issue we all found personally relevant, and we could envision solutions in which we could take part. This identification with an issue is key to creating a public—people actively involved in collaboratively solving a problem. As Kettering Foundation President David Mathews writes in *For Communities to Work*, Americans will act publicly when they "find a connection between the problems they hear about and their own sense of what is valuable" (Mathews 2002, 19). The point is made another way in a discussion of "public work" by Harry Boyte and Nan Skelton, when they describe the process of creating a sense of owning a problem: "When we help to build something, we experience it as ours" (Boyte and Skelton 1997, 12). In my case, seeing the connections that linked our campus problems, my personal concerns, and the proposed approaches to resolving the problems, enabled me to take our work seriously, in the belief that it was genuinely addressing campus concerns.

We also worked individually and as teams to organize the logistics of the forum. For example, I was responsible for recruiting a substantial number of community members to participate in the forum. This involved generating a list of community leaders, drafting a letter inviting them to our event, keeping track of those who agreed to participate, and updating my peers who were handling other group assignments. On the day of the deliberation, we served as moderators, recorders, and timekeepers.

A number of my friends attended our campus deliberation, and for many, it was the first time they could get a sense of what I was talking about when I said that I was a Democracy Fellow. They were amazed that students could organize and host such an event. Even those who, prior to the event, had complained bitterly about the three-hour time commitment the forum required, seemed to appreciate their exposure to deliberation. I gathered that students valued the "safe" space we were able to create between the student world and the administrative world. As one of my Democracy Fellow classmates, speaking to a reporter from the school newspaper, the *Old Gold & Black*, explained before the forum: "No one is going to have a name tag with the words 'Dean,' 'Doctor,' or even 'President' anywhere; that would detract from the value of the ideas presented" (Huff 2002).

More than 100 members of the campus and the community attended the forum. It was definitely a success. Even so, we knew we had made a number of mistakes and, in some instances, had chosen inefficient means to accomplish tasks. But, with the encouragement of our professors, we were willing to take responsibility for our decisions. In this way, our first attempt at forum organizing better prepared us for our second, an off-campus community forum on urban sprawl, hosted during our junior year.

We made a number of changes to ensure that the second deliberation ran more smoothly than the first. For example, we revamped our check-in/registration system to prevent the loss of valuable small-group deliberating time. Although a relatively minor detail, we found that attention to such details was important in creating a productive and meaningful event.

We adapted our issue guide from one published by the Kettering Foundation for the National Issues Forums, *A Nice Place to Live: Creating Communities, Fighting Sprawl* (1999). We felt that we needed to reframe the way that guide presented the issue so the material was more directly pertinent to the surrounding community of Winston-Salem. We carefully researched the issue and interviewed a number of community leaders, including the mayor of Winston-Salem, an executive of the Chamber of Commerce, and members of several neighborhood counsels. We also made the guide more accessible than our first guide, with summaries, action steps, and an issue map. Through our experience with the National Issues Forums books and from the response to our "Building Campus Community" guide, we learned that these components were vital for good forum participation.

As with the first deliberation, we split up in committees and handled logistics, recruitment, and publicity. While we were not able to get the number of participants we aimed for, I think the whole experience of trying to get the community to participate was a good one. It exposed us to a challenge we had not previously recognized.

I also believe that the issue book we created and the extensive research we completed, despite minor disappointments, were valuable to the community. For example, shortly after our community forum, a transportation planner from another county in North Carolina contacted me to ask about our forum. He requested copies of our materials, and solicited my sense of the community's interest in the issue of urban planning and sprawl. He had heard about the forum from a document circulated through the North Carolina Department of Transportation. I was pleased to correspond with the planner and glad to see that our learning experience was valuable to other people working on serious public problems.

Both deliberations showed us that community stakeholders and leaders were interested in hearing the public voice that emerges from forum work. For myself, I think that the challenges of forum organizing, issue framing, and moderator training will prepare me to work with others in community settings, perhaps even to take the lead in such activities.

Where Does Civic Knowledge Come From?

According to William Galston, recent studies are challenging the common scholarly notion that formal classroom-based civic education has no significant affect on civic knowledge (Galston 2001). Evaluations show that students in civic education classes have more fully developed civic values and attitudes than students who do not take such classes. I find this is true in my case, though of course I had the priming of my experience as a Democracy Fellow.

As a political science major, I took a number of American government classes and studied the systems of government, American constitutional law, and the intersections between religion and politics. These courses not only exposed me to basic civic knowledge, but they also allowed me to explore material both on my own and in meaningful ways with my peers, through group projects, class discussions, and in-depth research projects.

One class in particular, "Political Parties, Voters, and Elections," furthered my interest in both national and statewide elections. Offered in the semester leading up to the 2004 election, it provided an opportunity to discuss the upcoming elections and to keep abreast of current events and developments. Class readings focused on the policies, regulations, and laws that govern elections, the role of finances and political parties in elections, and trends in voter behavior.

One of our assignments was to research highly contested senate seats that had been vacated by Democratic senators. I turned to my home state of South Carolina as a research focus, and selected the senate campaign of State Secretary of Education Inez Tenenbaum. Through the course of my research, I learned about databanks like EMILY's List and the Web-based database of the Center for Responsive Politics, www.opensecrets.org. I retrieved updates on the election campaign, its key issues, and the public response from the online site of my local South Carolina newspaper.

At first, I was just working on a research project, but, gradually, I became excited about the race. When I spoke with my parents, I asked their opinions about it, and I frequently checked all of the candidates' Web sites for updates. I went so far as to download the "INEZ for SENATE" buddy icon for my America Online Instant Messenger Profile, a virtual campaign button, which appeared while I communicated with my peers in the online world.

Being an Inez supporter drew the attention of a number of my college friends who wanted to know who Inez was and why I felt the need to promote her cause. Even though the majority were not from South Carolina, they saw that I cared about the election. Such political activity seemed rare on campus, and I had the feeling that some of my friends saw it was possible to care about the election without necessarily joining a campus party-affiliated organization.

At the time, what I did seemed perfectly natural to me. But in retrospect, it is clear that I had come a long way from being a person who had little interest in her local political party. I would say now that through opportunities to deliberate and exposure to community action, I have come to appreciate the more formal perspective of electoral politics as well.

Combining Service Learning and Deliberation, in and out of the Classroom

Another political science course was also an important source of civic knowledge for me, a service learning course called "Citizen and Community." Taught by Dr. Harriger, the class was an extension of my deliberative work as a Democracy Fellow. It was designed to expose students to a public policy issue and then allow them to work closely with a community organization that was addressing it. We studied the issue of public education and spent a great deal of time analyzing current educational policies. Using a National Issues Forums guide, *Public Schools: Are They Making the Grade?* we held a class deliberation on public education and worked in teams to present different approaches to improving public education, one such example being the No Child Left Behind Act.

The service component of our class was directly linked to our classroom experience. We each played a role in aiding a Winston-Salem community organization, the Community Alliance for Education, to use a format promoted by the Study Circles Resource Center to conduct a series of deliberative study circle dialogue sessions on the subject of public schools. Some of us worked directly with the organization on planning for the event, others served as cofacilitators for the discussion groups. Facilitators completed a special training session and cofacilitated approximately eight hours of community dialogue. All students in the class attended the community forums either as facilitators or participants. Our in-class deliberations and discussions on improving public education prepared us to participate in the community dialogues with a working knowledge of relevant policies and procedures.

The study circle process employed in Winston-Salem challenged people to explore a range of views about a particular community problem by talking about their personal experiences. Discussants addressed how they saw the community problem, identified how they wanted the community to correct it, formulated an action plan, and then mobilized a group effort to address specific key concerns. Participating in this different type of deliberative dialogue gave me and the other fellows in the course the opportunity to see how community dialogue could be employed by a group to solve a specific problem. My dialogue group was made up of citizens who came to the study circle ready to identify their concerns about public education and to discuss how the community might resolve these concerns and communicate its views to school board leaders and other relevant governing bodies. Participants contributed on the basis of their own experiences with a wide variety of school problems, including busing and segregation. Even though I was a college student from another state, I would have felt comfortable contributing to such a group, and would have done so if I were not serving as a neutral facilitator. As it was, the experience of interacting with the group forced me to leave the comfort of the campus environment and face the reality of a failing public school system. I believe my work as a Democracy Fellow helped serve as a springboard into this wider public realm.

Hearing the group members talk about their experiences with the school system and its problems served to transform what I had seen as an abstract problem into a real problem. I believe that similar service-learning initiatives have the same potential to link traditional classroom learning to off-campus, real-life experiences. For example, many students see homelessness and poverty as abstract concepts. If we learn about these problems only through reading assignments, our understanding of them remains just that, part of our reading assignment. At the end of the day, they are still someone else's problem, and we can close the textbook and go play basketball.

Experiences like the study circle can make learning personal. The class essays we wrote on our community-forum experiences illustrate this point. One of our required class texts was Robert Putnam's influential book, *Bowling Alone*, which focuses on the concept of social capital. As a whole, our essays on the community-forum experiences reflected our belief that the forum process represented a strong example of social capital built through the formation of bonds and trust. Our experience doing forum work in the community helped us see what social capital looks like in the real world.

I would highlight two other aspects of meaningful service learning. First, I found that it offered helpful opportunities for reflection. In an article advocating spiritual reflection in service learning, Kent Roth maintains that organized reflection helps students see the impact of their service work on their communities, themselves, and societal issues on a larger scale (Roth 2003, 5). For me, having an opportunity to express my experiences through reflective writing was critically important because I have found that I learn and process information better through writing. Having the chance to reflect on the service-learning experience through the essay also helped make the experience a long-term memory—I can still recall a great deal about the forum series, including some of the stories and viewpoints of the teachers, parents, and community members who participated.

The second aspect of service learning I found important is, as the term itself indicates, the integration of service and learning. In the case of "Citizen and Community," the professor had a close working relationship with the Community Alliance for Education and could ensure that our involvement was genuinely beneficial to the organization. As others have noted, the coordination of a curriculum that involves students, teachers, and community agencies is essential to effective service-learning initiatives (Gibson 2001, 9 and Long 2002, 7). In my view, our service-learning experience was more meaningful because students were able to build on a preexisting bond between the professor and the agency.

However, I also agree with Hunter and Brisbin (2000, 626), who point out that service learning, even when coupled with classroom discussion, is "not a miracle cure for students' political apathy, civic disengagement, or lack of support for the values supporting pluralist participatory democracy." It is easy to make service learning one more assignment that turns into the thoughtless completion of mandatory service hours. I recall a friend who participated in a class with a community-service requirement that she was able to fulfill the week before the due date. In my own case, I found my service learning to be a complement to my experiences planning, organizing, and participating in forums and discussions with the Democracy Fellows, by providing an opportunity to see forums outside of the work we were doing. I was excited to learn that the skills we were learning did translate into meaningful solutions for real people.

Civic Learning Opportunities across Academic Disciplines

An important part of my undergraduate education has been the many classes I took outside of my academic majors. A number of my professors, including Harriger and McMillan, encouraged me to explore other disciplines and to pursue different interests. One of the most fulfilling of these classes was a course I took my last semester at Wake Forest, "Introduction to Sculpture," taught by a well-known sculptor and public artist. One of our projects was to create something using only one material and no adhesives. It probably is not a coincidence that the piece I created involved politics.

Driving around Winston-Salem prior to the 2004 presidential election and seeing campaign signs plastered everywhere gave me the idea of using campaign yard signs as my material of choice. Instead of taking signs from roadside areas, I went to the Democratic and Republican campaign headquarters and the headquarters of a Republican senate candidate. On the advice of a Democratic Party volunteer, I visited the recycling center of a small nearby town, where I obtained quite a few metal frames without endorsements. My curiosity led me to the police station to check with the police about the policies on posting political yard signs in the city limits.

My project was an installation of signage and frames set in the grass outside of the campus's arts building. I destroyed many of the paper signs, twisted many of the metal frames into long rods stemming from the ground, and stacked signs and frames on top of each other to create a small heap of signage and metal.

I was nervous about what my classmates would say in the critique period during which we discussed each other's work. At first, the class was uncharacteristically quiet. Then a few started to voice their hesitancy to discuss what they saw. Then someone remarked that seeing the piece forced us to talk about politics, a subject that people often try to avoid in discussion.

Depending on their relation to the state of North Carolina, my classmates felt connected to or disconnected from the sculpture. One of them remarked that the piece meant more to her because she knew the candidates and so was able to analyze the messages implied by the placement of the campaign endorsements and slogans. Others said they were reminded how little they knew about the elections, the candidates, and the campaign messages.

For me, my "political project" forced me to think about the political dimensions of art. I saw that an artist has the power to express a certain message without explicitly saying anything. Dialogue is then stimulated among and between spectators who are trying to tease out the meaning of the artist's message. The political project was also an opportunity for me to express how I felt about politics and the electoral process. In constructing my work, I realized that I still had a lot of bitterness toward our political system with its emphasis on money and negative campaigning. At the same time, I appreciated the chance to express my views in a nontraditional manner and to stimulate dialogue through art.

Would I have created such a piece had I not been a Democracy Fellow? Maybe not. In all, I feel that my political art demonstrates that a strong liberal arts curriculum complete with opportunities in interdisciplinary studies, interactive teaching, and innovative cocurricular activities is instrumental in ensuring that students are well rounded, see connections in their course work, and are on track to becoming responsible citizens (Colby et al. 2004, 52; Mallory and Thomas 2003, 15-16; and Thomas 2004, 44).

Preparing for Citizenship

I sometimes become upset with myself when I notice that I am starting to forget the amendments, court cases, and important historical dates I learned in high school and college. At these times, I tell myself that my college experience has helped me develop civic perspectives and skills, which in the long run are likely to prove more important to me.

I know that working with the Democracy Fellows for four years helped foster important participatory civic skills. Many of these skills are identified in a report by the Campaign for the Civic Mission of Schools (*The Civic Mission of Schools*). The skills that I feel I significantly developed included the abilities to engage in dialogue with those who hold different perspectives; to manage, organize, and participate in groups; to participate and contribute to community problem-solving efforts; to use nonelectoral means to voice opinions; and to develop and utilize strategic networks for public ends. Organizing a community forum and working as a group to accomplish a challenging task has proven to me that students can solve problems that have an impact on them and are willing to work with others to do so. In fact, I saw this often on my campus, where students banded together to start organizations, raise money, and donate their time and talents to problems ranging from AIDS in Africa to racial tensions on campus.

Through repeated exposure to democratic and deliberative processes, I believe that I have also developed many of the civic dispositions described in the report of the Campaign for the Civic

Mission of Schools, dispositions like tolerance and respect for others, and a desire to be involved in and attentive to community and civic matters. For example, while I do not agree with the political views and ideas of all of the Democracy Fellows, I continue to respect and learn from them. Now we can have civil conversations on sensitive issues, and we can work together to solve tough problems. Despite our differences, we are linked by a common concern for our democracy and a desire to be influential in our learning and living environments.

Obviously, the Democracy Fellows experience was more than a one-time exposure to deliberation in a classroom. Our initial classroom deliberations were only the starting point for the development of additional skills and the pursuit of more in-depth opportunities. Instead of just participating in a forum or two, I was able to help organize forums. Our work did not stop at deliberating with materials handed to us; we were able to create our own materials and, with guidance, took responsibility for everything from framing the issues to writing and designing our issue books. Further, not only have I participated in forums, I have moderated forums, and eventually I was able to teach others how to moderate small-group discussions.

Thus, what could have been a very basic classroom exposure to a National Issues Forums issue book turned into an array of other opportunities. My experience was enhanced by the ability to build on what I learned in the classroom, and my learning became more meaningful because I was able to take more responsibility for my education and make contributions to our group effort using my skills and talents.

The skills I learned in class and working with the Democracy Fellows prepared me to work on other projects, both on and off campus. For example, I was able to put my community organizing/mobilizing skills into practice when I cochaired a student-organized multicultural women's summit on our campus in fall 2004. Part of our work was to raise the funds for speakers and workshop facilitators by applying for grants, petitioning the dean's office, and seeking the financial support of local small businesses. We hoped to offer a campus event that would reach out to our off-campus community, specifically the minority population. I feel that we were successful. More than 200 members of the Winston-Salem and Wake Forest communities attended our summit and keynote event.

Even though I never ran for student government office, I participated in many activities in which I interacted with administrators to help make important decisions for the campus. For example, on the Board of Investigators and Advisors (part of student government's Judicial Affairs division), I had the opportunity to serve in a leadership position as a student advisor and investigator for judicial hearings. The position helped me practice advocacy, critical thinking, and public skills; and to work with professors and administrators and a wide range of students to uphold the ethical and moral fabric of our university. Being a member of the board was important to me because it involved meaningful work within the campus-governance system and helped prepare me, I believe, to be active in my community after leaving the sheltered world of the university campus.

While opportunities like meaningful service-learning experiences, campus leadership positions, community relationships, and a strong liberal arts curriculum added to the development of my civic knowledge and skills, I reiterate the powerful impact of learning "civics" in both traditional environments like my "Political Parties, Voters, and Elections" course and in a nontraditional class like our Democracy Fellows first-year seminar. Through the traditional class, I became interested in knowing what was going on with my political party in my home state of South Carolina, and I am more motivated to stay informed.

At an early point in my college career, I was largely uninterested in the political world outside of my immediate surroundings. I believe that participating in nontraditional political activities, like the Democracy Fellows project and the service-learning project of which I was a part, is leading me to an acceptance of and increasing interest in the traditional modes of politics.

I want to close with four observations:

First, it was important for me that I did not feel like a research subject in the Democracy Fellows project. Although I knew I was a part of a study, I never felt like a guinea pig; our learning environment always seemed to focus on what we were learning and the important work we were doing. I think that creating a shared opportunity to learn together is very powerful and puts both professor and student in nontraditional roles. The concept of students being active producers of knowledge is discussed in Paulo Freire's influential text *Pedagogy of the Oppressed*. Boyte and Kari express a similar sentiment: "Adults who work with young people in the field of youth development need to engage in public work with young people, both challenging and learning from them" (Boyte and Kari 1996, 4).

Second, participating in the Democracy Fellows program and engaging in the Wake Forest and Winston-Salem communities helped me realize a good deal about myself and about how I work with others. I now know that I am willing to step in and get tasks done if I feel that others will not, but I am also aware that I tend to refrain from involving myself in major controversies and disagreements, even when I should speak up. I also know that even though I prefer to work "behind the scenes" and avoid attention, I am fully capable of taking on leadership roles and talking in public.

Third, some of my most vivid college memories involve my interaction with the other Democracy Fellows. Even though we did not have as much time to get to know each other as we would have had in a club or social organization, I had the opportunity to talk to and learn from people that I probably would never have talked to had we not had the shared Democracy Fellow experience. I developed genuine relationships with a few of the fellows and found that I could talk to them about controversial campus issues and ask for their opinions.

Fourth, while I now wish I had done more on campus—volunteered more; gone to more campus events, lectures, and forums; taken more classes for a broader perspective on issues; more often placed myself in situations involving people or topics I had little knowledge of—I am sure that my experience as a Democracy Fellow was key in my developing awareness of the world outside of the classroom and of my developing desire to take an active part in shaping it. As I try to understand how my future career choices can contribute to my vision for a more engaged society, it is clear that the lessons that began in my Democracy Fellows seminar have had a strong (and perhaps lasting) impact on me. Put simply, I am confident that my undergraduate experiences and my exposure to democratic dialogue will continue to influence my decision making and my understanding of citizenship.

Allison N. Crawford *is currently a student at the University of Georgia School of Law. She is a graduate of Wake Forest University where she studied political science and English.*

References

Bennett, Stephen L. and Linda M. Bennett. "What Political Scientists Should Know About the Survey of First-Year Students in 2000." *PS, Political Science and Politics*, 34 (2001): 295-299.

Boyte, Harry C. and Nancy N. Kari. "Young People & Public Work." *Wingspread Journal* (1996): 4.

Boyte, Harry C. and Nan Skelton. "The Legacy of Public Work: Education for Citizenship." *Educational Leadership*, 54 (1997): 12.

Campaign for the Civic Mission of Schools. Available at: http://civicmissionofschools.org/site/resources/civiccompetencies.html.

Colby, Anne, Thomas Ehrlich, Elizabeth Beaumont, and Jason Stevens. "The Role of Higher Education in Preparing Undergraduates for Lives of Civic Responsibility." In *New Directions for Civic Engagement: University Avenue Meets Main Street*, ed. Kathleen Ferraiolo. Charlottesville, VA: University of Richmond, 2004.

Galston, William A. "Political Knowledge, Political Engagement, and Civic Education." *Annual Review of Political Science*, 4 (2001): 217-234.

Gibson, Cynthia. "From Inspiration to Participation: A Review of Perspectives on Youth Civic Engagement." The Grantmaker Forum on Community and National Service/ Carnegie Foundation. (November 2001): 9. Available at: www.gfcns.org/pubs/Moving%20Youth%report%20REV3.pdf.

The Harwood Group. *College Students Talk Politics*. Dayton, OH: Kettering Foundation, 1993.

Hess, Diana. "Developing Strong Voters Through Democratic Deliberation." *Social Education* 64 (September 2000): 293.

Huff, Scott. "Fellows Pursue Campus Discourse." *Old Gold & Black*. October 3, 2002.

Hunter, Susan and Richard A. Brisbin. "The Impact of Service Learning on Democratic and Civic Values." *PS, Political Science and Politics*. 33 (2000): 626.

Hurtado, Sylvia, Mark Engberg, Luis Ponjuan, and Lisa Landerman. "Students' Precollege Preparation for Participation in a Diverse Democracy." *Research in Higher Education* 43 (April 2002): 168.

Levine, Peter and Mark Hugo Lopez, "Youth Voter Turnout Has Declined, by Any Measure." *The Center for Information and Research on Civic Learning and Engagement Fact Sheet* (September 2002): 1.

Long, Sarah. *The New Student Politics: The Wingspread Statement on Student Civic Engagement*. Second edition. Providence, RI: Campus Compact, 2002.

Mallory, Bruce L. and Nancy L. Thomas. "When the Medium Is the Message: Promoting Ethical Action through Democratic Dialogue." *Change, The Magazine of Higher Learning*, 35 (September/October 2003): 15-16.

Mathews, David. *For Communities to Work*. Dayton, OH: Kettering Foundation, 2002.

Roth, Kent. "Deepening the Commitment to Serve: Spiritual Reflection in Service Learning." *About Campus* (January/February 2003): 5.

Thomas, Nancy L. "Educating for Citizenship in a Diverse and Interdependent Society." In *New Direction for Civic Engagement: University Avenue Meets Main Street*, ed. Kathleen Ferraiolo. Charlottesville, VA: University of Richmond, 2004.

Afterword

Who Else Cares?

David Mathews

Deliberation and the Work of Higher Education is part of a growing body of work showing that some faculty members, administrators, and students are thinking about the role that higher education should play in our democracy. I am pleased to see this interest, but it raises some challenging questions. In a nutshell, the central question is, other than the authors and their immediate audience, who else cares? Does this torrent of books and reports mean that a great many people in colleges and universities have come alive with concern about the role of citizens in a democracy and their responsibilities to this citizenry? And if that is so, what is motivating them? Are academic institutions today in touch with the citizens who are angry about being shut out of the political system? Is there any connection between the quest for a more "engaged" university and the efforts at public engagement going on in government agencies, schools, and civic organizations?

Just look at the books that have been published by Kettering Foundation Press in the last few years. Two faculty members at Wake Forest University, Katy Harriger and Jill McMillan, who have a chapter in this volume, also have authored a book describing a four-year experiment in which a group of students was exposed to deliberation-based democracy in the classroom and through direct experience. This experiment had a profound effect on the undergraduates involved; it also altered the way the faculty members see their own work. Harry Boyte, who has written about faculty members who want a deeper engagement with the public, would probably say that Harriger and McMillan found a measure of the "public happiness" that many scholars feel is missing in their careers. Boyte's colleagues, Nan Skelton and Nan Kari, predated the Wake Forest book with a volume on what happened when they took their students into a nearby immigrant community and together founded the Jane Addams School for Democracy—where everyone could learn the meaning of democracy through collective or public work. And Scott Peters and his colleagues in extension have written about turning their scholarly research into a public craft that builds community.[1]

The titles within this body of work tell a story of *Academics and Public Life* and of attempts at *Engaging Campus and Community*. The most provocative of the titles is the one for a collection of essays by contributors to Kettering's *Higher Education Exchange*. They chose *Agent of Democracy*![2]

The authors in *Deliberation and the Work of Higher Education* care about the role of citizens in a democracy and what people can do to make democracy work as they think it should. Americans want to be able to make a difference in the electoral system, but they are discouraged when districts are gerrymandered to invalidate their votes or when moneyed interests have an undue influence. They want to be able to shape their future, beginning in their communities, but they are frustrated by a conventional politics that doesn't have a meaningful role for them to play. People sense they are being pushed out of the political system and, even though prone to throw up their hands with frustration, they care enough to be angry.

These authors believe democracy depends on citizens, and their distinctive take on democracy is reflected in their references to public deliberation and public work. Public deliberation isn't a technique for group dynamics. It helps put the public back in the public's business by giving people a concept of democracy they

---

[1] Katy J. Harriger and Jill J. McMillan, *Speaking of Politics: Preparing College Students for Democratic Citizenship through Deliberative Dialogue* (Dayton, OH: Kettering Foundation Press, 2007); Nan Kari and Nan Skelton, eds., *Voices of Hope: The Story of the Jane Addams School for Democracy* (Dayton, OH: Kettering Foundation Press, 2007); and Scott J. Peters et al., eds., *Engaging Campus and Community: The Practice of Public Scholarship in the State and Land-Grant University System* (Dayton, OH: Kettering Foundation Press, 2005).

[2] Harry C. Boyte, *Going Public: Academics and Public Life* (Dayton, OH: An Occasional Paper of the Kettering Foundation, 2004) and David W. Brown and Deborah Witte, eds., *Agent of Democracy: Higher Education and the HEX Journey* (Dayton, OH: Kettering Foundation Press, 2008).

can experience. Making decisions to shape our collective future brings us face-to-face with differences about what that future should be like. And these differences are moral. That is, they are more than differences in interests that might be compromised, bargained away, or resolved through rational arguments. Putting the public back into the public's business requires living with these differences without letting them spark the violence often associated with moral disputes. Deliberation involves recognizing different moral concerns and treating them all fairly. And it turns moral absolutes into practical political options by asking, if this concerns you, what do you think we should do? Deliberation doesn't treat moral concerns as *relative*, but rather *in relation* to the other things people hold valuable by asking them to weigh the consequences of various options for action. Deliberating makes people aware that differences over what is truly most important are often as much within them as individuals as between them as a citizenry.

The experience of deliberation also shows the connection between collective decision making and collective action (or public work) and the norms that are associated with democracy—freedom, equality, respect for others, and justice. The experience enables people to see that these norms are not simply abstractions. Citizens can't work together effectively without them.

Kettering's publications aren't alone in exploring the claims that various concepts of democracy have on higher education. A 2004 report by the Pew Partnership for Civic Change, *New Directions in Civic Engagement*, argues for "why higher education must take a more active, engaged role in local communities." And the Center for Information & Research on Civic Learning & Engagement (CIRCLE) released a report in 2007 on college students' attitudes toward politics; these students seem interested in being involved and engaged in their communities. The American Association of State Colleges and Universities (AASCU) has an impressive American Democracy Project whose goals include increasing the number of graduates who are engaged as citizens. And Public Agenda's 2007 study of public attitudes toward colleges and universities is part of this body of work because it uncovers a wide range of public concerns, some of which bear indirectly on democracy, such as the importance of preparing students to live and work with other citizens.[3]

Other related publications include those in various disciplines that suggest democracy has implications that reach into the academic core of higher education.[4] Consider *Democracy and Disagreement* by Amy Gutmann and Dennis Thompson, whose discussion of deliberative democracy has had a significant impact on political theory. They argue democracy depends on open deliberations about issues with moral implications, which means democracy is inimical to predetermined conclusions—however compelling the moral imperatives may be. Their book also implicitly raises questions about the role of political science in democracy and resonates with an article Claire Snyder wrote for the *Higher Education Exchange* in which she recounts the democratic impulses that led to the founding of the American Social Science Association.[5]

---

[3] Abby Kiesa et al., *Millenials Talk Politics: A Study of College Student Political Engagement* (College Park, MD: Center for Information & Research on Civic Learning & Engagement, in collaboration with the Kettering Foundation, 2007); Pew Partnership for Civic Change, *New Directions in Civic Engagement: University Avenue Meets Main Street* (Charlottesville, VA: Pew Partnership for Civic Change, 2004); "About ADP," American Association of State Colleges and Universities, http://www.aascu.org/programs/adp/about/default.htm (accessed November 2, 2007); John Immerwahr and Jean Johnson, with Paul Gasbarra, Amber Ott, and Jonathan Rochkind, *Squeeze Play: How Parents and the Public Look at Higher Education Today* (San Jose, CA: Public Agenda for the National Center for Public Policy and Higher Education, 2007).

[4] I have written about these publications in David Mathews, "Listening to the Public: A New Agenda for Higher Education?" in *Higher Education for the Public Good: Emerging Voices from a National Movement*, ed. Adrianna J. Kezar, Tony C. Chambers, and John C. Burkhardt (San Francisco: Jossey-Bass, 2005), 71-86.

[5] Amy Gutmann and Dennis Thompson, *Democracy and Disagreement* (Cambridge, MA: Belknap Press of Harvard University Press, 1996) and R. Claire Snyder, "The Civic Roots of Academic Social Science Scholarship in America," *Higher Education Exchange* (2000): 5-16.

Despite such democratic impulses in academic disciplines, there are inevitable tensions in a society that depends heavily on expert knowledge, yet makes citizens, who aren't necessarily experts, the sovereign political power. No one has done more to identify the tensions between professional routines and democratic practices than William Sullivan in his work at The Carnegie Foundation for the Advancement of Teaching.

The most explicit study I have seen linking democracy and higher education comes from Russia. It was conducted by the Foundation for Development of Civic Culture in collaboration with the Department of Political Science and Sociology at Moscow State Pedagogical University. Although the study reports that the Russian public expects more education for democracy from its universities, it also reports promising developments. The most important may be a "de-ideologized" curriculum. In various other ways, the university system is said to promote democratic values, such as freedom of speech. It seems that there may be some interest within the Russian academy for creating a more democratically relevant system of higher education.[6]

Who Is Paying Attention—and to What?

To see how widespread this interest is on U.S. campuses, researchers at the Kettering Foundation, Matt Johnson and Halima Sow, did a quick review of what outside observers and people inside the institutions are saying about higher education.

Financial Pressures and Accountability

One of the dominant concerns reflected in the literature is consistent with the findings in the Public Agenda study: more

---

[6] Foundation for Development of Civic Culture, with Department of Political Science and Sociology of the Moscow State Pedagogical University, *University Students and Deliberation: Higher Education and Democratic Challenges in Russia, Report on Stage 1. The Status Quo: Where We Are with Higher Education's Civic Mission* (Moscow: Russian Federation, 2007).

than half of those surveyed now see colleges and universities as businesses that care mainly about the bottom line. People aren't convinced, however, that these institutions are doing enough to keep costs down. Rising costs limit access, another public concern, so institutions are pressed to be better managers of the resources they have.[7]

Given the cost pressures, much of the literature has to do with finance. Some examples: *Cost Containment in Higher Education, Analyzing Costs in Higher Education*, and *Economic Challenges in Higher Education*. This emphasis is so dominant it has prompted a critical response. In his book *Universities in the Marketplace*, Derek Bok warns explicitly against *The Commercialization of Higher Education*. Nonetheless, rising costs and consumer pressures have resulted in greater emphasis on "accountability," defined largely in managerial and financial terms. For instance, the federal government, a major source of revenue, is one of those pressing for more performance data to ensure this accountability.[8]

The accountability trend's hold on higher education is well entrenched. It reminds me of a meeting I attended in 1976 with a group of prominent intellectuals, including Margaret Mead, Charles Frankel, and E. O. Wilson, and leaders in higher education, including Pat Graham, Sam Proctor, Roger Heyns, and Frank Newan. The objective was to take stock of what was on the agenda of colleges and universities. We found that the "new egalitarianism" of the 1960s was being challenged by a coming "managerial revolution."

---

[7] Immerwahr and Johnson, *Squeeze Play*, 3-5.

[8] Walter A. Brown and Cayo Gamber, *Cost Containment in Higher Education: Issues and Recommendations*, ASHE-ERIC Higher Education Report, vol. 28, no. 5 (San Francisco: Jossey-Bass, 2002); Michael F. Middaugh, ed., *Analyzing Costs in Higher Education: What Institutional Researchers Need to Know*, New Directions for Institutional Research, no. 106 (San Francisco: Jossey-Bass, 2000); Charles T. Clotfelter et al., *Economic Challenges in Higher Education* (Chicago: University of Chicago Press, 1992); and Derek Bok, *Universities in the Marketplace: The Commercialization of Higher Education* (Princeton, NJ: Princeton University Press, 2003).

In a 1973 article in the *Chronicle of Higher Education*, Harold Enarson, president of The Ohio State University, made an observation that rang true at the meeting:

> There is a tempting heresy loose in the land. Very simply, it is the dangerous notion that state universities are simply another agency of state government, a unit to be policed, regulated, and whipped into a bureaucratic mold. In this view, the university is simply a production unit in the knowledge industry, a kind of specialized factory processing human beings for strictly utilitarian ends.... Make no mistake about it. In state after state, a managerial revolution is steadily under way.... The new articles of faith are control, coordination, efficiency, and something called "accountability."[9]

Today, these articles are no longer new, and they have far more champions than the federal government.

Concerns about what the new values would do to higher education's traditional role were palpable by the mid-1970s. The warning went out: colleges and universities were in danger of forgetting that they were once part of powerful democratic movements and that their values were shaped by those movements.

Today, many continue to be concerned. Boards of trustees, as representatives of the citizenry, might be expected to share these concerns about the mission of their institutions. Yet, if the literature is any indication, trustees pay more attention to what happens within their institutions than to the institutions' role in society.

Social Justice and Diversity

While much of the literature on higher education has focused on fiscal issues, a good deal of attention has also been paid to aberrant student behavior on campus (racial conflict, drug and alcohol abuse, and student violence). Perhaps out of concern for this behavior and the widespread public perception that the country has lost its

---

[9] David Mathews et al., *The Changing Agenda for American Higher Education* (Washington, DC: Government Printing Office, 1977), 71.

moral certitude, colleges and universities are emphasizing moral education and building good character.[10]

The premise in much of the literature that the Kettering researchers examined seems to be that democracy requires individuals with a strong sense of moral responsibility. So there is a tendency to equate democracy with moral precepts. Service learning is very popular, and proponents believe it promotes greater acceptance of differences in race, gender, and sexual orientation. The importance given to creating such diversity on campuses is reflected in statements that rank it as a "key component to educational excellence in the 21st century."[11] On many campuses, moral education translates into advocacy for social justice. At some institutions, moral education has a decidedly religious grounding, although there are highly contested interpretations of what is "moral."

It's not surprising that these different views on morality have fueled ideological conflicts. Some critics have speculated that the ideological battles on campus may be contributing to hyperpolarization in the country's political system, raising the question of whether higher education really promotes intellectual diversity. A number of efforts have been launched to combat what some see as faculty indoctrination and others see as academic freedom.

What Kind of Democracy Does Higher Education Serve?

Now back to the questions I began with, questions about who else cares. Our researchers' cursory survey of issues on campuses doesn't show a complete neglect of concerns about democracy.

---

[10] Although the dominant themes in the literature have to do with business issues or issues of social justice and diversity, it would be a mistake to conclude that either is the main concern of typical faculty members or students. Faculty, for instance, are more likely to be concerned with how prepared incoming students are. And the typical student is more likely to be concerned with schoolwork or finding a job.

[11] Debra Humphreys, "The Value of Campus Diversity: The Emerging Research Picture," *Diversity Digest* 4, no. 3 (Spring/Summer 2000): 1.

But it doesn't suggest a strong connection between the concerns of citizens and the issues that command the greatest attention at colleges and universities either.

If academic leaders were asked whether they care about the role their institutions play in our democracy, I am sure they would say that the very existence of their institutions is a service to democracy, although they wouldn't all define democracy in the same way. Champions of social justice and diversity would most certainly say that their efforts were at the heart of democracy because democracy can't function without justice and respect for differences. Fair enough.

It would be unrealistic to expect every institution to think of democracy as a citizen-centered system of self-government that relies on deliberative decision making to inform the collective actions citizens need to take to shape their future. But it isn't unrealistic to expect colleges and universities to pay more attention to the public's problems, such as people's frustrations in trying to make a difference in the political system and their often unrealized ambitions to build more livable communities. These concerns of citizens, however, don't appear to register with the academy as they have in other moments in history—when the American Revolution turned campuses into "seminaries of sedition," when agrarian and labor distress revitalized the land-grant movement, and when the civil rights movement stimulated more than a decade of student activism and campus reform.[12]

Nonetheless, this sensitivity to the plight of citizens and their role in democracy hasn't completely disappeared from campuses. And where it has lodged is interesting. For instance, who would have predicted that faculty members, pressured to publish in the conventional confines of their disciplines, would be leading the charge for a more publicly relevant form of scholarship? I have enjoyed meeting with faculty groups at the University of Minnesota, Pennsylvania

---

[12] Louis Leonard Tucker's book on Yale is titled *Connecticut's Seminary of Sedition: Yale College* (Chester, CT: Pequot Press, 1974).

State University, and Kansas State University, among others, and I have found many professors are as determined as Scott Peters and his fellow extension educators to return to the democratic roots of their disciplines. I have been encouraged that students like those at Wake Forest, Central State University, Hofstra University, Franklin Pierce University, and Fordham University respond with character-istic idealism when given the opportunity to experience democracy in its most basic and direct form. And I suspect there is potential support for a college curriculum reuniting the liberal arts with the civic arts—the arts of citizenship—even though we are supposed to be living in a consumer-oriented, job-driven environment. In fact, this book includes accounts of connections already being made between the humanities, classical rhetoric, teacher education, and the civic practice of public deliberation.

There was a time when academics saw the need for connecting the work of citizens and the work of their institutions. They had to document what they were doing to make this connection and demonstrate the impact of their efforts. As this and other books illustrate, that is being done. I hope that this outpouring of books and reports will encourage other faculty members who share the concerns of these public scholars; other students who are looking for experiences with a democracy they can practice now; and other citizens who want more from higher education than career training.

Still, there is an additional challenge. Demonstrating impact is one thing; engaging others in a broader consideration of the full implications of democracy for higher education is something else. And if these efforts in higher education don't engage a wider audience, defensive tendencies (already evident in academe) will grow. To prevent this from happening, a connection has to be made with the self-interests of those whose attention is now more narrowly focused or is directed elsewhere.

I don't believe there is any group of citizens that is deaf to the concerns of their fellow citizens. Yet I don't think they can be reached by preaching to or arguing with them. They have to be engaged in terms of their own self-interests. The critical issue is how to get those concerned with accountability, for instance, to broaden their notion of accountability and consider what research has documented in detail—the sidelining of citizens and the general weakening of civic life. This problem is profound:

> American democracy is at risk. The risk comes not from some external threat but from disturbing internal trends: an erosion of the activities and capacities of citizenship.... Although some aspects of civic life remain robust and some citizens still participate frequently, Americans should be concerned about the current state of affairs. The risk is not to our national survival but to the health and legitimacy of our shared political order.[13]

Frankly, I don't know how to do what I am proposing. I suspect that the problem described in this analysis won't get much attention until there are more opportunities to discuss the true self-interests of higher education—discussions that include citizens both inside and outside academe. Meeting financial pressures is not negotiable; neither is meeting the expectations of individual students who know full well that their careers depend on getting a sound college education. At the same time, according to the Public Agenda study *Squeeze Play*, leaders of our major civic, governmental, and economic institutions want colleges and universities to benefit society as a whole, not just individuals. Maybe that is an opening for a broader conversation about self-interests. And maybe there is a way to expand on the current interest in social justice, diversity, and service learning. Most students want a meaningful life as citizens. When they experience the full meaning of citizenship, as they did at the campuses cited in this book, that experience resonates with an instinct deep within them. The positive effects are obvious in the way students interact with other people, beginning on campus. That is surely an opening for a broader conversation.

---

[13] Stephen Macedo et al., *Democracy at Risk: How Political Choices Undermine Citizen Participation and What We Can Do About It* (Washington, DC: Brookings Institution Press, 2005), 1.

As readers reflect on the reports in this volume, I hope they will consider the question of who else cares. If colleges and universities were to become merely cogs in the machinery of a knowledge industry, it would be an incredible loss. The forces that have prevented this from happening in the past have come largely from outside institutional walls. They have come from external imperatives that have inspired academic responses. That is why the question of who else cares is so important.

David Mathews *is president of the Charles F. Kettering Foundation. He served as Secretary of the Department of Health, Education, and Welfare in the administration of President Gerald Ford. Between 1969 and 1980, he was president of The University of Alabama. He has written extensively on education, political theory, southern history, public policy, and international problem solving. His newest book focuses on the relationship between the public and public education:* Reclaiming Public Education by Reclaiming Our Democracy *(Kettering Foundation Press, 2006). He serves on the board of a variety of organizations, including the Gerald R. Ford Foundation, National Issues Forums Institute, and Public Agenda.*

This powerful collection reveals hidden public possibilities in higher education. Created by a group of faculty members drawn from diverse settings who have been in intense conversation about their experiments in deliberation for several years, *Deliberation and the Work of Higher Education* testifies to the messy, complex, but also often exhilarating process of "going public." Their stories show how deliberation and public work can help make classrooms come alive with new energy and student learning; can make campus cultures create more open, vital public spaces on campus; and can help higher education make distinctive contributions to the broader movement for renewal of America's democratic narrative.

HARRY C. BOYTE, CODIRECTOR
Center for Democracy and Citizenship

Both faculty and students in American higher education say they are way too busy, so teaching and learning strategies that serve many different purposes are more valuable than ever. This thoughtful collection of essays describes in candid and practical terms the ways that deliberation both inside and beyond the classroom can be used to support students' development as responsible citizens, while also building clarity of thought; rhetorical skill; effective writing; habits of careful, open-minded reflection; communication across differences; substantive knowledge; and community bonds. It's hard to imagine a richer bounty.

ANNE COLBY, SENIOR SCHOLAR
Carnegie Foundation for the Advancement of Teaching

KETTERING
FOUNDATION
PRESS

ISBN# 978-0-923993-25-2

51595

9 780923 993252